THE NOVELS OF SIMONE DE BEAUVOIR

THE NOVELS OF
Simone de Beauvoir

ELIZABETH FALLAIZE

ROUTLEDGE
London and New York

First published 1988 by
Routledge
11 New Fetter Lane, London EC4P 4EE
29 West 35th Street, New York, NY 10001

Printed in Great Britain by
Billing & Sons Ltd, Worcester

Typeset by Pat and Anne Murphy, Highcliffe-on-Sea, Dorset

British Library Cataloguing in Publication Data

Fallaize, Elizabeth
    The novels of Simone de Beauvoir.
    1. Fiction in French. Beauvoir, Simone
    de — Critical studies
    I. Title
    843'.912
    ISBN 0-415-02294-0

Library of Congress Cataloguing-in-Publication Data
ISBN 0-415-02294-0

Contents

For Alice

Preface

I have been lucky enough to be able to complete the writing of this book in Paris, in 1986–1987. My thanks are due to the University of Birmingham for allowing my request for an extended leave of absence, and I would like to record my gratitude to Professor Colin Burns and to all my colleagues in the French department for their support of my request.

In Paris, I have greatly appreciated the encouragement of Barbara Watkinson, Carrie Tarr and Johanna Dunlop, and I would like to thank Michelle Léonard for her help in obtaining various materials. Diana Knight was an ever-dependable source of help in moments of crisis; I am very grateful to her for the afternoons she spent reading chapter drafts and for the helpful and positive discussions she had with me. I am also grateful to François Noudlemann for his advice on the chapter he found time to read for me.

The groups of students who have read Beauvoir's texts with me over the years since 1979 have been a great source of stimulus and pleasure. More recently, I have enjoyed and benefited from working with Jill Wharfe, who shared with me the experience of interviewing Simone de Beauvoir in July 1985. Most of the questions which I asked, and the replies on which I draw here, relate to the later fictional work. Beauvoir encouraged us to return for further questions on other aspects of her fiction, but all such plans were cut short by the news of her death nine months later.

My children have had to bear with my frequent absences. Emma Topp and Karen Swanson filled the gap with never failing good humour and reliability; my grateful thanks go to them both. Finally, I owe an enormous amount to Michael Driscoll, whose generosity in terms of time and advice has as usual been completely unstinting.

Elizabeth Fallaize

Key to Abbreviations

Page references to the texts by Beauvoir which I use most frequently appear in brackets in the text immediately after quotations. For further publication details of the editions used, please refer to the bibliography.

Abbreviation	English title of work	Edition
ADD	*America Day by Day*	Morihien
AMM	*All Men are Mortal*	Gallimard
ASD	*All Said and Done*	Penguin
BO	*The Blood of Others*	Penguin
FOC	*Force of Circumstance*	Penguin
LBI	*Les Belles Images*	Fontana
MDD	*Memoirs of a Dutiful Daughter*	Penguin
MND	*The Mandarins*	Fontana
OA	*Old Age*	Penguin
POL	*The Prime of Life*	Penguin
SCS	*She Came to Stay*	Fontana
TEA	*The Ethics of Ambiguity*	Gallimard
TSS	*The Second Sex*	Penguin
TWD	*The Woman Destroyed*	Fontana
WTS	*When Things of the Spirit Come First*	Fontana

Introduction

The fact is that I am a writer. (. . .) A woman writer . . . someone whose whole existence is governed by her writing.

Simone de Beauvoir[1]

This study of Beauvoir's five novels and two collections of short stories is primarily focused on Simone de Beauvoir as a writer of fiction. This is not to deny, of course, the importance of her philosophical essays, or the seminal place that *The Second Sex* has earned in contemporary feminism, or the fascination of her autobiographical writings. All these elements have served as a basis for readings of her fiction in the past, and will serve to some extent in my own, but I want to consider them principally in relation to another optic, which is: given the 'meaning' or central problematic which Beauvoir intended her text to convey (and which in every case she has made perfectly explicit in her autobiographical writing and in interviews), what narrative strategies does she employ to impose and channel this meaning? Given the interaction of form with meaning, how do these strategies function and themselves affect the meaning of the text?

I investigate with particular interest the relation of narrative strategies to the sexual politics of her writing. Though Beauvoir herself denied the existence of a specifically 'feminine' writing, she recognised that she wrote as a woman. Asked by Alice Jardine in 1977 whether her books could have been written by a man, she replied, 'No, certainly not. I have never read a really good novel written by a man where women are portrayed as they truly are. They can be portrayed externally very well (. . .) but only as seen from the *outside*. But from within . . . only a woman can write what it is to feel as a woman, to be a woman.'[2] This is something which Beauvoir only came to see fairly late in her writing career, opposed as she was to any essentialist notion of what it is to be a woman. What are the effects on her writing of the fact that she conducted most of her writing career in a highly masculine context and tradition? I want to examine in particular the effects on the construction of women characters, and on the narrative power allocated to them, within the general context of an examination of narrative authority and the construction of gender roles.

The idea of this study and the way in which it has been conceived have not, of course, emerged from a vacuum. It has been strongly influenced by years of teaching Beauvoir's texts to enthusiastic students, and by gaps collectively perceived in the existing literature. 'Is there room for another book on Simone de Beauvoir?' a fellow reader at the Bibliothèque Nationale recently enquired of me. The assumption behind this question seems to be that there is only one thing to be said about Beauvoir — presumably that she wrote *The Second Sex*. Simone de Beauvoir studies effectively began — leaving aside the reactions to her work which appeared in newspapers — with Geneviève Gennari's *Simone de Beauvoir* published in French in 1958. Putting the accent on Beauvoir as a disciple of existentialism and the author of *The Second Sex*, Gennari examined the four novels Beauvoir had published up to that date as an interlocking whole with her essays, thereby setting a trend still marked in approaches to Beauvoir's fiction. The first study to appear in English was Elaine Marks's *Simone de Beauvoir: Encounters with Death*, a thematic study of Beauvoir's fictional and autobiographical writing published in 1973. Since those pioneering studies, a number of paths through Beauvoir's considerable body of work have become increasingly well-trodden. The majority of the studies dealing with the fictional work have given at least as much attention to her essays and/or autobiographical writings (following the pattern set by Gennari). Thus Francis Jeanson in his *Simone de Beauvoir ou l'entreprise de vivre* (1966) places considerable emphasis on autobiographical factors, whilst Madeleine Descubes in *Connaître Simone de Beauvoir* (1979) examines the work in order to approach the personality of its author; others, like Robert Cottrell's *Simone de Beauvoir* (1975) and Terry Keefe's *Simone de Beauvoir; a Study of her Writings* (1983), look at the fiction in the context of all Beauvoir's writings. Only Keefe has so far been able to include all the published fiction, since the early *When Things of the Spirit Come First* remained unpublished until 1979.

The fiction has also been examined in other thematic studies (another on death by J. Audet published in 1979 and Claire Caryon's study of *La Nature chez Simone de Beauvoir* 1973), and in a more limited way by critics with exclusively political or philosophical concerns (such as Anne Whitmarsh's *Simone de Beauvoir or the Limits of Commitment*, 1981, and Hazel Barnes's much earlier *The Literature of Possibility, a Study in Humanistic Existentialism*, 1961). A new trend began in 1975 with Jean Leighton's *Simone de Beauvoir on Woman*, in which she applies some of the theoretical elements of

The Second Sex to the fiction, to conclude that the fiction is sadly wanting. Readers looking at Beauvoir's fiction for either a confirmation of *The Second Sex* or, in a quite ahistorical spirit, for a reflection of contemporary feminist thinking, have in general shared this sense of disappointment — see for example Mary Evans's *Simone de Beauvoir: A Feminist Mandarin* (1985).[3] Some of the best feminist work on Beauvoir has been done on *The Second Sex* (see my Chapter 1) and is emerging in article form on the fiction.[4]

Within this body of work, the focus on theme and content has meant that where the fiction has been dealt with, relatively little attention has been paid to its formal literary properties (with the notable exception of Anne-Marie Lasocki's *Simone de Beauvoir ou l'entreprise d'écrire* (1971), which deals with Beauvoir as a writer in her autobiographies and fiction). In looking at content in relation to form, my hope is to focus more attention on Beauvoir as a writer. Beauvoir did not see writing as one activity amongst others. She writes in *The Prime of Life* (POL p. 666):

> Whence does it come, no less urgent now at fifty-five than it was when I was twenty, this extraordinary power of the Word? (. . .) Words, without doubt, universal, eternal, presence of all in each, are the only transcendent power I recognize and am affected by (. . .). Perhaps the most profound desire I entertain today is that people should repeat in silence certain words that I have been the first to link together.

The power of the word makes literature into a powerful and privileged activity for Simone de Beauvoir. She takes language as a weapon against death, against time, against the isolation of the individual; language 'reintegrates us to the human community'.[5] As such, words are not to be used lightly; the novelist's task, for Beauvoir, is to 'recreate an imaginary world which reveals meaning'.[6] Words are not to be piled up in a way which does not relate to the real world: 'I have never denied that words do not exactly mimic reality — but I do say that words are our only means of communication and that we must try to establish a reality through words even though we know what traps words can hold out for us.'[7] Communication of a meaning which relates to the real world is thus a primary function of literature for Beauvoir. She sees herself as a writer who 'has something to say' about the real world, but, as she underlined in a debate on literature in which she took part in 1965, 'having something to say does not mean owning an object which the writer can carry home in a bag and then spread on the table before searching round for words to describe it'. The writer discovers meaning through writing: 'this is why any work of literature is essentially a search for meaning'. Before writing, the author 'did not know what book would be produced; starting out simply with a line of enquiry, the result, for the author, is always something unexpected. And this is why the distinction between form and content is no longer applicable; the two are inseparable.'[8]

Narrative structure for Beauvoir ('the way of telling a story') is thus inseparable from the story it tells: 'the way of telling it is the rhythm of the search itself, the way of defining it, of living it'.[9] Her interest in the American novelists of the 1930s — especially Dos Passos, Hemingway, Faulkner — led her to pay particular attention to the problem of 'point of view', that is: the question of who speaks a narrative (an external narrator? a character?), and what powers they are given as a speaker; and the question of whose perspective is adopted by the speaker (the question formulated by theorist Gérard Genette as 'Who sees?', as opposed to the question of 'Who speaks?').[10] The principle of subordinating the external narrator's voice (where there is one) to the perceptions of the characters, is one which, once she had adopted it in *She Came to Stay*, Beauvoir never departed from. However, there are considerable changes in the way in which narrative voice is handled, in particular in the number of voices in any one text, in the powers allocated to them and in the hierarchy established between them. In examining these changes, I want to look at the effect on meaning and on expectations set up by the text about the reader's position, and to ask from what changes in assumptions and attitudes they spring. There is an evident relation with historical events taking place during the years in which she produced these texts, and which she herself saw as determining in their effects on her and her work: in particular, the outbreak of the Second World War, the German occupation of Paris, the Cold War and the drama of decolonisation in France, especially in the Algerian War.

If my starting-point, therefore, is the narrative economy of the text, this is in direct relationship to meaning. Narrative structure and voice will play a greater part in my discussion of a text such as *Les Belles Images*, where language itself and the construction of myths through words is a primary concern, than in texts like *The Mandarins*, where there is a dense and complex weight of political and personal preoccupations. In order to move between form and meaning, and to appreciate the situation of the fictional texts in historical terms, the reader requires a grasp of the movement of Beauvoir's intellectual preoccupations. The first chapter therefore offers an introduction to the broad lines of this development, and to some of the terminology which she uses. In the following six chapters each of Beauvoir's five novels and two short-story cycles is examined in turn, in order of their publication; although this order distorts the chronology of composition in the case of *When Things of the Spirit Come First*, it has the advantage of allowing me to take the two short-story cycles together. Each of these chapters can to a large extent be read independently. In the final chapter, however, I adopt a broad focus to discuss overall developments in the fiction and offer some interpretations of the pattern of narrative strategies which I have identified.

I give relatively little biographical information; the reader is directed to the biographical notes at the end of the volume for some indications that I have found useful in a reading of the fictional texts.

Notes

1. *Force of Circumstance*, p. 664.
2. Alice Jardine, 'Interview with Simone de Beauvoir', p. 233. In 1984 Beauvoir also told Hélène Wenzel: 'Of course a woman will mark her work with a femaleness, because she's a woman and because when one writes one writes with one's entire being. So a woman will write with her whole being, and therefore with her femaleness too' (interview with Wenzel published in 1986).
3. Carol Ascher's *Simone de Beauvoir: a Life of Freedom* (1981) is another eloquent expression of the difficulties for contemporary feminists of working on Beauvoir. Compare Toril Moi's remark that 'Whether we like it or not, Beauvoir remains a mother figure for modern feminists, and as such is treated with as much ambivalence as any Kleinian mother could wish for: love and hate mingle in our readings.' See Moi's article, 'She came to stay' (1986).
4. For example, in the special number of *Yale French Studies* (1987) devoted to Beauvoir.
5. Quotation from *Que peut la littérature?* (What Can Literature Do?) (1965), pp. 88–91. My translation.
6. See 'My Experience as a Writer' in Francis and Gontier, *Les Ecrits de Simone de Beauvoir* (1979), p. 445. No review of the literature on Beauvoir would be complete without a reference to this extremely useful volume which, despite some confusions of dates, gives an indispensable chronological list of all Beauvoir's writings up to 1977 together with details of the history of their composition and reprints many interviews and short texts

by Beauvoir hitherto unpublished or difficult to locate.

    7. Quotation from a 1968 interview in the Norwegian *Vinduet*, reprinted and translated into French in Francis and Gontier (1979), p. 233. My translation into English.

    8. Quotations from *Que peut la littérature?*, pp. 83–85.

    9. *Que peut la littérature?*, p. 85.

    10. In *Figures III* (1972), p. 203.

1

The Radicalisations of Simone de Beauvoir

Born in 1908, Simone de Beauvoir was brought up in a conservative bourgeois milieu, and received a conventional Catholic education. As a child she expected to marry, possibly her cousin Jacques, and to lead the discreet and respectable life of the bourgeoisie. Instead she became, in turn, an existentialist, a feminist, a Marxist, a Maoist sympathiser, and an outspoken critic of the class into which she was born and of the institution of the family. Her thinking never ossified behind any of these labels, however, always remaining open to the next leap forward. The story of her intellectual life is the story of a succession of radical transformations.

One of the earliest of these was the abandonment of her religious belief; after a childhood period of religious fervour fostered by her mother, Beauvoir was able to tell herself by the age of fourteen that 'I no longer believe in God' (MDD p. 137). The calm with which she faced this revelation gave way to panic only when she eventually grasped the logical consequences of her position: 'One afternoon, in Paris, I realised that I was condemned to death. I was alone in the house and I did not attempt to control my despair: I screamed and tore at the red carpet' (MDD p. 138). Her father's open atheism had eased his eldest daughter's passage from Catholicism. A change in Georges de Beauvoir's circumstances after the First World War, occasioning the family's move from their apartment on the boulevard Montparnasse, above the café de la Rotonde, to a smaller and cheaper one in the rue de Rennes, also made it easier for his daughter to pursue her education. He announced to his two daughters, ' "My dears, you'll never marry; you'll have to work for your livings" ' (MDD p. 176). After her studies at the Cours Désir, a narrow and unstimulating educational

7

institution for the daughters of the bourgeoisie, Beauvoir
eventually made her way, via a spell at the Institut Catholique and
the Institut Sainte-Marie, to the Sorbonne and the prestigious
Ecole Normale. Working on Leibniz and preparing herself to take
the *agrégation* (postgraduate examination for teaching posts in the
lycées and universities) in philosophy in 1929, Beauvoir studied
alongside Lévi-Strauss, Merleau-Ponty, Nizan, Maheu and,
eventually, Jean-Paul Sartre. Her encounter with Sartre, her
success in the *agrégation* and her escape from the family home to an
independent room rented from her grandmother made 1929 a
capital year in Beauvoir's life.

Despite her new independence, and the contact which she had
had through her studies with ideas and philosophies, she failed,
however, in her own words, 'to face the weight of reality' (POL
p. 15). In their 'spiritual pride' she and Sartre saw themselves as
the proponents of a 'radical freedom', living lives over which they
had total personal control (POL pp. 15–16). Occupying herself
fully with her writing, with the beginning of her teaching career (in
Marseilles in 1931 followed by Rouen in 1932), and with her
relationship with Sartre, Beauvoir assumed that life would always
submit itself tamely to her will. Beyond a vague conviction that
society required remoulding, she took no interest in politics,
despite her friendship in Rouen with her Trotskyist colleague
Colette Audry. Visiting Berlin, where Sartre was studying phenomenology in 1934, it was Husserl, rather than the activities of the
Nazis, who retained her attention. The discovery of Husserl laid
the base for the discussions which Beauvoir had with Sartre
throughout the 1930s, and which in turn eventually led to their
essays on existentialism published in the early 1940s.

In the meantime, Beauvoir approved the election of the Popular
Front in 1936, though she said she would not have voted even had
women had the right to do so.[1] The Spanish Civil War (1936–38)
affected her more deeply, through her friendship with Stépha and
Fernando Gerassi (POL p. 275), but she still found it hard to
believe at the end of the 1930s that a world war could be approach-
ing. When Daladier returned from Munich after the infamous
Franco-British attempt at appeasement of Hitler, she was, she
admits, 'delighted, and felt not the faintest pang of conscience at
my reaction' (POL p. 336). But there were limits to how long she
could continue to see world events from a purely individualistic
point of view. 'Spring 1939', she writes in *The Prime of Life*,
'marked a watershed in my life. I renounced my individualistic,

anti-humanist way of life. I learned the value of solidarity' (POL p. 359). A few sentences later Beauvoir writes, 'History took hold of me, and never let go thereafter' (POL p. 359).

In Beauvoir's own account of her life, then, the Second World War is presented as an important turning point in her intellectual development, and it is certainly true that the war and the German occupation politicised her attitudes. But when she describes herself as having discovered history, she means more precisely that the historical situation — the historicity — of the individual was now evident to her. She had no truck, however, with the notion of history as a grand design, as *All Men Are Mortal*, completed in 1945, emphatically shows. Despite the closer connection with the Communists which Beauvoir and Sartre had during the Resistance, there was no question of their accepting the Marxist doctrine of historical materialism. The name of the Resistance group which Sartre and Beauvoir briefly tried to set up in 1941 after Sartre's return from captivity, 'Socialisme et liberté' (Socialism and freedom), captured in a formula their political position — one which they were to hold to in one way or another for the rest of their lives, though Beauvoir always kept the emphasis on freedom.

It was to the notion of freedom that both turned with a vengeance in their essays published in the 1940s. The discussions which they had carried on in the 1930s, and continued by correspondence during the period of Sartre's mobilisation, bore their fruit in Sartre's *Being and Nothingness*, published in 1943.[2] It can be disconcerting to note the extent to which Beauvoir's essays of this period take *Being and Nothingness* as their basic reference point. However, there are two points to be made here: the first is that Beauvoir had played the role of discussant and critic of the theories at the base of Sartre's essay over a period of ten years or so. She was as familiar with them as if they had been her own, and had worked over every page of the manuscript with Sartre.[3] What her actual contribution may have been seems impossible to assess — but one thing is clear, and this is the second point to be made, and that is that Beauvoir did not agree with Sartre on every point.[4] She naturally tends to stress in her essays the ideas of *Being and Nothingness* with which she is in full agreement, but the fact is that her own essays tend to have emphases rather different from those of Sartre.

Being and Nothingness starts out from Descartes' *cogito*: the individual consciousness is at the centre of each of our worlds; we control everything that we are through the consciousness. Consciousness is held to be 'transparent': there is nothing in it that the individual has not chosen. We are all, therefore, responsible for what we are, for all our attitudes, our emotions, our behaviour. We cannot look to any notion of a Maker, any preconceived notion of human nature to explain what we are. Nor is there any such thing as the unconscious, simply a mass of habits and tricks which Sartre calls bad faith and which we develop to help us cope with the enormous burden of freedom. A great deal of the essay is in fact devoted to how we try to escape from our freedom — by invoking various forms of determinism ('I couldn't help it'), by trying to pretend that we are no more than the role which we play in life (teacher, waiter, parent, etc.), or by trying to pretend that we have the fixed nature of objects — and bad faith, or inauthenticity, is made to appear almost as a more natural activity than the authentic recognition of our freedom.

A welter of terminology was created, much of which Beauvoir adopted. The consciousness itself is labelled 'being-for-itself', the world of things with their fixed natures is named 'being-in-itself', and the ambiguous mode of being in which the for-itself is perceived by another consciousness is named 'being-for-others'.[5] Despite the fact that the existence of others is seen as an essential condition of existence for the consciousness, the existence of others in the world is in fact one of the major limitations on individual freedom which *Being and Nothingness* concedes. The natural desire of the consciousness, according to Sartre, is to attempt to possess the world around it; through the mastery of the 'look', the consciousness bestows meaning on the inert world about it, and it is unwilling to brook the presence of another for-itself who not only competes in the bestowal of meaning but threatens to convert the consciousness itself into an object, through the power of its own look. The basic relation of consciousnesses is thus conflictual.

Being and Nothingness is essentially an *ontological* essay — that is, it attempts to lay a philosophical basis for the *existence* of freedom. A moral dimension does arise from the notion that we are only authentic when we recognise our own freedom and set up our own project, but *Being and Nothingness* has nothing to say about what the content of that project should be. In the essays which Beauvoir wrote in the early 1940s she took up the concept of existential freedom, as set out in *Being and Nothingness*, and explored it both for its moral potential and in order to develop the ways in which relations between consciousnesses could be something other than conflictual. In 'Idéalisme moral et réalisme politique' (Moral Idealism and Political Realism, published in 1945 in *Les Temps*

Modernes), for example, she tried to show that morality is not a collection of universal imperatives but a constituent element of our every action. In the sense that any action is designed to bring about an aim, the individual engaged in action necessarily posits his or her aim as good. New values will arise for the individual from each new action and new situation. This view of morality shows the traditional dichotomy between idealism on the one hand and realism on the other to be false, since morality arises from the reality of action. It also vitiates the traditional conflict of ends and means; means are not just the mechanics of bringing about a desired aim, but are themselves invested with meaning. They will affect the end, just as the end will dictate the means; ends and means form an indissoluble whole.

The authentic individual project will derive, then, not from any externally created values, but from the individual's reflection and action. It will necessarily take into account the basic fact of individual freedom. In this perspective, action by the oppressed or the enslaved in pursuance of improvements of their situation is not seen by Beauvoir as being just about the results that might be obtained, but as an affirmation of the individual's power to achieve that aim. Thus the achievements of the 1789 Revolution, she argues, would not have had the same meaning had they been granted by the king.

What can we do or should we do about others who are not in a position to exercise their freedom? In *Pyrrhus et Cinéas* (1944), Beauvoir points to the difficulties of helping others. Since only the individual can choose, and invest his or her project with meaning, we can never help anyone fix their aims, and we can only even attempt to help them achieve those aims if we are perfectly sure that we act as they intend.[6] Both the themes of morality and the question of our relation with others are raised in Beauvoir's longest existentialist essay, *The Ethics of Ambiguity* (1947). Like the earlier essays, it argues that 'morality is the triumph of freedom' (TEA p. 64, my translation). It introduces a cautious distinction, however, between freedom and power. Whereas my freedom is infinite, my power may be limited. If I find myself, for example, faced by a locked door, my freedom simply consists of deciding what to do about it. I can always retain my freedom, Beauvoir argues, if I regard obstacles as giving new and different possibilities to my future. The existence of others is clearly a possible obstacle, but Beauvoir takes up a positive attitude towards this:

to be free does not mean having the power to do absolutely anything; it means being able to go beyond the situation towards an open future; the existence of other freedoms is a defining factor of my situation and is even the condition of my own freedom. (TEA p. 131, my translation)

Even though, therefore, it is unjustifiable in general to intervene in another's project, we must intervene in the case of someone whose freedom has been blocked, because freedom is not an individual but a universal value.

The positive note struck here by Beauvoir is also evident in her whole definition of the 'ambiguity' of the individual's situation in the world. This situation is defined as ambiguous for two reasons: first because the consciousness sees itself as subject, in control of the universe which it takes as its object, and yet paradoxically the consciousness constantly experiences the fact of being viewed by other consciousnesses as object. Secondly, because the consciousness, the for-itself, constantly yearns towards an impossible synthesis with the in-itself, towards a state in which it would gain the reassuring fixity of objects whilst still retaining its freedom. It is this impossible desire which led Sartre, at the end of *Being and Nothingness*, to describe man as a 'useless passion'. Beauvoir comments directly on this statement on the last page of *The Blood of Others*, where she writes: 'if only I dedicate myself to defend that supreme good (. . .) Freedom — then my passion will not have been in vain' (BO p. 240). In *The Ethics of Ambiguity*, she characterises the constant movement of the consciousness towards the in-itself not as a useless failure, but as the triumphant movement of the unveiling of meaning. To take a further example from the fiction, the opening pages of *She Came to Stay* in which Françoise walks the dark corridors of the theatre are an eloquent demonstration of the triumph and excitement which the power of the for-itself to bestow meaning on the world around it holds for Beauvoir. Equally, the existence of others becomes more than an obstacle; in the same novel she shows, through the relationship of Françoise and Pierre, the possibility of 'reciprocity' between human beings: 'in the moment that you acknowledge my consciousness, you know that I acknowledge yours too. That makes all the difference' (SCS translation adapted, p. 303).

When Beauvoir came to write the third volume of her autobiography in the 1960s, her position on morality and freedom had changed considerably. She criticises her own essays for their lack of historical context and materialism, and points out that her abandonment of individualism had not advanced very far.[7] 'I was in error', she wrote in *Force of Circumstance* (1963) 'when I thought I could define a morality independent of a social context' (p. 76). Nevertheless, the distinction made in these essays between freedom and power, and Beauvoir's concern with the responsibility of individuals to involve themselves in the liberation struggles of others, shows that the notion of the 'situation' had begun to bite. As Sartre and Beauvoir became increasingly aware of the circumstances which might hinder a given individual from assuming his or her freedom, they developed the notion of the situation — the sum of the factors with which the individual has to engage in the bid to assert his or her freedom and create meaning. By the end of the 1940s Sartre had begun work on his study of Genet in which, moving much closer to both Marxism and psychoanalysis, he posited the situation as strongly limiting individual freedom.

Beauvoir herself, meanwhile, had discovered from 1946 onward a 'situation' which exerted a limitation and oppression of the individual beyond anything she had previously contemplated: the situation of being a woman. Since women are often described as being 'unfeminine' or 'unwomanly', says Beauvoir in her introduction to *The Second Sex*, it would seem that the female biological function is not enough to define what society means by 'woman'. What then, she asks, does this label mean? The whole of *The Second Sex* is really an answer to this question, but the short answer is this: 'woman', in the sense of the social construction of femininity, is a situation.[8] In 1946 Beauvoir began work not on the biology which eventually figured as the opening topic of the final published volume, but on the myths. Man, she saw, had invented 'woman', had invented Eve the temptress and Mary the holy virgin, had invented woman as idol and servant, had invented in fact every image of woman that might conceivably serve him. Man had invented woman for man. Spurred on by the unexpected richness of the mystifications she was uncovering, Beauvoir began to enlarge her study of women's situation beyond its constitution through myth: history, biology, literature, education, socialisation within the family, marriage, maternity, all were investigated for their contribution to Beauvoir's primary thesis, that woman is not born but made.

Throughout each of the sections a single constant appears: whether she considers the way the female sex as a whole has been theorised about (as for example in psychoanalytic theory), or whether she considers the way an individual woman relates to an individual man, Beauvoir discovers that women do not accede to the subjectivity which is the crux of freedom for existentialism. Woman is cast out from the reign of the subjective consciousness, and 'finds herself living in a world where men compel her to assume the status of the Other' (TSS p. 29). Women are posed as object, not subject, as deviation, not the norm. Worse still, women themselves connive at this situation. Succumbing to the temptation which all consciousness experiences to flee their freedom, women's story is often the story of their failure to assert themselves as subject and to take up the burden of freedom. In the existentialist moral perspective which Beauvoir is applying, this state of affairs means that women are cut off from the possibility of creating their own authentic values, cut off from any justification of their existence. Though society bears a heavy responsibility for the encouragement it offers women to remain in this situation, it is in the hands of women themselves, in Beauvoir's view, to bring about change.

It is already apparent that *The Second Sex* does not err on the side of over-indulgence towards women. It does not, either, offer any support to the idea of 'female difference', except in so far as this is socially constructed and can be changed. This becomes clear from the section of the book devoted to biology, which has proved one of the most difficult for modern feminists. In it, Beauvoir conducts an investigation of women's anatomy, to reach two conclusions. The first is that women's bodies are organised to a high degree as a direct function of our reproductive role. A significant impact on our daily lives and on our behavioural characteristics is made by our reproductive cycle. The second conclusion is that, important as these biological effects may be in the constitution of women's situation, nevertheless they cannot possibly be used as a justification for the hierarchy of the sexes and in no way pre-determine women to play the role of the Other.

The problem with this section is that the language and emphases of the argument tend to weight the first conclusion rather than the second. Women's bodies emerge as a problematic, crisis-ridden element of their situation, and an element, moreover, for which Beauvoir seems to have a personal distaste.[9] This distaste is also apparent in the section on maternity. Pregnancy seems to Beauvoir to be a positive incitement to women to sink into the passive state of being-in-itself. After the birth, the mother–child relationship is described not as a source of joy and fulfilment but as a battleground of tensions and conflicts. The only answer Beauvoir can see to these problems is for children to be brought up collectively.

The role of mother, like that of wife, is seen by Beauvoir as part of the mythology used to confine women to the home and prevent them from exercising their freedom. Love is a great danger for women, as is particularly apparent from the portrait Beauvoir draws of the woman who makes a cult of love (the *amoureuse*). Knowing that she has failed in the attempt to be autonomous, the *amoureuse* appoints a man as her saviour and aspires to authentic existence not directly for herself but vicariously, through a union with a male consciousness which she does perceive as subject. This perverse struggle towards authenticity is both severely castigated and warmly sympathised with by Beauvoir: 'there are few crimes that entail worse punishment than the generous fault of putting oneself entirely in another's hands' (TSS p. 677). It is difficult not to agree with Dorothy Kaufmann-McCall when she argues that this section betrays Beauvoir's personal struggle with the temptations she so graphically describes.[10]

The roles women are called on to play are thus fraught with danger, for Beauvoir. It is they, more than any biological or psychological determinism, which create women's situation, block their freedom and encourage them to remain locked in femininity. The only way out, for Beauvoir, is the refusal of these roles; in concrete terms this means taking up paid work outside the home and fighting for the liberalisation of contraception (not made freely available in France until the 1970s). In the longer term Beauvoir puts her faith in socialism as the means by which a society will be created in which both men and women could be free. There were problems with both of these solutions, and Beauvoir later abandoned her position on the automatic benefits of socialism for women. Her position on women and 'femininity' however, was not to change much. Far from being the key to a new way forward for humanity, the traditional values and roles of women seem to be viewed by Beauvoir as something to be cast off with all possible speed; the future lay in economic independence, in paid work outside the home, in the assumption of freedom. In short, femininity is a form of bad faith, and the future lies in being more like men. Feminists have pointed out that whereas Beauvoir's new woman would wrest masculine values from the male preserve, there is no talk in *The Second Sex* of change in men or of men adopting any traditional feminine values.[11] When the partisans of 'female difference' emerged in the 1970s, with their emphasis on the unconscious and on the search for a feminine language, Beauvoir continued to argue that it is 'almost antifeminist to say that there is a feminine nature which expresses itself differently'.[12]

It can be seen then, that though the discovery of women's situation was a completely new departure for Beauvoir, that her study of women was inscribed within the existentialist perspectives which she had espoused earlier. Its approach, with its dismissal of Freud and bare reference to Marx (though she spends some time on a refutation of Engels' *Origins of the Family*), still reflects a deep suspicion of theories which she regarded as deterministic. Nevertheless, as Toril Moi has argued, *The Second Sex* does not try to account for women's situation purely in the ontological terms of *Being and Nothingness*; there is a materialist emphasis in the analysis which takes women's situation as partially constituted by male power structures exercised through the historical and social dimensions which had been notably missing from both Sartre and Beauvoir's earlier essays.[13] By the end of the 1940s Sartre, politically in the wilderness after the failure of his attempt to work with a political grouping tied neither to the Soviet Union nor to the United States, had begun re-reading Marx in an attempt to find a conciliation between the subjective basis of existentialism and Marxist materialism. In 1952 he began working closely with the French Communist Party, not so much because of any change in his thinking or in the practice of the Communist Party, but because of a growing inability to stomach what he saw as the hypocrisy of the bourgeoisie, abrogating its own humanism and democratic principles in events such as the Henri Martin affair.[14]

Though Beauvoir had not participated in Sartre's political activities, she had been influenced in the period of the Cold War by her visits to the United States, from 1947 onwards. Her visits convinced her that democracy in America was little more than a sham, and she was shocked by American racism, conformism and anti-intellectualism. She was also deeply disturbed by the American 'happiness ideology' — the false optimism which refuses to admit that everything is not for the best in the best of worlds — and which she denounced in its French form in *Les Belles Images* twenty years later.[15] She had been reluctant to follow Sartre down the path of Marxism and the abandonment of morality, but in 1952 came into contact with a new influence, that of Claude Lanzmann, a member of the *Temps Modernes* team 17 years younger than Beauvoir, with whom she became closely involved in July 1952. Lanzmann, who strongly approved Sartre's move towards the Communist Party, challenged Beauvoir 'to give explanations when I had been used to asking for them; every day, I was put in the position of having to challenge my most spontaneous reactions, in other words, my oldest prejudices. Little by little, he wore away my resistance, I liquidated my ethical idealism and ended up by adopting Sartre's point of view for my own' (FOC p. 302).[16] Though she never became a Marxist in the strict sense of the term, she adopted a broadly Marxist framework for her article on right-wing ideology written for *Les Temps Modernes* in 1954, and Marxism left its mark on her view of alienation and exploitation in the capitalist system.[17]

In 1956 she published an enthusiastic essay on China, written after a six-week visit there in 1955. However, it was the colonial wars of the 1950s which effectively pushed Beauvoir into political activism. In 1954, when the French were defeated by the Viet Minh at Dien Bien Phu, Beauvoir felt 'radically cut off from the great mass of my compatriots (. . .). For years I had been opposed to the official governments of France; but I had never before been in a position where I found myself rejoicing over a defeat' (FOC pp. 314–15). Then came the Algerian War, from 1954 onwards. Reading all the articles and dossiers on the French atrocities in Algeria sent to *Les Temps Modernes*, Beauvoir became revolted by the indifference of the French general public to the tortures their army was carrying out on their behalf. She involved herself in meetings, petitions, speeches; she acted with Gisèle Halimi in defence of Djamila Boupacha, a young Algerian member of the FLN who had been tortured by the French. When peace eventually came, in 1962, she wrote in *Force of Circumstance* that victory 'came too late to console us for the price it had cost' (FOC p. 658). The result of the Algerian War was radical for Beauvoir's thinking: 'the horror my class inspires in me has been brought to white heat by the Algerian War' she wrote in 1963 (FOC p. 665).

Sartre had broken off his working relationship with the Communists in 1956, disgusted by the reaction of the French Party to the Soviet invasion of Hungary. He and Beauvoir were resigned to political isolation, and Beauvoir had accepted once and for all the existence of horror and tragedy in the world. She concluded *Force of Circumstance*, the volume of her autobiography completed in 1963 (and with a suitably materialist title — literally from the French, 'The Force of Things'), with the statement that looking back on her childhood, and on the promises which she had made to herself then about the life she would lead, she had been tricked ('j'ai été flouée'). Taken up by the press as a confession of the disappointments of old age, this phrase in fact was designed to indicate the gap Beauvoir perceived between the expectations of a happy world which a privileged bourgeois childhood had led her to have, and the reality that had been kept from her, the fact 'that the world is a dreadful place, and that one cannot be happy in isolation'.[18] The diseases of malnutrition, hunger, torture and massacres were not part of her upbringing, but by the 1950s they composed an essential element of her world.

Beauvoir was 55 when she completed *Force of Circumstance* in 1963, but her radicalisations were by no means complete. The political isolation in which she and Sartre found themselves was suddenly broken by the events of May 1968. They supported the students protesting against hierarchical subordination and the power of the technocrats; their revolt seemed to Beauvoir and Sartre to be a new form of revolution in which the impetus was not the demand for material goods but for power. The students, Beauvoir writes in *All Said and Done*, 'saw that in our dehumanised world the individual is defined by the object he produces or the function he fulfills: they rebelled against this state of affairs and they claimed the right to decide for themselves what part they should play' (ASD pp. 463–64). The groups of students and young teachers whom they supported, largely of Maoist inspiration, gave Beauvoir and Sartre a new political impetus and allowed them to return to the notion of morality as action, which they had tried to abandon in the 1950s.

In a sense, they were repeating the political commitment of the early 1950s, but this time to a position left of the Communist Party. Sartre tried to create a direct link between the intellectual and the masses, putting his skills at the service of the Lens miners or the Renault car factory workers. Beauvoir investigated an 'accident' which had taken place at the Rochel factory in Méru, to the northwest of Paris, in which three women had been killed and 55 badly burned. The management of the factory had been so negligent of safety matters that Beauvoir concluded it could not be called an accident, and denounced the nature of 'bourgeois justice' which could give the factory owner a one-year suspended sentence.[19] During the early 1970s both Beauvoir and Sartre supported banned revolutionary papers, notably *La Cause du Peuple* and *L'Idiot International*, of which Beauvoir assumed the directorship for a few months. In a letter to *Le Monde* of 19 October 1970,

Beauvoir wrote that the system 'only tolerates news which serves it (. . .). Despite the courts, I say with my comrades of *L'Idiot International* that we shall pursue the combat for freedom through the combat for the freedom of the press'.[20] In *All Said and Done* (1972), Beauvoir declares, 'In spite of certain reservations (particularly my lack of blind faith in Mao's China) I do sympathise with the Maoists. They assert themselves as revolutionary socialists in contrast to the revisionism of the USSR and the new bureaucracy set up by the Trotskyists: I share their rejection of these things' (ASD p. 478).

The end of the 1960s and the beginning of the 1970s were an extremely active period in Beauvoir's life. Quite apart from the 1968 radicalisation, Beauvoir had opened her eyes to a new 'situation' — that of old age, which she decided to study in an essay which would be 'the counterpart of *The Second Sex*, but dealing with old people' (ASD p. 146). *Old Age (La Vieillesse)*, published in French in 1970, is indeed constructed along lines similar to *The Second Sex*, investigating in a first part how biology, anthropology, history, sociology and literature construct old age, before looking at the way the individual experiences old age, how he or she interiorises their relationship with time, with the body, with others. The thesis from which the study begins, that old age is above all a socio-cultural phenomenon, the meaning of which varies according to the social context, is also parallel to *The Second Sex*. However, *Old Age* has a much stronger social and economic emphasis than *The Second Sex*, and a much more highly politicised approach; in her introduction, Beauvoir argues that the deplorable circumstances of the old in modern Western society owe nothing to chance — they are the inevitable consequence of the way in which capitalist society exploits its workers. The living conditions of the old are the proof that reforms are of little use, 'for it is the exploitation of the workers, the pulverisation of society, and the utter poverty of a culture confined to the privileged, educated few that leads to this kind of dehumanised old age' (OA p. 13). The treatment meted out to the elderly 'makes it clear that everything has to be reconsidered, recast from the very beginning' (OA pp. 13–14).

Beauvoir herself was an excellent example of her own argument that a far more privileged old age is available to an intellectual, and to the rich, than to the manual worker who is deprived of the means (financial, cultural, often physical in terms of health) of making use of the freedom theoretically made available to the retired. In her sixties Beauvoir remained as engaged as ever in the struggles of her times. In the early 1970s Beauvoir found herself approached by members of the newly formed Mouvement de Libération des Femmes (MLF, the French women's movement) and asked to join their campaign on abortion. The contact was decisive; more than twenty years after publishing *The Second Sex*, Simone de Beauvoir publicly declared herself to be a feminist. She told her friend and fellow militant Alice Schwarzer in an interview in *Le Nouvel Observateur* in 1972:

> At the end of *The Second Sex*, I said that I was not a feminist because I thought that the solution to women's problems would be a socialist development of society. I meant, by feminist, fighting for women's demands independently from the class struggle. Today, I would keep the same definition: I would call feminist women or even men who fight to change women's situation, of course in liaison with the class struggle, but nevertheless outside it, without totally subordinating this change to change in society. And I would say that today I am a feminist of this kind. Because I have realised that, before the socialism of which we dream comes about, we must fight for the concrete situation of women. And besides, I have realised that, even in socialist countries, this equality has not been achieved. Women must therefore take their future into their own hands.[21]

Campaigning on abortion, contraception and battered women, involving herself in the Bobigny trial of a seventeen-year-old girl on trial for abortion, becoming president of Choisir (campaigning on abortion and contraception) and of the Ligue du Droit des Femmes (set up to combat discrimination and fight for women's rights), setting up a regular column in *Les Temps Modernes* on everyday sexism ('le sexisme ordinaire') and launching with other Marxist feminists the journal *Questions féministes*, Beauvoir engaged in a feminist practice which would scarcely have been possible in the isolation in which she found herself at the time of writing *The Second Sex*.

However, it was indeed the practice rather than the theory which had basically changed, as some of Beauvoir's dialogues with the new feminists revealed. Her dialogue with Betty Friedan (in which Friedan is left rather comically gasping) left no doubt as to Beauvoir's distance from the kind of reformist position adopted by Friedan; emphasising the 'very strong relationship between the economic struggle and the feminist movement', Beauvoir declared that a few token women in high places would do nothing at all to bring about change: 'if society is to be changed, it must be done not from the top, but from the bottom'. To Friedan's enthusiasm for wages for housework, Beauvoir replied, 'No woman should be authorised to stay at home to raise her children. Society should be totally different. Women should not have that choice, precisely because if there is such a choice, too many women will make that one.' Arguing that 'as long as the family and the myth of the family and the myth of maternity and the maternal instinct are not destroyed, women will still be oppressed', Beauvoir concludes that childcare and housework should not be regarded as a private but as a community responsibility. Instead of focusing on the joys of motherhood, we should be focusing on the child: 'The liberation of children is a very interesting area. Now, the child becomes the object of the parents.'[22]

Two years later in an interview with Alice Jardine (carried out in 1977 but published in 1979), Beauvoir remarked that the Friedan interview was an example of the 'we want to be just like men' attitude: 'that is, men as they are today, when in truth we need to change the society itself, men as well as women, to change everything'. Feminism, Beauvoir told Jardine, 'is one way of attacking society as it now exists'.[23] Giving women equality with men would of necessity, Beauvoir thinks, revolutionise society in its entirety and change the nature of relations between people. Thus, feminism for Beauvoir in the 1970s remains closely tied to the social revolution she had evoked at the end of *The Second Sex*, even if her idea of how change is to come about has become far more voluntarist and specifically feminist.

The series of interviews which Alice Schwarzer carried out with Beauvoir between 1972 and 1982 are an excellent guide to Beauvoir's thinking on feminism over a ten-year period going up to within four years of her death. In 1972 Beauvoir states firmly that women's liberation is tied to the class struggle, though she admits freely that she is unsure how the two forms of oppression can be articulated on a theoretical level. The suppression of capitalism is a necessary, but not sufficient, preliminary to women's liberation; the suppression of capitalism is not the suppression of the patriarchy, as long as the family structure remains. 'I think that the family must be suppressed.'[24] By 1976, Beauvoir is less certain of the theoretical primacy of the class struggle, not only in relation to women but in relation to other oppressed groups such as immigrant workers or regionalists. There is also some change perceptible in her attitudes to men, to sexuality and to language. The end of *The Second Sex* had looked forward to a glorious era of co-operation of equals between men and women, and early in the Schwarzer interviews Beauvoir makes it clear that she is personally keen to work with men on feminist problems. By 1976 she is impatient in a discussion with Sartre at his refusal to accept that men cannot be admitted to women's groups, and she describes all heterosexual relations as a potential trap for women. If she were to rewrite her memoirs in 1976, she says, she would 'like to tell women how I have lived my sexuality, because this is not an individual but a political issue. At the time I didn't do it because I hadn't understood the size and importance of the issue.'[25] On the question of language, Beauvoir remains constant in her rejection of the search for a specifically feminine writing, but concedes that language has been tainted with patriarchal elements which it is important to remove.

In the 1980s Beauvoir remained a controversial figure with the publication of her book on the last ten years of Sartre's life (*La Cérémonie des Adieux*, 1981, translated as *Adieux: A Farewell to Sartre*) and her edition of Sartre's letters to her (*Lettres au Castor et à quelques autres*, 1983). In an interview in *Libération* in March 1983, commenting on the posthumous publication of Sartre's *Cahiers pour une morale*, Beauvoir gives her view on morality: in an alienated society, such as our own, it is impossible to be moral. The only possible moral attitude is to seek to act in such a way as to create a world in which inequality would not exist, in which morality would become possible. 'Of course this is utopian, but it's in the right direction.'[26] Simone de Beauvoir died on 14 April 1986, aged 78.

Notes

1. French women were not given the right to vote until 1944.
2. For Sartre's letters to Beauvoir during the war, see Sartre, *Lettres au Castor* (1983).
3. The book was dedicated to her, as was Sartre's second major philosophical tome, published 17 years later, *Critique de la raison dialectique* (1960).
4. In a 1982 interview with Alice Schwarzer, Beauvoir points to these differences of opinion and gives as an example her opposition, in discussions with Sartre prior to the publication of *Being and Nothingness*, to the weight he gave at that time to the notion of freedom as opposed to the weight of the situation. See Schwarzer, *Simone de Beauvoir aujourd'hui*,

p. 114. See also Margaret Simons' discussion in 'Beauvoir and Sartre: The Philosophical Relationship' (1987).

5. A detailed explanation of these concepts is to be found in Mary Warnock, *The Philosophy of Sartre* (1965) and in A. C. Danto, *Jean-Paul Sartre* (1975).

6. See *The Prime of Life*, pp. 549–50, where Beauvoir also makes it clear that she used her essay to try to 'reconcile Sartre's ideas with the views I had upheld against him in various lengthy discussions', and *Force of Circumstance*, pp. 75–77.

7. Full accounts of these essays can be found in Terry Keefe, *Simone de Beauvoir: A Study of Her Writings* (1983) and in Anne Whitmarsh, *Simone de Beauvoir and The Limits of Commitment* (1981).

8. In the following discussion the term 'woman' (as opposed to 'women') is used to denote the social construction of femininity.

9. See Mary Evans, *Simone de Beauvoir: A Feminist Mandarin* (1985), p. 66, for a discussion of Beauvoir's attitude towards biology. Evans comments that 'women's biology is only problematic to men' (p. 64). See also the excellent article by Dorothy Kaufmann-McCall, 'Simone de Beauvoir, *The Second Sex* and Jean-Paul Sartre' (1979), which argues that Sartre's influence is heavily apparent in Beauvoir's rejection of the female flesh.

10. See Kaufmann-McCall (1979), pp. 216–21.

11. See for example Evans, *Simone de Beauvoir: A Feminist Mandarin*, p. 57; and Judith Okely, *Simone de Beauvoir. A Re-Reading* (1986), p. 98. Okely's chapter, 'Re-reading *The Second Sex*', is a stimulating one which offers an anthropological angle on Beauvoir's essay.

12. From Alice Jardine's 'Interview with Simone de Beauvoir' (1979), p. 230.

13. See Toril Moi's 'Existentialism and Feminism: the Rhetoric of Biology in *The Second Sex*' (1986). Focusing on Beauvoir's sections on biology, Moi shows that Beauvoir silently recognises the body as a material constitutive element of human consciousness — thus in effect denying the Sartrean categorisation of the body as for-itself, as pure facticity.

14. See *Sartre. Un film réalisé par A. Astruc et Michel Contat* (1977), pp. 90–91, where Sartre points to the Martin affair, to the demonstrations against the visit to France of the American General Ridgeway and to the arrest of one of the demonstrators Jacques Duclos in 1952 as determining factors. He also declares that reading Henri Guillemin's *Le Coup du 2 décembre*, a book that brought together letters and other documents of members of the right wing who prepared the coup, had 'showed me what a sewer the bourgeois heart can be' (my translation, p. 91). The filmscript is a good introduction to the development of Sartre's ideas over his lifetime.

15. See Beauvoir's *Amérique au jour le jour*, pp. 30–31, where she describes the 'smile propaganda', and p. 69, where she argues that 'many things would be different for Americans if they would only admit that unhappiness is not *a priori* a crime' (my translation).

16. Beauvoir's relationship with Lanzmann also awoke in her an idea of what it meant to be a Jew — in later years she showed considerable sympathy with the Jewish people, writing, for example, the preface to

J.-F. Steiner's *Treblinka* in 1966, and to Lanzmann's *Shoah* in 1985. In 1975 she accepted the Jerusalem Prize, in order to mark her solidarity with Israel.

17. When I asked Beauvoir in 1985 what Marxism had represented for her she replied:

> it has been very important, it has left its mark on my view of the world on exploitation, on alienation, ideas which I remain close to and which result in my rebellion against all regimes based on the exploitation, the alienation of human beings. But of course, I am not a Marxist in the strict sense of the term.

18. Interview with Caroline Moorhead (1974), p. 11.

19. See her article in *J'Accuse*, 15 February 1971, and reprinted in Francis and Gontier (1979), pp. 475–81.

20. Letter reprinted in Francis and Gontier (1979), p. 88. My translation.

21. *Le Nouvel Observateur*, 14 February 1972, pp. 47–54. My translation. Interview reprinted in Schwarzer, *Simone de Beauvoir Aujourd'hui*, pp. 27–51.

22. Friedan, 'Sex, Society and the Female Dilemma' (1975), pp. 14, 18, 19, 56.

23. Jardine, 'Interview with Simone de Beauvoir' (1979), pp. 226–27.

24. Schwarzer, *Simone de Beauvoir Aujourd'hui*, p. 41.

25. Ibid., pp. 81, 87.

26. *Libération*, 30 March 1983, p. 27. My translation. This position is almost identical with the one expressed by Robert in *The Mandarins* in 1954, but rejected by Henri. See my Chapter 5.

2

She Came to Stay

'I had written a real book (. . .) I had become, overnight, a real writer. I could not contain my joy' (POL p. 556). After all the manuscripts which she had abandoned or judged not worthy of submission to a publisher, after the rejection of her short stories, the publication of *She Came to Stay* in 1943 at last provided Beauvoir with concrete evidence that she had achieved her ambition to become a writer. She had spent four years on the manuscript. Begun in 1937, it was the product of the early years of the Second World War and of the period immediately preceding it in which Beauvoir's stubborn refusal to countenance the idea of war gradually gave way by the spring of 1939 to a sense of shame at her own egotistic individualism in the face of the fate of Hitler's victims; the writing also covered the period of Sartre's mobilisation and imprisonment, and the German occupation of France. The novel was eventually completed in the summer of 1941 at a time when Beauvoir and Sartre were actively engaged in an attempt to form a Resistance group.

When Beauvoir submitted her manuscript to the publishers, in October 1941, Sartre was only just beginning his monumental *Being and Nothingness*, yet in the end *Being and Nothingness* (dedicated to Beauvoir) was published a month or so before *She Came to Stay*, in the summer of 1943. The two works have a number of themes in common, and the coincidence of their publication dates has often led to the novel being treated as above all a fictional demonstration of some of the main tenets of *Being and Nothingness*. Whilst the fact that the novel was completed before Sartre's essay was begun establishes that this view of the novel is, in literal terms, impossible, it has nevertheless to be said that Sartre's essay was the end product of a system of ideas which Sartre had been elaborating and discussing with Beauvoir since 1933.[1] A philosopher by training, Beauvoir was inclined to seek a philosophical explanation of most phenomena, and the reading of the novel in terms of *Being and Nothingness*, carried out by philosophers such as Hazel Barnes, has its attractions; however, it by no means exhausts the text.[2]

In giving the novel an epigraph from Hegel ('Each consciousness pursues the death of the other'; unfortunately omitted in the English translation) Beauvoir clearly directs the reader to interpret her depiction of a triangular relationship as an examination of the problem of the threat which the existence of other consciousnesses in the world poses to our own need to affirm ourselves as consciousness. Yet the trio described in the novel was not invented by Beauvoir to exemplify this existentialist dictum; on the contrary, the central experiences of the story draw directly on Sartre and Beauvoir's attempts to set up a trio with Beauvoir's former pupil Olga Kosakievicz, to whom the novel is dedicated.[3] Beauvoir was not, therefore, dealing with abstractions but with the emotions of a crisis which she herself had experienced; the epigraph directing the reader towards the metaphysical is undermined by the more coded dedication to Olga, signalling (privately in 1943, publicly after the appearance of *The Prime of Life* in 1960) the emotional crisis at the origin of the text. Within the narrative itself Françoise adopts philosophical rather than emotional terms in her analysis of her reactions to the trio (the word 'hatred' is used, but 'jealousy' is largely avoided); however, the reader is often tempted to interpret in psychological terms. This oscillation between the demonstration of philosophical perceptions and the playing out of a psychological crisis forms an ambiguity central to the text. At times, the philosophical construction appears to be a sophisticated attempt to explicate and rationalise a highly charged psycho-sexual conflict.

The history of the trio is viewed largely through the eyes of Françoise Miquel, the 'Beauvoir' figure. Beauvoir was acutely conscious of questions of narrative technique; she was enthusiastic about the writings of Hemingway, Dos Passos and Faulkner, published in the late 1920s and 1930s, and was particularly interested in their use of new narrative techniques marked by the influence of the cinema and by behaviourism.[4] Hemingway's use of narrative modes privileging the character's viewpoint was particularly well suited to the existentialist emphasis on the individual consciousness as the basis of all meaning and value. In the spring of 1939, when Beauvoir was working on her novel, Sartre published his famous attack on François Mauriac in which he claims that Mauriac has no real claim to be a novelist because he uses a godlike omniscient narrator who overtly manipulates and judges the characters, switching in and out of the characters' point of view at will, summarising their speech for them and making the reader a party to information to which the characters are denied access.[5] Many of these points, inspired by the experimentation of the American writers whom Sartre and Beauvoir admired, appeared new and revolutionary.

Taking to heart the precept that technique is a function of the moral and metaphysical stance of the writer, Beauvoir sought for her novel a technique which would posit the characters as free beings, in charge (at least in appearance) of their own destinies. In fact, *She Came to Stay* is the only one of Beauvoir's novels not to include sections of first-person narrative voiced by a character; the whole text is instead kept within the remit of an external narrator, but the presence of this narrator is kept relatively covert. Though the narration is voiced in the third person, it is always focused through the characters and purports to describe only the views and perceptions of the character acting as focus. Summaries of events are avoided, and there are frequent long dialogues in which the reader has direct access to the character's voice. However, there is also an extensive use of free indirect speech which inevitably involves an element of distancing from the characters and from what they can be supposed to have actually said or thought. Time is strictly divided into chunks of characters' consciousness, with no overt attempt at filling in the gaps. Since Françoise is the character acting as focus for the narrative in 14½ of the 18 chapters, it is her perceptions which largely shape the text; however, there is a switch of focus to Elisabeth, in 2½ chapters (pp. 62–85, 213–24, 380–84), and to Gerbert for a brief 20 pages (pp. 252–72). The intention behind these switches of focus was to allow external views of Françoise, who otherwise would be seen by the reader only from the inside (in other words, only as being-for-itself, and never as being-for-others).[6] However, an interesting second effect of these changes is the creation of a narrative trio, Françoise – Gerbert – Elisabeth, which offers an intriguing double of the other trio, Françoise – Pierre – Xavière. Both trios consist of two women and a man, and both are the source and expression of Françoise's struggle towards self-assertion.

The first two chapters of the novel originally described Françoise's childhood and adolescence in the affluent sixteenth arrondissement of Paris, but Beauvoir removed them on Galli-mard's advice.[7] In doing so, she removed virtually the only parts of the text which posed the characters as social products, subject to the influences of family, educational institutions and social class. The virtual absence of these elements in the final text contributes strongly to the impression of the characters' freedom as they float on the margins of society, free of all domestic ties. Beauvoir declares herself to have been 'bowled over' in the 1930s by Dos Passos and his presentation in his trilogy *U.S.A.* of his characters both as individuals and as 'purely social phenomena' (POL p. 137); she describes how she and Sartre would amuse themselves by applying Dos Passos' techniques to descriptions of their own conversations (see POL p. 137). However, this element is strikingly absent from *She Came to Stay*, and the use of multiple narrative points of view is not exploited to introduce a social element.

The historical situation of the characters is kept similarly low-key throughout the greater part of the text, before suddenly assuming importance in the last chapter. The war, which formed the context of the actual writing of the book and which Françoise keeps at bay in her own mind for as long as possible, suddenly becomes a reality. Trapped in wartime Paris with the theatre closed and Pierre no longer beside her, Françoise sees only a void stretching into the future. She plunges into immanence, her life 'a flaccid substance into which she expected to sink at every step. The past alone retained reality, and it was in Xavière that the past was incarnate' (SCS p. 391). Windows are blacked out, curtains drawn over the café doors; the images of claustration present from the beginning of the novel intensify, suggesting the enclosure of the past and present, as well as those of the boundaries of the individual consciousness and of the emotional confines of the trio. The whole history of the trio and of Françoise's gradually mount-ing frustration, which eventually breaks out into destruction, can be read as an expression of the gathering sense of doom of 1937–39, and of the destruction on the horizon. In *The Prime of Life*, after describing the beginning of her work on *She Came to Stay*, Beauvoir writes, 'I now passed through one of the most depressing periods of my whole life. I refused to admit that war was even possible, let alone imminent. But it was no use my playing the ostrich; the growing perils all around crushed me beneath their weight' (POL p. 319). The obsession with the threat of an Olga or a Xavière can be seen as a way of playing the ostrich and refusing to deal with the greater threat of a war. In Beauvoir's later novels, historical realities figure more directly.

If social and historical pressures are conspicuous by their apparent absence, until exploding in the destruction of the murder, the characters are in contrast bound hand and foot by metaphysical and psychological constraints. The smooth and apparently solid edifice of the life which Françoise appears to have built for herself begins to crack with the arrival of the adolescent Xavière. Why is Xavière able to challenge Françoise's entire conception of herself and of her relationship with Pierre? A number of responses to this can be elicited from the text. In existentialist terms, Xavière is simply a representation of the implicit challenge that all other consciousnesses constitute to our own. We wish to see ourselves as pure subjectivity, sovereigns in a world in which other people are primarily objects in our own reference system. However, in certain circumstances, such as when we discover that we have been observed unawares, or when we see that another person is judging us, we become aware of our status as objects in the world of other people. We feel that our sovereign status at the centre of our own world is threatened.[8]

Françoise does not immediately perceive Xavière in these terms; on the contrary, she views Xavière as securely lodged in a subsidiary niche in Françoise's plans. Françoise will be the teacher and master of Xavière's new life in Paris, financing her and organising her social and cultural education, and assuming the kind of Pygmalion role which men traditionally play for women. It is only gradually that Françoise becomes aware of a solid core of resistance to her somewhat imperialistic projects; Xavière clearly demands more of her time than Françoise is willing to give, Xaviere shows signs of wishing to capture Pierre's attention for herself to the exclusion of Françoise, and Xavière undermines Françoise's value-system by refusing to respect Françoise's work or Françoise's scrupulous attempts to behave honestly and unselfishly. Xavière is endowed with a character ideally suited to her incarnation of the challenge of the 'other'; she is capricious, obstinate, egotistic and nihilistic. As a fully fledged individual, Xavière would be detestable, and perhaps insignificant — but she is not a fully fledged individual, has not crossed the threshold into adulthood. She poses the classic adolescent challenge to the adult world of Françoise.

In metaphysical terms, Xavière incarnates the challenge that any consciousness presents; in psychological terms she plays out with Françoise a drama akin to that of the adolescent girl's struggle with the mother, her attempt to secure the attention of the father figure, Pierre, for herself. Françoise in her turn (whom Beauvoir endows with her own mother's name) displays the classic mother's determination to view the adolescent as a child; to her, Xavière's head is 'almost like a small boy's' (SCS p. 12), and her eyes are 'the frank blue eyes of a child' (SCS p. 28). All the warmest scenes between the two women in the early part of the book depend on Xavière adopting the role of 'no more than a fond ingenuous little girl' (SCS p. 33). When Françoise promises to arrange Xavière's removal to Paris, Xavière abandons herself on Françoise's shoulder, 'looking at her, with eyes shining, parted lips; mollified, yielding; she had abandoned herself completely. Henceforth Françoise would lead her through life' (SCS p. 30). Here, the domination which Françoise seeks, and the childlike trust and admiration which she asks of Xavière, are clearly evident.

Yet, however much Françoise may wish to see Xavière as a child, she is increasingly forced to recognise that there is also a more adult Xavière, a 'supple, feminine Xavière' (SCS p. 47). She cannot help but see that 'the blue dress fitted revealingly over a slender, rounded body, and the delicate youthful face was framed by sleek hair' (SCS p. 47). The significant element of this pseudo-oedipal triangle comes precisely from the hesitations and the ambiguous attitudes of the adolescent Xavière to the adult female role which she will shortly be called upon to assume. The portrait of female adolescence which Beauvoir gives in *The Second Sex* (1949) seems to have been strongly influenced by her relationship with Olga Kosakievicz, and by her fictional portrayal of Olga in Xavière.[9] In *The Second Sex* adolescence is presented as a crucial period in which the girl, who has until this point considered herself as an autonomous individual, perceives that with her passage into womanhood will come a subsidiary social status and an expectation that she will adopt a docile behaviour pattern. She oscillates between desire and disgust, between independence and submission:

This is the trait that characterizes the young girl and gives us the key to most of her behaviour; she does not accept the destiny assigned to her by nature and by society; and yet she does not repudiate it completely; she is too much divided against herself to join battle with the world. (*The Second Sex*, p. 375)

Beauvoir underlines the ambivalent attitude of the adolescent girl to her body and sexuality. Discovering that she is an object in the world, the girl may devote a narcissistic cult to her body but simultaneously be revolted by the idea of male desire. Beauvoir sees this attitude as being frequently expressed through self-mutilation: 'The young girl may gash her thigh with a razor blade, burn herself with a cigarette (. . .) These sado-masochistic performances are at once an anticipation of the sexual experience and a protest against it' (TSS p. 377). The whole portrait of the adolescent girl in *The Second Sex* is thus built on the girl's attitude to sexuality and to the feminine roles which she will shortly be expected to play. In *She Came to Stay*, Xavière is constructed in exactly the same way. Oscillating between childhood and womanhood, Xavière alternately feels a violent repulsion for the expression of bodily needs such as sleep — 'The very thought of being subject to natural needs disgusts me' (SCS p. 59) — and preens her body in the sanctuary of her room, in which she is the 'supreme deity' (SCS p. 132). Her unease about sexuality is displayed in her interest in all ambivalent forms of sexuality (for example the androgynous personage living in their hotel) and in her violent reaction of self-disgust to her first night of lovemaking with Gerbert. Beauvoir's theory about the practice of self-mutilation as a means of translating unease about the body and sexuality can be perceived at work in the novel in the long episode where Xavière burns her hand with a cigarette in a nightclub. The episode is particularly interesting for the way in which it brings together the themes of adolescence, emotional and sexual conflict and metaphysical rationalisation.

Xavière burns herself slowly and deliberately, in an intense moment of self-absorption. She presses the cigarette to her hand 'with a bitter smile curling her lips. It was an intimate, solitary smile, like the smile of a half-wit; the voluptuous tortured smile of a woman possessed by secret pleasure' (SCS p. 284). The sexual — masturbatory — image, which suggests both the adolescent refusal of sexual relations with others and an intense sexual pleasure, takes on a metaphysical dimension as Françoise, disturbed by the smile, feels face to face with the hostile presence of another consciousness: 'behind that maniacal grin, was the threat of a danger more positive than any she had ever imagined' (SCS p. 285). The reader is thus offered Françoise's ontological interpretation, yet it is clear that the scene also revolves around the emotional and sexual conflict between the two women. After the first burn Françoise decides that she has been allowing Xavière to assert her feelings at the expense of Françoise's own. Françoise has repressed her jealousy and hatred, has not dared to assume her own feelings, and has created 'a void within herself' (SCS p. 288). Xavière, meanwhile, in Françoise's view, has enshrined her feelings and asserted them with such audacity that she is rewarded by Pierre's passionate interest. Françoise has to sit through a long and amorous tête-à-tête between Xavière and Pierre; when Pierre eventually notices Françoise's distress and lays his hand on hers, Françoise feels 'dense vapours of hatred' emanating from Xavière (SCS p. 290). Moments later the latter again begins to burn herself beneath Françoise's gaze, and again loses herself, in Françoise's phrase, in 'maniacal pleasure' (an expression given a strongly sexual flavour in the French by the use of the term *jouissance*; SCS p. 292). Françoise feels with intensity that her sovereign status at the centre of her own world has been abolished. Metaphysical and sexual crisis combine; Françoise is at her most vulnerable to Xavière's challenge when Xavière posits herself as a woman at Françoise's expense. The tension mounts to intolerable proportions and snaps as Françoise breaks into a long and uncontrollable bout of sobbing — clear evidence, if any were needed, of the powerful emotional dimensions of the episode.

Because Xavière is seen from the outside only, Françoise's interpretation of Xavière's fundamentally adolescent behaviour as a metaphysical challenge dominates the text. It is only from Xavière's own pronouncements that we sometimes glimpse the situation from a point of view more sympathetic to her — her dislike, for example, of Pierre's intense verbality, or of Françoise's attachment to a regular pattern of work; her feeling of inadequacy, the difficulties of coping with the violent and contradictory emotions which sweep over her, and her desire to challenge the values which the older couple establish. Her lack of gratitude at Françoise's suggestion that she might train to become a secretary or a beautician is not hard to understand, especially when Françoise herself is involved in much more interesting work. Had the novel included Xavière's point of view, the philosophical argument of the text might well have been subsumed into a classic adult/adolescent conflict, with all the emotional and sexual elements which that entails. The dominance of Françoise's point of view, and the absence of Xavière's voice, are the underpinnings of the metaphysical interpretation of the conflict which the author directs us to in the text.

The reader, then, has to share Françoise's perception of Xavière; despite the emphasis which Françoise increasingly places on the metaphysical challenge which she sees Xavière as representing, Françoise's perception of Xavière is also strongly marked by Xavière's corporality. Her clothes, her hair, her expression are continually evoked, with the result that Xavière's sexuality is constantly foregrounded in the text. This is in sharp contrast to the virtual silence which Françoise maintains about her own appearance. In Françoise's eyes, Xavière frequently undergoes chameleon-like changes, appearing at one moment puffy-eyed, tousled and with blotchy skin, only to emerge a few moments later with shining eyes and hair, and clear pearly skin. These abrupt transformations reflect not only Françoise's uncertainty about Xavière, but Xavière's own ambiguous, contradictory attitude to the roles she has to play.

Françoise finds the idea of Xavière as a sexual being extremely distasteful. When she realises that Pierre views Xavière as a woman, she is overwhelmed by the fear that Pierre 'with his caressing masculine hands, would turn this black pearl, this austere angel, into a rapturous woman' (SCS p. 208). Pierre, she fears, would gain Xavière's surrender and Xavière would 'end up there like anyone else. For a moment she frankly hated him' (SCS p. 209). The strength of this reaction suggests that Françoise's desire to keep Xavière as a child, as a nonsexual being, derives from more than a wish to keep Xavière for herself.[10] The emergence of Xavière's sexuality, and of the rivalry which it creates, brings to the surface Françoise's uncertainty about her own relationship to femininity, and her uneasy rapport with her own sexual and physical being. Her lack of sexual confidence is indicated right from the opening scene of the novel, in which Françoise recognises that she is attracted by the younger Gerbert, but assuming humbly that her feelings are unreciprocated, decides to make no move in his direction, pretexting her relationship with Pierre even though she knows this to be no obstacle. Later, the uneasy relationship which she maintains with her physical being is further highlighted by the plethora of references to her reluctance to dance, and by her refusal to pay more than a minimal attention to her appearance. ' "She never looks at herself," Xavière had said. It was true. Françoise was heedful of her face only in so far as she took care of it as something impersonal' (SCS p. 146).

As happens so often in the text, the metaphysical and the psycho-sexual again come together here; Françoise's lack of awareness of her being-for-others, of how she appears to other people in the world, is damaging to her awareness of herself as a sexual and gendered being. To think of herself as 'no-one', as 'a naked consciousness in front of the world' (SCS p. 146) is to fail to perceive herself as body and as a woman. As the crisis intensifies, and Françoise is gradually forced to recognise her existence in the world on the same terms as other people, she begins to see that 'whether she liked it or not, she too was in the world, a part of this world. She was a woman among other women' (p. 146). The juxtaposition of these two statements is striking. The discovery of being-for-others, of her social existence, is a rediscovery of corporality, and hence of sexuality and gender. Françoise's illness at the end of the first part of the book signals the re-emergence of her awareness that she is not pure consciousness, that she also has a corporal existence — but here she experiences the temporary pre-eminence of the body in passive terms as she retreats with relief into illness.

In the second part of the book, Françoise is impelled to face the challenge which Xavière represents, and to eventually destroy her in an extreme act of self-assertion. But before she can do this she first carries out another, more primary act of self-assumption by initiating the sexual relationship with Gerbert which she had refused to consider at the beginning of the book. Her choice of Gerbert is important from a number of points of view. It underlines the development which she has undergone and it ensures that this is an act which Françoise herself has to initiate and take full responsibility for (in view of the evident respect in which Gerbert holds her). More significant still, however, is the relation in which Gerbert stands to Xavière and to Pierre. In terms of the latter, Gerbert is a Pierre-approved figure (idolising and resembling Pierre almost to the point where he can be considered a kind of stand-in for him); initiating a sexual relationship with Gerbert in no way constitutes a challenge to Pierre.[11] But the most significant aspect of Françoise's choice of Gerbert is that he is also Xavière's lover; the rivalry between the two women impells Françoise into her act of sexual assertion and allows her to beat Xavière on her own ground. When Pierre points out that Xavière would commit suicide if she knew of Françoise's relationship with Gerbert, Françoise thinks with triumph of the 'daily ration of soothing lies' which she will allot to Xavière. 'Scorned, duped, she [Xavière] would no longer dispute Françoise's place in the world' (SCS p. 378).

Françoise gains enormous strength from this rediscovery of herself as a sexual being (sex is noticeably absent from the accounts of the time which she spends with Pierre). She is no longer the defeated creature who retreated into illness at the end of the first part of the novel, but a woman with enough confidence to face the renewed threat which she perceives in Xavière on her return to Paris. Almost at once, however, Françoise is reminded that she has to contend not with 'a vague image' but with 'hair far fairer than any memory', with 'lips opened in a completely new smile', with 'a presence in the flesh that had again to be faced' (SCS pp. 289–90). Now Françoise no longer wants to play the mother–child roles: 'Xavière's deliberate childishness aggravated her' (SCS p. 390). In the final chapter of the book, which immediately follows the Françoise–Gerbert episode, the tone mounts dramatically. Françoise perceives Xavière as feeling 'something far more than a childish and capricious hostility: a true female hatred' (SCS p. 392). She transforms her image of Xavière from the 'silky golden girl' to the 'bitch crouching behind the door in her nest of lies' (SCS p. 399). When Xavière discovers, as Françoise has longed, almost planned for her to do, that Françoise and Gerbert are lovers, that both Gerbert and Pierre prefer Françoise, Françoise's triumph is turned on its head by Xavière's construction of her behaviour: 'You were jealous of me because Labrousse was in love with me. You made him loathe me, and to get better revenge, you took Gerbert from me' (SCS p. 405).

Here, a new aspect of the threat which Xavière poses to Françoise is revealed. Xavière seizes the power of the word and claims the right to narrate Françoise's story in her own terms. Françoise, who has always hated the idea of 'no longer being anything but a figment of someone else's mind' (SCS p. 7), can no longer tolerate Xavière's challenge; she has to be destroyed both in the word and in the flesh. Françoise will destroy Xavière's image of Françoise as jealous and treacherous, will assert herself in order to defend her self-image, the reflection in the mirror which now concerns her urgently and 'which there had been a long enduring attempt to rob her of' (SCS p. 406). She will act to maintain her own view of herself as involved in an innocent idyll with Gerbert ('The wind was blowing, the cows were rattling their chains in the stable, a young trusting head was leaning over her shoulder'; p. 406) and as the woman to whom Pierre had given a parting look of tenderness at the Gare de l'Est (see p. 401).

The murder is a deeply rewarding act for Françoise. On the

metaphysical level, she asserts her sovereignty at the centre of her own world, asserts her being-for-itself in the face of the challenge of a hostile consciousness. She crushes the claim of another to narrate her story.[12] On the psycho-sexual level, she destroys her rival, preserves her newly rediscovered confidence in herself as a woman, and establishes herself as the sole recipient of both the male characters' love and esteem. Despite her need for male approval, she carries out the murder without the knowledge of Pierre, and she displays a total independence of ethical norms. She discovers, in a word, her own power. Readings of the text based purely on the metaphysical element are not adequate to deal with Françoise's act. As Hazel Barnes acknowledges, there is no actual justification for the murder in purely existentialist terms; Françoise ought simply to have accepted the consequences of her acts and lived with her own view of them no matter what interpretation of them Xavière might offer.[13]

In any interpretation of the murder, it is clear that it is also caught up with the relationship of Françoise with Pierre. Pierre posits their relationship as an exception to the existential difficulties of all relationships, of which he sees the stumbling block as the fact that 'everyone experiences his own consciousness as an absolute. How can several absolutes be compatible?' (SCS p. 302).[14] Pierre and Françoise theoretically escape this difficulty by mutually acknowledging each other's consciousness and freedom, thus attaining a balance (*réciprocité*) between them. Friendship is impossible, Pierre explains, without this balance and voluntary renunciation of sovereignty. It soon becomes clear, however, that this renunciation is anything but balanced. While both characters take pleasure in repeating the idea that the two of them form an indissoluble unit, Pierre does not allow this to interfere in any way with his own desires and projects. Françoise, on the other hand, takes the idea almost literally:

> Pierre was speaking, his hand was raised, but his gestures, his tones, were as much a part of Françoise's life as of his. Or rather there was but one life and at its core one entity, which could be termed neither he nor I but we. (SCS p. 44)

Central to this concept of their indivisibility is the way in which the two recount to each other their every moment. 'Nothing that happened was completely real until she had told Pierre about it' (SCS p. 17); Françoise is dependent on Pierre turning her life into a series of 'clear, polished, completed moments' which 'became moments of their shared life' (SCS p. 17). This efface-ment of herself in favour of the verbalised 'Françoise' which she and Pierre create is an abdication of Françoise's desire to bestow meaning herself on the world around her, to carry out her 'mission' to bring the whole world to life (SCS pp. 2, 12). She has an unshakable belief in the power of words, and Pierre is posited as the master manipulator of language, the inheritor of the silver tongue (*bouche d'or*) of Saint John Chrysostom (SCS p. 109). Françoise is a true disciple and is lulled into a sense of false security which saps her independence. In the final chapter of the text, the absence of Pierre and his verbal construction of her makes Françoise especially vulnerable to Xavière's onslaught, and especially determined to believe in the version of herself which she constructs from Pierre's letters. Her desire that Xavière should read the letters is a pointer to the significance she places on them.

The 'balance' between herself and Pierre is thus fraught with danger for Françoise. The crisis over Xavière is actually highly salutary in so far as it forces Françoise into a brutal recognition that she does not form an indissoluble unit with Pierre and that she must take responsibility for herself. Whilst Françoise makes the classic female mistake of trying to merge with Pierre and share his view of Xavière, Pierre unashamedly sets out to use his verbal skills to master the women who attract him. He explains to Françoise that he wants to make Xavière love him in order 'to dominate her, to enter into her world and there conquer in accord-ance with her own values. He smiled. "You know that this is the kind of victory for which I have an insane need"' (SCS p. 164). Despite her need to see Pierre as an extension of herself, Françoise sometimes perceives Pierre as a sheer incarnation of masculinity. As he tries to force a public admission of love from Xavière, Françoise sees 'a man fighting desperately for his masculine triumph' (SCS p. 203). A few pages later, jealousy of Gerbert again arouses his domineering instinct and he becomes a prey to a 'dangerous mechanism of which he was not master' (SCS p. 208). He loses interest in Xavière once she is 'at my disposal from night till morning, repentant, full of good-will, almost loving'; then 'she suddenly lost all importance for me' (SCS p. 377). Pierre's almost caricatural masculinity (a faithful echo nevertheless, one suspects, of Sartre's attitude) is strongly associated with his gift for words ('I told her stories about our travels . . . All of a sudden she said to me: "I'm having a wonderful time with you"'; SCS p. 128);

words act as a tool of seduction and domination for him in the best Don Juan tradition.

This is in marked contrast to the way in which Françoise is 'masculinised' and distanced from 'feminine' models of behaviour. Thus Gerbert mentally congratulates Françoise on 'so often unashamedly wearing down-at-heel shoes and caught stockings' and on not being 'given to coquetry, to headaches, to abrupt changes of mood' (SCS p. 252) — all characteristics, it is clearly implied, which one might expect in the general run of women. In the scene immediately before they make love, Gerbert remarks to Françoise that 'You can't do anything with a female; you can't go walking, you can't get drunk, or anything. They can't take a joke, and then, besides, you always have to make a fuss of them or you always feel you're in the wrong' (SCS p. 366). Françoise's ironic response to these remarks draws the ultimate accolade: ' "Oh you! You're like a man!" he said warmly' (SCS p. 366). Françoise is thus simultaneously posed as an attractive woman (since Gerbert is about to express his desire for her) and one who is above 'feminine' behaviour. We have already seen the effects of this distancing in the conflict with Xavière; it is also strikingly evident in the tensions set up in the text between Françoise and Elisabeth.

Elisabeth appears to incarnate everything which Françoise fears becoming. In existentialist terms, Elisabeth plays the masochist role in her relationships — she is involved with a man who is not committed to her and whose vacillations control her life. Obsessed by the mirage of how she appears to others ('a different dress, a different woman'; SCS p. 64), she is unable to believe in herself, in her own activities and values: 'She knew that in no way would she ever reach the authentic ideal of which her present self was only a copy. Never would she know anything other than these shams' (SCS p. 215). In terms of the analysis Beauvoir made later in *The Second Sex*, Elisabeth falls into the traps of narcissism, and of attempting to live through others — traps which Beauvoir sees women as particularly vulnerable to, and as limiting their capacity as artists. Elisabeth becomes the first of a line of women in Beauvoir's fiction who are not permitted to succeed as artists, or even to believe in themselves as painters or writers. 'Her pictures! Pigment spread on canvas so as to give the appearance of pictures; she spent her days painting in order to convince herself that she was a painter, but it was still nothing but a lugubrious game' (SCS p. 217).

Françoise nourishes a mixture of pity, revulsion and fascination towards her: 'She must not be like Elisabeth,' she tells herself (SCS p. 153), and only a few pages later we are told: 'Françoise did not want to lie to herself like Elisabeth' (SCS p. 159). Although the two women have been friends since their schooldays (a theme strongly developed in the excised first two chapters) and have a number of things in common (Elisabeth paints and Françoise writes, both are devoted to Pierre, both are involved in triangular relationships), Françoise finds the thought that they may be in any way alike unbearable. She classifies Elisabeth as 'a perennial adolescent', who constantly compares herself to others, and remodels herself accordingly (SCS p. 135). 'You are certainly not like Elisabeth,' Xavière tells Françoise, and reassured by this unsolicited remark, Françoise is able to reply cautiously, 'I am in a way' (SCS p. 135), explaining that the void which Elisabeth experiences at the heart of herself is the void which everyone experiences. Elisabeth is credited with such low self-esteem that even the sections of the text in which the narrative is focused through Elisabeth herself confirm this idea that her existence is built on a void which she is unable to succeed in filling. The distaste which Françoise feels for the character also suffuses not only the parts of the narrative focused through Françoise, but those focused through Elisabeth. Since Elisabeth also presents Françoise with considerable sympathy, the extent to which the values of the narrator and those of Françoise coincide becomes particularly evident.

Elisabeth is clearly marked out for disapproval and punishment — but why? Elisabeth's failings serve to highlight Françoise's lack of narcissism, her confidence in her own projects and her strong relationship with Pierre. Yet Elisabeth's dependency on Claude also serves as a clue to Françoise's more subtle dependency on Pierre; her doubts about herself as a painter remind us that Françoise does not seem to be making much progress with the novel about adolescence she is writing (the theme of which is another pointer to the importance of the theme of the adolescent girl in the text). She also raises the question of women and sexuality. 'You know my principles,' Elisabeth tells Françoise early on in the novel. 'I'm not the sort of woman who is taken. I'm a woman who does the taking. That very first evening, I asked him to spend the night with me. He was flabbergasted' (SCS p. 40). Far from sharing the idea that a woman might take the sexual initiative, Françoise is disturbed by it. When she eventually contemplates suggesting to Gerbert that they make love, she recoils at the thought that she will be imitating Elisabeth: 'The blood rushed to her face; she remembered Elisabeth — a woman who takes — and she loathed the thought' (SCS p. 368). Françoise is eventually rewarded by the tender, romantic scene with Gerbert. Elisabeth, in contrast, is subjected to a humiliating sexual episode with Guimiot, who goes about 'his job as a male' with 'the fingers of an expert, endowed with a skill as precise as those of a masseur, a hairdresser, or a dentist' (SCS p. 84). Sensuality is presented as a trap for Elisabeth, binding her to Claude and allowing her to be humiliated by men; Françoise, in contrast, declares that 'pure sensuality does not interest me' (SCS p. 42) and is careful to let Gerbert know that 'it wasn't just sensuality that made me want to be in your arms' (SCS p. 373). In *The Prime of Life* Beauvoir remarks that she disliked the kind of eroticism to be found in a novel like Malraux's *Man's Fate* (published in 1933) but admired Hemingway's lovers, who 'when they gave themselves to desire, to pleasure, it bound them together in their totality' (POL p. 138). This admiration for Hemingway's portrayal of sexual experience is significant in the sense that positive sexual experiences for women tend to be bound up with emotions and words in Beauvoir's fiction; pure sensuality is often presented as a danger for them. However, it is also interesting to note Beauvoir's automatic reference here to representations of sexual experience by male writers.

When Françoise and Elisabeth have parallel experiences, Elisabeth's always becomes the negative one. She represents a negative image of woman, a kind of narcissistic sensual femininity from which Françoise recoils and from which she congratulates herself on escaping. The trap represented by Elisabeth is as real a danger to Françoise as the conflict with Xavière, even if it is one which is apparently more easily disposed of. To claim that the novel is a powerful depiction of conflicts about certain models of femininity, and certain aspects of female experience, is not to deny the existentialist framework of the text, nor to devalue the philosophical interpretation of it. Earlier commentators, aware that the text could be open to multiple readings, have sometimes attempted to safeguard the philosophical reading. Thus Merleau-Ponty writes, 'The drama of *She Came to Stay* could be expressed in psychological terms: Xavière is a flirt, Pierre desires her, Françoise is jealous. This would not be inaccurate. It would simply be superficial.' Brian Fitch hastens to agree with Merleau-Ponty, adding that such an interpretation would be not only superficial but 'against the intentions of the author'.[15] One need not agree with Merleau-Ponty that psychological phenomena are a kind of 'superficial' manifestation of ontological anxieties (though the schema he suggests above is indeed a simplification and takes no account of Elisabeth); in fact it is rather the reverse process (psychological phenomena giving rise to a rationalised philosophical discourse) that can be argued to be at work in the text. However, rather than establishing hierarchies of interpretation, it is probably more useful to say that one of the central interests of the text is in fact the way in which these two sets of codes are interlocked. Fitch's reference to the 'intentions of the author' is a reminder of the power that authorial directives on meaning can exert, though in fact in *The Prime of Life* Beauvoir is clear about the 'cathartic' role which the writing of the novel played for her. Her throat dry as she wrote, the murder was not a simple exigency of the plot for Beauvoir but, she says, 'the motive force and *raison d'être* behind the entire novel' (POL p. 340). Beauvoir herself was thus in no doubt about the strength of the emotions fuelling her fiction.

The novel displays a profound anxiety about the behaviour roles open to women. As an adolescent, Xavière oscillates between adopting a submissive cajoling femininity, and experiencing waves of rebellion and self-disgust. Elisabeth, herself blocked at an adolescent stage, lacks the confidence to do any more with her life than model herself on those around her. Françoise, despite her apparent assurance, experiences considerable difficulties: she has become dependent upon Pierre, and her pride in the codes by which she has determined to live, her desire to be a woman without coquetry or artifice, leave her struggling with her sexuality, vulnerable to the fear that the selfishness and capriciousness of a Xavière are more attractive to Pierre and Gerbert than her own surrogate masculinity. Though she emerges strong at the end of the novel, triumphing over both herself and Xavière, she has to have recourse to a violent act to do so. Erupting in the final pages of the novel, this violence can be seen as a substitute for the narrative power which Françoise both strongly desires and fears achieving. For as Martha Noel Evans has recently argued, doubts about femaleness and femininity in Beauvoir are closely connected to doubts about the right to write at all.[16] Just as Elisabeth, strongly locked into a female world, cannot be a 'real' artist, and as Beauvoir herself did not believe herself to be 'a real writer' until the publication of *She Came to Stay*, Françoise has been content to form a narrative duo with Pierre. In the last chapter she has stopped work on her novel, and allowed the narrative initiative to be seized from her by Xavière. The murder represents both the wresting back of the right to narrate her own story, though still in tandem with Pierre, and the violence of her desire to do so.

The fracturing of the narrative focus of the text into three is a figuration of this failure of narrative power. Yet in the end, Françoise dominates the narrative trio just as she eventually dominates the trio she forms with Pierre and Xavière through the murder. Elisabeth's brief narrative does not undermine Françoise's; indeed, the contrast it establishes between Elisabeth's failure and Françoise's success in filling the void at the heart of existence, in finding a workable mode of female behaviour, reinforces the impression of Françoise's strength. Both Gerbert and Elisabeth's narratives tend to support Françoise's views, and both build an image of her as strong and attractive. Thus the narrative trio falls into line behind Françoise; her verbal construction of herself is maintained and Xavière's is expunged from the face of the earth. In thematic terms, a victory is achieved in the word and in the flesh, despite the doubts about femininity and writing which dictate that Françoise's act of liberation bears the criminal face of murder. As a narrative strategy, the use of a triangular focus does not reappear in Beauvoir's novels, though Françoise's habit of narrating as a duo with Pierre might be seen as the basis of the dual narrative focus (one male, one female) used in the next three novels. In later texts, the doubts about the female and the feminine, together with the obsession with words and with women's relation to them, become almost constants. In *She Came to Stay*, the desire of the strong female character to cling to the authority of the male word and to distance herself from undesirable models of femininity remains strong.

Notes

1. See Contat and Rybalka, *Les Ecrits de Sartre*, pp. 85 – 86, and my Chapter 1.
2. See Hazel Barnes, *The Literature of Possibility*, pp. 121 – 36.
3. See *The Prime of Life* (p. 227 onwards) for Beauvoir's own account of Sartre's passion for Olga, which lasted from March 1935 to March 1937, and its effects on the lives of all three. Beauvoir's affair with Bost (the model for Gerbert) is omitted from her account.
4. See Anne-Marie Celeux, *Jean-Paul Sartre, Simone de Beauvoir: Une*

expérience commune, deux écritures, for a discussion of the impact of these writers on Beauvoir's and Sartre's early fiction.

5. See 'M. François Mauriac et la liberté' in Sartre, *Situations I*.

6. For an explanation of these terms see my Chapter 1.

7. They can be read in Francis and Gontier, *Les Ecrits de Simone de Beauvoir*, pp. 275–316.

8. This twin aspect of the individual's existence in the world constitutes one of the central ambiguities of existence for Beauvoir. She explores it in particular in *The Ethics of Ambiguity* (1947).

9. See the chapters entitled 'The Young Girl' and 'Sexual Initiation' in *The Second Sex*.

10. Nancy Friday, in her analysis of mother–adolescent daughter rivalry in Chapter 5 of *My Mother, Myself*, describes the Freudian view of this rivalry as stemming from the return in adolescence of highly charged feelings initially originating from the Oedipus complex experienced by the four-, five- or six-year-old girl, but not resolved at that stage. 'Alas,' writes Friday, 'the entire literature and folklore of the oedipal conflict is written from the child's point of view.' She goes on to describe the mother's usual response as to try not to admit the rivalry she feels, and to try to insist on treating her daughter as her 'little girl' (p. 168).

11. Carol Ascher's assertion that Françoise is 'deeply angry with Pierre' and that this is why she makes love with Gerbert is not easy to substantiate, though any reader might feel that Françoise *ought* to be angry with Pierre. See *Simone de Beauvoir: A Life of Freedom*, p. 57.

12. Harold Wardman develops this idea of Françoise's desire to be the omniscient narrator of her own life in his 'Self-Coincidence and Narrative in *L'Invitée*'. Also to the point is Brian Fitch's remark that the problem with Pierre and Françoise's relationship is their passage through language (*pace* Keefe). Fitch compares the couple with the hero of *Nausea*, who grasps the fact that a choice has to be made between living life and narrating it. See *Le Sentiment de l'étrangeté chez Malraux, Camus et Simone de Beauvoir*, p. 159.

13. Barnes, *The Literature of Possibility*, p. 136.

14. I have altered the English translation's version of the French *conscience* from 'conscience' to 'consciousness'. What is at stake here is not the moral imperative of the English 'conscience', but the phenomenon of our own awareness of our existence.

15. Merleau-Ponty, *Sens et Non-Sens*, p. 63. My translation from the French. See Fitch, *Le Sentiment de l'étrangeté*, p. 172.

16. See Martha Noel Evans, 'Murdering *L'Invitée*: Gender and fictional narrative'.

3

The Blood of Others

The principal characters of *The Blood of Others* make a discovery which marks them off from the world of *She Came to Stay*, and which is quite simply the fact of the insertion of their personal lives in their own time, their own period of history. In a play on the word 'history' which is insistently exploited in the text, Hélène exclaims, 'I was watching the March of History! It was my personal history' (BO p. 230).[1] This discovery not only conditions the thematics of the text and its narrative structure, but opens up the topography of the novel and brings a wider network of characters into play. For all this, however, the anxieties exhibited in *She Came to Stay* about the nature of our relations with others, and about the roles women play, are just as present, manifesting themselves in the obsessive imagery of blood and guilt, of nausea and the odour of corruption which permeate the text.

The discovery which the characters make is one which Beauvoir herself had reluctantly been led to make in the immediate pre-war years, when she was still working on *She Came to Stay*. The subject of her first novel, however, was not easy to conciliate with her new conviction, and it was only with *The Blood of Others*, begun in the autumn of 1941 and written entirely during the period of the German occupation of France, that Beauvoir was able to approach the theme of the individual's responsibility to the community. To convey the conversion of her characters, she constructed a complex narrative framework in which the destinies of Jean Blomart and Hélène Bertrand are recounted in parallel, each character serving as the narrative focus or source of narration in alternate chapters, each eventually coming to the same conclusion by different paths. The insertion of the individual into history, the fundamental interrelation of the personal and the political, is underlined not only by having a number of characters independently arriving eventually at the same conclusion, but by treating the theme simultaneously in a limited interpersonal context (Jean's fears at intervening in Hélène's life) and in a wider political context (Jean's uneasy abstinence from political action in the run-up to the Second World War). The conclusion of the novel, which is essentially brought about by a change in the character's attitudes as much as by a change in their actions, is retarded until the end of the novel by a disjunction between the personal and political levels, which are not allowed to coincide until the final chapter.

The narrative strands of the two principal characters are far from having equal weight in the novel. Blomart's narrative encloses the one focusing through Hélène, since it begins and ends the novel, and occupies seven chapters, in comparison to Hélène's six. In addition, the chapters are of very uneven length, with the result that Blomart's narrative in fact covers a third again as many pages as Hélène's. Much of this extra space is taken up with the evocation of the political atmosphere and dilemmas of the 1930s; the political dimension is noticeably absent in the narrative focusing through Hélène until the occupation of Paris in 1940. Blomart's narrative also deals with the majority of the subsidiary characters, and has to cover much wider time spans (as much as a decade or more in Chapter 1). The most fundamental difference between the two narratives, however, is the infinitely more complex narrative situation which characterises the chapters in which Blomart is both voice and focus.

On the level of time, first of all, two sequences soon become evident in these chapters. The first is that of the spring night during the German occupation (1942 or 1943) during which Blomart must decide whether to authorise an act of sabotage which will be dangerous for his Resistance group and is certain to lead to the execution by the Germans of innocent hostages. The novel opens late in the evening with the posing of this issue, and ends when Blomart gives his decision in the last line of the novel, at about 6 a.m. the following morning. Though the whole of his narrative — and the whole novel — is thus in one sense the preparation of this decision, relatively few of the events narrated by Blomart are located at this time level. The last chapter certainly operates entirely at this level (because it is the chapter of resolution) but more typical is the first chapter, in which only the first page and a half and the last two paragraphs record events taking place during this single night; the rest of the chapter follows Blomart's thoughts back to his childhood and traces his life up to the death of Jacques, in Blomart's early twenties.

The account of this past, from boyhood to the present, provides the second chronological sequence — intercut, however, by present reflections arising from the past. The most anguished of these are presented in italics in the text and often refer to events which have not yet been narrated (the first, for example, on page 11, interrupts the account of an event which takes place when Blomart is eight to refer forward both to Jacques' death, more than ten years later, and to Hélène's injury, the circumstances of which are not made clear until the penultimate chapter). The italic passages form a heightened, emotive commentary on the narrative, and serve in particular to connect the series of deaths in the novel — those of Louise's baby; of Jacques; of Hélène; of those held by the Germans in prison and in concentration camps; of the innocent French hostages who may be shot in reprisal for the sabotage Blomart is about to authorise. The commentary, and the connections it makes between these deaths, carries the burden of the underlying thesis of the text set out in the epigraph, that 'Each of us is responsible for everything and to every human being.' It also prepares the conclusions that Blomart eventually draws from this position. But the passages in italics are not the only commentary of the 1940s Blomart-narrator. The whole of the narrative in these chapters is firmly embedded in the voice and perspective of the 1940s Blomart. Other characters only appear in so far as Blomart presents and interprets them. Though dialogue in direct speech is often presented, there are also many passages in which other characters' remarks are presented in free indirect speech, or simply recalled in summary and directly commented on by Blomart. The narrative in these seven chapters is thus overtly dominated by the voice of the 1940s Blomart, and oriented towards the problematic of Blomart's guilt in the face of the death of Hélène and of the decision he must take.

This subjectivity is hardly lessened by the fact that Blomart as narrator refers to his past self in the third person as well as in the first. Though Blomart the child had perceived himself as pure subjectivity, the 1940s Blomart is only too well aware that he is also being-for-others, an object which other people can contemplate and, above all, categorise and judge (as Blomart's son, as a bourgeois, as a coward). The chain of memories from the past begins with a reminder of this double face of the individual:

> He was present, but at first he did not know it. I see him now,
> leaning against a window in the gallery. But he did not know
> it, he thought that only the world was present. (. . .) He did
> not know that through the fanlight, when they raised their
> heads, the workmen could see the solemn, fresh face of a
> middle-class child. (BO pp. 8–9)

Thus, when Blomart the narrator is viewing his younger self in terms of object in the world, in terms of a social classification, as he does in this quotation, he presents himself in third-person terms; when viewing himself as subjectivity, he uses the first person ('I felt the lukewarm liquid slip down my throat'; BO p. 11). The effect of this technique is consequently to reinforce by yet another means the idea that our lives are lived as both subject and object, as personal experience and yet inserted in a wider social and political perspective. The techniques employed in *She Came to Stay* to indicate this double perspective are thus considerably extended in *The Blood of Others*, where not only is Blomart observed from the outside by Hélène's narrative, but also himself includes this perspective in his own narrative. It remains subjective, nevertheless, since he cannot be objectively certain of his own being-for-others.[2]

Blomart is the dominant narrative power of the text; this status derives not only from the fact that his narrative is the longest, and is voiced by himself, but from the fact that the central argument of the text is made to rest heavily on the interpretation which Blomart gives to the account of his past, an account covering the period from his boyhood, located towards the end of the first decade of the century, to the early 1940s when Blomart can be presumed to be in his early thirties. In his reconstruction and interpretation of this, Blomart the narrator thus focuses on a series of events which he presents as having both shaped his life and as echoing the central problematic of guilt and responsibility. The first of these, and one of the most obscure at first sight, is the death of Louise's baby. Blomart the child is aware from an early age of a sense of social guilt, associated with the contrast between the sunny, comfortable apartment in which he lives and the dark, grimy workshop below, where 'other people's work' makes his privileged life style possible (BO p. 8). But if the world of work has at least some meaning for him, the world of poverty and misery does not. He lives in a world of flowers and apples, holidays and adventure stories, which is rudely disrupted by the monstrous event of the death of Louise's baby and the visit to the one-room flat in which the dead child lies in its cot. The power of this event in the novel derives both from its autobiographical origins, and from the multiple significance with which it is invested in the text.[3] It represents in one the discovery of poverty and social inequality ('behind every door there was a room in which a whole family lived'; BO p. 11), of the finite nature of death ('I was crying, mother was talking, and the baby remained dead'; BO p. 11), and of the inability of the individual to cross the frontiers of another's consciousness and live their suffering as they do ('the sin of shedding my own tears and not hers'; BO p. 12). Social, moral and existential guilt well up together and find their expression, as so often in Beauvoir's writing, in nausea and a refusal of food (cf. in this novel, Hélène's refusal of food in the black market restaurant, Denise sweeping her food from the table on to the floor, Hélène vomiting in the German lorry). The most humiliating aspect of the crisis for Blomart, however, is the fact that, when pressed by his father, he does eventually eat his soup. The shame and guilt of the child at this gesture which seems to him to be a betrayal of Louise, is expressed by the nauseating feeling of the lukewarm liquid slipping down his throat.

The dialectic set up between the mother and the father in this incident, the mother representing a recoil from action, the guilt-induced desire to retain as much purity as possible by doing nothing, and the father representing the nauseous pragmatics of action, sets the pattern of Blomart's subsequent oscillations. Breaking with his father and with his social class by joining the Communist Party and working his printer's apprenticeship, Blomart is able to ease his sense of social guilt. But one form of guilt is replaced by another as he measures first the pain which his decision has caused his mother, and later his responsibility for the death of Jacques, the second traumatic death in the chain. Seesawing back to the other pole, aghast at the unintended effects of his own actions, he becomes a pacifist and engages in an apolitical syndicalism which he sees as minimising the effects his own actions are able to have on others.

On the political level, this flight into noninterventionism, arrived at by the end of the first chapter (and set in the early 1930s), is maintained right up to its reversal in the ninth chapter (set just after the fall of France in 1940). However, it is always a position under pressure. From its inception, it is subject to criticism both from the comments of Blomart the narrator, and from the remarks made by other characters such as the sceptical Marcel or the committed communist Paul. We are, in addition, constantly reminded that the premise of Blomart's withdrawal is in no way a rejection of the basic postulate of the text expressed in the Dostoyevsky quotation: 'Each of us is responsible for everything and to every human being.' On the contrary, he is so penetrated by his sense of responsibility that he dare not undertake an action whose consequences are unforeseeable and for which he would nevertheless bear responsibility. In the second chapter of his narrative, he is able to maintain this position with confidence; by the third (Chapter 5) the rapidly worsening world situation (Austria and Czechoslovakia have been overrun by Hitler) leaves him isolated and vulnerable. By the fourth section (Chapter 7) his position has become untenable; he becomes increasingly convinced that his respect for the values in which he believes may in itself bring about the defeat of those values by fascism. Mobilisation is the deliverance which enables him to put off any further self-questioning and simply to carry out orders.[4] This prepares the final stage, recounted in Chapter 9, where Blomart reverses his position on intervention and abstention. The fall of France and the German occupation provide the final impetus for this reversal, imminent since Chapter 7. Instead of arguing that he cannot pay with the blood of others, cannot send innocent people to their deaths, he now argues that all his decisions are bought with the blood of others, whether it is to enter the war against Germany (thus spilling the blood of French soldiers) or not to enter it (allowing the blood to be spilled of those killed in concentration camps). Both positions derive from a sense of total responsibility.

On the political front, therefore, the dialectic between action and withdrawal is exposed as a false one by Chapter 9; but this discovery is curiously forestalled by events in Blomart's personal life, in which his refusal to enter the life of Hélène parallels his political noninterventionism. In this personal context, the results of this refusal to involve himself become dramatically clear to him at a much earlier stage of the novel than on the political level; the abortion episode of Chapter 5 leads him to abandon his position and accept involvement with Hélène, accepting that to abstain from action is as much an act which will have consequences for others as to intervene. 'Whatever I did, I was in the wrong' (BO p. 112). This statement closely parallels his arguments in Chapter 9 that French blood must be spilled because 'all means are bad'

(BO p. 190) and that 'whatever one did, one was always wrong' (BO pp. 189–90). Why is it, it needs to be asked, that his conclusions on the personal level, reached so much earlier in the novel, fail to feed over at that stage into the more generalised political context? It is noticeable that the two strands function independently, and that both reach crisis and then reversal in the face of concrete unpalatable evidence of the consequences of abstentionism — the abortion scene on the one hand, the sight of occupied Paris on the other. In both cases this evidence brings no new element to Blomart's thinking; it simply tips the scale one way rather than the other, since the premiss of both options is total responsibility.

The answer is that the earlier reversal reached on the personal level does not transfer into the political context quite simply because it is shown not to work. Indeed, Blomart is constantly faced with the problems it entails — the difficulties of coping with the reactions of Paul and Madeleine to his relationship with Hélène, the unease his own lack of emotional involvement causes him, the godlike status with which his control of the situation invests him in Hélène's eyes. Blomart's attempt to involve himself to the hilt in Hélène's happiness by lying to her — since he finds himself to be the arbiter of her happiness whether he will or no — does not in the end avert the break between the two of them, nor Hélène's suffering. The point here is that Blomart has not yet taken into account the extent to which his notion of responsibility towards others constitutes an invasion of their freedom; this is the notion that he is forced to consider on both the personal and political levels in the last chapter, and which requires two different sets of arguments to resolve.

Blomart's guilt at sending Hélène to her death is easily resolved as Hélène claims responsibility for her own acts: 'You had no right to choose for me,' she declares (BO p. 237); and indeed it is their joint failure to accept the notion of the responsibility of each partner in a relationship to respect the freedom and autonomy of the other which is made to lead to the breakdown of the couple at an earlier stage. This assertion of responsibility by Hélène frees Blomart by implication from his earlier sense of guilt towards Jacques and Madeleine (who also had the right to choose for themselves). However, the notion of the respect of the freedom of others will not serve to justify the death of the hostages, since Blomart clearly violates their freedom and removes all possibility of their deciding for themselves on their fates. After Hélène's death,

Blomart has to find this argument for himself, and does so on the last page of the novel, where he argues that his action is justified because it is committed in the name of freedom: 'that supreme good which makes innocent' (BO p. 240). This justification is bolstered by Blomart's acceptance of the fact that a clear conscience is a luxury he can no longer permit himself; he has to bear 'my crimes and my guilt which will rend me eternally' (BO p. 240). Setting a high value on 'personal scruples' has been progressively revealed in the text to be mere bourgeois individualism, even neuroticism. ' "You're too interested in yourself" ', Denise tells him and Blomart reflects: 'Those words strike home. It is perhaps because I am bourgeois that I must always be thinking about myself' (BO p. 221).

The arguments for an absolution of guilt in the case of Hélène and in the case of the hostages thus in the end have to be separated out. Interventionism proves futile and arrogant on the personal level; on the political level, it is found to be the only way forward. Yet the two issues are constantly interlinked in the novel and are resolved in a single movement. Though the political issue is virtually settled in the ninth chapter, where Blomart sets out the detailed arguments in favour of sabotage action and the spilling of French blood, the ultimate philosophical justification — acting in the name of freedom — is saved until the end, where the personal and political are subsumed into one. There is thus a strong *emotive* link made between the two; ultimately, it is implied, commitment to the wider community and a strong authentic relation with another individual go hand in hand. In the case of Hélène, of course, the attainment of an unselfish love and the adoption of a political commitment are shown even more schematically to go hand in hand.[5]

The Blood of Others is thus undoubtedly a love story with a happy ending, despite — or even because of — the death of the heroine. Is it, however, a *roman à thèse*, as it has so often been written off as?[6] It is certainly possible to extract from the novel a more or less consciously defined ideology. Sartre's *Being and Nothingness* provides a doctrinal intertext to which *The Blood of Others* quite specifically relates; overlaying this, the Dostoyevskian notion of responsibility remains, as has been seen, an unquestioned absolute of the text. Yet this is not in itself sufficient to make of *The Blood of Others*, to borrow Susan Suleiman's terminology, an 'authoritarian' text. In Suleiman's model, the *roman à thèse* formulates a system of absolute values in an insistent and unambiguous manner; in its fictional universe 'right' and 'wrong' can be clearly and categorically distinguished.[7] If this is true of *The Blood of Others* at the most basic level of the text (the thesis of responsibility), it is less evident that it applies to the central problematic which is made to derive from these assumptions. Blomart's conclusion that he is justified in spilling the blood of others in the name of freedom is certainly formulated at the end of the book in an unambiguous manner. The fact that his evolution in this direction is echoed in the text by the characters of Hélène and Marcel is also a reductionist factor; even more insistent is Blomart's interpretative discourse (the italic commentary) which repeatedly exposes the 'meaning' of events. But this meaning is not posed as absolute and definitive. Intervening in another individual's freedom is shown to be futile in the case of Hélène; even in the case of Resistance action, the argument for intervention is only arrived at after a series of refusals and hesitations. More importantly still, the arguments *against* the eventual solution are presented as serious and weighty ones. Some are left unanswered in the text — this is in particular the case of the point put forward by Blomart in his pacifist phase that there can be no point in struggling for man's happiness and dignity if human life is to be treated as a cheap resource: 'If men were simply material to be wastefully handled, why worry about their future? If massacres and tyranny carried so little weight, how important were justice and prosperity?' (BO p. 132). In a more general way, the problems posed by defending a value by temporarily transgressing it are indicated to be enormously complex. Blomart is certainly not posited as the innocent champion of 'right'. On the contrary, he remains ambivalent about his final choice and accepts almost as an inevitability that he may be wrong. To sum up, if the position Blomart arrives at at the end of the novel is unambiguously posed as the best one in the circumstances, it is shown to be the result of a choice between two evils, rather than as a choice between right and wrong. Blomart's is a manichean solution to an extreme situation.

The final chapter of the novel presents the most marked features of a 'closed' text, with its attempt to provide an absolute justification of a specific case (the 'supreme good' of freedom). It is essentially the ending of the novel which lends the most weight to Blanchot's conclusion (in 1945) that the text does not escape the *roman à thèse*. Otherwise, his argument that, unlike the hero of *Nausea* who Blanchot sees as discovering eventually a truth he already half-knew, Blomart undergoes a road-to-Damascus conversion which will guide him through the rest of his life, seems to me to be quite without foundation. If an ultimate value in this text had to be found, it might well be the moral integrity with which Blomart reassesses each new situation in which he finds himself, and which is compared to the fixity of a Gauthier: ' "I am a pacifist".' He had given a definition of himself once and for all, he had only to act in accordance with his own idea of himself, neither looking to left or right' (BO p. 119).[8] To explain why, despite this argument against fixity and in favour of examination of every new situation on its merits, Beauvoir still felt the need to justify Blomart's position with reference to the absolute value of freedom, we need to recall the extreme nature of this specific case, and the climate in which not only the characters of the novel but the author herself were caught up.

Like André Malraux who wrote — and published — his novel about the Spanish Civil War before the war was over, Beauvoir wrote her novel entirely during the period of the German occupation of France, completing it more than a year before the liberation of Paris. Since the value system of the novel ultimately depends on freedom eventually being achieved (otherwise the deliberate provocation of the death of the hostages would appear too great a sacrifice), the whole novel is in effect an act of faith in the future freedom of the French. However, within this context, the assassination of German soldiers in which Blomart's group engages was one of the most controversial forms of action of the Resistance, and it is not surprising that Beauvoir felt the need to put the case strongly. Beauvoir describes in her memoirs the change in political climate which came about in occupied Paris in the summer of 1941. The first year of the occupation had been marked by only sporadic acts of resistance and sabotage, but with Hitler's invasion of the Soviet Union in June 1941 and the Communist Party's entry into active resistance, the number of bombs, train derailments and other acts of industrial sabotage grew rapidly. From August onwards the Communist Party set up special groups to execute German soldiers; German reprisals in the form of execution of French 'hostages' began the same month. Reaction to this form of action was mixed; some quarters claimed that it only fed German and Vichy propaganda and that those engaged in resistance were 'terrorists' (hence Marcel's ironic remark to Blomart that he is now heading a 'terrorist movement'; BO p. 216). De Gaulle gave instructions against it, and even some of the Resistance press found the reprisals too high a cost to pay; only the Communist Party continued systematically with this policy, though it is not clear that even they were deliberately setting out to provoke the death of hostages as Blomart does.[9]

Besides the general justification offered by the concept of fighting for freedom, the text offers a panoply of detailed arguments in favour of active resistance. In the scenes in which Blomart convinces first his financial backers and then his comrades, he argues the need to establish through action a body capable of holding out until the end of the war; the need to shake the French from the passive acceptance of occupation and indoctrination; the responsibility to ensure that the high risk to activists is compensated by highly visible and effective forms of action; the need to accept the risk that in acting against the Germans they may be working in the interests of bourgeois capitalism, of what he sees as Anglo-Saxon imperialism. 'Anything is better than Fascism' is his argument here (BO p. 190). The pacifist case is disposed of by the portrait of Gauthier, the pacifist turned collaborator (see pp. 186–87); the fate of the Poles, the fate of those in prisoner-of-war and concentration camps is constantly raised as a reminder that the relative comfort and security of occupied Paris is only the more acceptable face of Nazi domination. Thus, Beauvoir's choice of the Resistance as a context in which her characters could play out the drama of history versus History, and as a sufficiently extreme situation to weight the balance of Blomart's thinking towards commitment whatever the cost, led to her producing an unmistakably committed novel. In the climate of 1941–43, it is virtually unthinkable that she could have written about the Resistance in a noncommitted way, though she could have made the argument for commitment without taking it to the extremes of arguing that there must be 'blood, newly shed, between us' (BO p. 224).[10]

The theme of commitment, the consequence of the discovery of 'History', is explored not only in Blomart's narrative, however, but also in the second narrative of the novel, the one focusing through the character of Hélène Bertrand. The existence of Hélène's narrative is in itself evidence of the dialogism of the novel; although it echoes the theme of responsibility and commitment through Hélène's own development, there is no italicised interpretative commentary as in Blomart's chapters — indeed Hélène does not have the authority of a narrative voice in the way that Blomart does. Despite the absence of a first-person narrator — a fairly covert external narrative voice is employed — Hélène's chapters strike a more intimate note than Jean Blomart's, largely because there is much less attempt to cover large stretches of time (each of the first three chapters covers only a few hours of Hélène's life, less than a single day), and because there is a much greater concentration on personal relationships.

The historical perspective intervenes in Chapter 8 where Hélène, in a prefiguration of the break with Jean in the following chapter, makes her abruptly terminated visit to him during the phony war. Beauvoir used her own visit to Sartre at Brumath (see *The Prime of Life*, pp. 426–32) as the basis for this chapter — with the significant difference that her own visit was not interrupted. In Chapter 10 the detailed description of the exodus from Paris in June 1940, and Hélène's experiences on the road, are equally based on Beauvoir's own experience.[11] A detailed picture of living conditions in occupied Paris emerges from the chapter: the hunger and cold suffered by most inhabitants, the darkness and silence of the capital, the transport difficulties, the curfew, the success of the haute couture houses (in one of which Hélène works), the black market restaurants, the fate of the Jews, the ambivalence felt by Parisians towards their occupiers, especially in the early days when the latter appeared polite, correct and disturbingly like tourists. In these chapters the deliberate attempt to offer a portrait of an era shown to affect the development of the characters is in marked contrast to the ahistorical construction of *She Came to Stay*.

Beauvoir's own experience is abruptly left behind, however, in the last part of the chapter, where Hélène is briefly tempted by collaboration. Throughout the novel Hélène is characterised as strongly individualistic; it is this individualism, combined with a mood of nihilism resulting from her break with Blomart, which allows Hélène to view working with the Germans with indifference. Through Hélène, Beauvoir is able to discredit, without ever descending to a black-and-white portrait of a collaborationist, the kind of historicist arguments which Hélène mechanically repeats to herself. By entrenching herself in the 'realist' attitude that the Germans are the future masters of Europe, and that the French will simply have to learn to adjust to this fact, Hélène can dismiss Nazi atrocities as 'the necessities of history' (BO p. 212). When she sees the posters informing the French that a saboteur has been executed, she tells herself briskly, 'Well, doubtless one has to go through that stage' (BO p. 209).[12] But this flight into escapism is halted when, on the dance floor, Hélène catches a glimpse of herself in a mirror as others would see her, held in the arms of a German officer. As suffering floods back into her carefully preserved empty shell, she abandons the pretence that she can stand outside the collective situation and begins the climb back to responsibility. There can be few such charitable portrayals of the collaborationist temptation by a writer in the other camp.

The final chapter of Hélène's narrative records her conversion as she witnesses one of the large-scale raids on the Jews carried out by French police. Solitude, frustrated love for Jean and existential nausea disappear as Hélène begins working with Blomart's resistance group: 'Now she was no longer ever alone, no longer useless and lost under the empty sky (. . .). The shell had burst open; she existed for something, for someone' (BO p. 235). Thus in the end, Hélène's destiny parallels Jean's. However, the Hélène of the last chapters, whose essential function appears to be to release Jean from his sense of guilt, is an anesthetised version of the vigorous character of the earlier chapters.

From the beginning of her narrative it is clear that Hélène embodies a number of illusions which she is destined to lose in the course of the moral and political education which she receives in the book. She represents an extreme individualism which will have no truck with the needs of others; she incarnates a sense of unreflecting irresponsibility underlined by her childish traits (delight in the new bicycle, affection for the dog cemetery and the zoo, fondness for chocolate and brightly coloured drinks). These traits are echoed in her romantic expectations of men. She wants a man to consider her as unique and to find 'each beat of her heart and the slightest of her sighs' of 'infinite significance', just as she had imagined God to consider her when she was a child (BO p. 43). But at the same time this man must have no need of others, must be strong and unassailable; Paul does not fit the bill because beneath an outer shell Hélène perceives 'an innocent mollusc, just like the one she discovered in herself' (BO p. 49). Blomart, on the other hand, appears to Hélène as completely autonomous, with 'no desires, no needs; he was not dependent on anyone or anything, not even on his own body' (BO p. 88). His attractiveness is increased in Hélène's eyes by the evident fact that he has no need whatever of her and refuses to see her. When she does eventually wrest a relationship from him, her illusions about his status and invulnerability are not destroyed by closer acquaintance; so removed from ordinary mortals is he that she can hardly believe he has a mother; on the intellectual level she regards him 'as if I had been God the Father,' Blomart recalls (BO p. 71). On the sexual level she closes her eyes in Blomart's arms 'with a docile and rapt expression' (BO p. 105) and communicates her desire to be 'all his' (BO p. 106) in a coy and submissive phrase which is far removed from Françoise's assumption of responsibility in a similar situation. She accepts trustfully the lie that Blomart loves her, and, as a result, feels justified in every detail of her physical existence: 'the colour of her hair, the shape of her nose, everything had become important since it was now the face that he loved' (BO p. 135).

Eventually, Hélène herself begins to wonder if this cult of Blomart is sufficient to justify her existence: ' "I have Jean," Hélène repeated to herself. She looked at Jean. Only him. Was that enough?' (BO p. 145). After the couple break up, she admits that her love was an egotistic one which took no account of her lover's needs and which excluded in its absolutism any possibility of friendship between them. But love still retains a tremendously high status in the book; far from learning that love is not all, Hélène is eventually rewarded with this prize in return for her adoption of what are, after all, Blomart's values. Despite her adulation of Blomart, the earlier Hélène had clung obstinately to her pursuit of happiness, and though the values to which she is eventually converted may be less egotistic, there remains a sense in which the character has been made to abdicate her own position. This is all the more apparent because the character's individualism and romanticism are by no means entirely negatively coded. The happiness she finds in the last chapters where she feels 'light and fully herself as on the finest evening of her childhood, when she rested in the arms of a paternal God' (BO p. 233), bears a strong resemblance to her earlier romantic ideal, especially in its evocation of the security of childhood and of a God-figure. Blomart's anxious concern for her well-being (BO p. 234), followed by the emotional vigil at her deathbed, is also the literal — if tragic — incarnation of her desire to have each of her heartbeats followed with emotion by the man she loves. Thus, though the romanticism of the character appears to be under attack, the structures of the text in fact support it and reinforce the romanticism already noted in the emotive link made in the text between the personal and the political.[13]

Hélène's romanticism is closely interwoven with her zest for life and appetite for happiness; above all, she is valorised for the strength of her desires and the determination with which she pursues them. This is in strong contrast to the emotional vacuum which paralyses Blomart for the majority of the book. 'I'm thin-blooded,' he admits. 'I've never been capable of passion. I dither about between my guilty conscience and my scruples' (BO p. 104). On a less conscious level there is a strong suggestion in the novel that an unresolved Oedipus complex might have placed a stranglehold on Blomart's emotions and be at the origin of his guilt complex (see for example pp. 124–25, where Blomart assumes his mother cannot love his father and that it is he himself who 'she loved most dearly'). At the end of the book Blomart decides that 'at least it is possible to know what one wants; one must act for what one wants' (BO p. 190). This is one lesson he might have learned from Hélène.

The initial phase of Blomart and Hélène's relations, in which Hélène pursues and Blomart retreats, emphasises Hélène's strength of will, and the open and vigorous manner in which she conducts her campaign allows her to escape from the stereotype of female guile.[14] 'Never had I met a woman so ignorant of feminine wiles,' remarks Blomart in patronising amusement (BO p. 74). The presentation of Hélène's body — largely through Blomart's eyes — supports this image of naturalness, of health and vigour, of a body inhabited by strong appetites and desires, her sunburned legs are constantly swinging (see e.g. pp. 67, 70), her gaze is bold (BO p. 57), her cheeks glowing (BO p. 58). Her eyes 'searched the horizon to wrest from it all its promises; her legs, eager to spring forward, trembled with the effort to control them' (BO p. 69). These descriptions function in part as a stimulus to Blomart's guilt, in their stark comparison to the pinched nostrils and laboured breathing of Hélène's body as she approaches death. However, her coltish body and lack of feminine wiles are an indication not only of the character's authenticity and appetite for life, but also of an adolescent, almost prepubescent quality. Hélène is catapulted brutally into womanhood in the abortion scene, in which the blood of aborted childbirth is also made to suggest the blood of first menstruation:

> My poor child, my poor little child. How young she was! She liked chocolate and bicycles and she went forward into life with the boldness of a child. And now she lay there, in the midst of her red woman's blood, and her youth and her gaiety ebbed from her body with an obscene gurgling. (BO p. 100)

The whole scene is marked by a sense of disgust evident in both characters' reactions to the idea that beneath Hélène's 'childish skin was that thing which she fed with her blood' (BO p. 97), a description which evokes the mix of guilt, blood and disgust so characteristic of the novel. Grotesque and caricatural details such as the powdered 'unwashed flesh' and unsterilised nail-scissors of the semi-senile abortionist who admits, 'I can't see an inch in front of my nose' (BO p. 101) abound in the scene. The disgust at the abortion is projected back by Blomart into his imaginary representation of the scene in which Hélène became pregnant: 'It was already dark outside; women passed on their lovers' arms, women with the red laughter of women. Hélène had had a lover, a dirty beast, who had slipped his hand under her dress. He hurt her: she is going to suffer, and she is a child' (BO p. 97).

Hélène's passage into 'womanhood' is thus connected by Blomart to the colour red, symbol of the blood of death, of menstruation and of childbirth; to pain (the 'sharp woman's pain' which Hélène undergoes; BO p. 98); to humiliating and painful sexual experience (with the 'dirty beast' who had 'hurt' her); and to a generalised sense of disgust at female bodily functions.[15] The nine references in five pages of the abortion scene to 'red' or 'blood' give a new dimension to the central thematic of 'the blood of others'; when one recalls that Beauvoir considered the title 'The Other Sex' for her essay on women demonstrating how man had constituted woman as 'the other', and that she and Sartre were using the equivalence of 'woman/the other' between themselves, it becomes evident that *The Blood of Others* can be read as 'The Blood of *Women*'.[16] It is after all Hélène who has to shed her blood twice over in the novel, both times as a result of her passion for Blomart. Blomart himself specifically links the two nights when Hélène's blood flows ('how long was that night, as long as this one is short'; BO p. 99).

Both of these nights are marked by death — the second by that of Hélène and the first by that of the foetus. The foetus is represented only as 'that thing in her womb' (BO p. 97) and as the bloody contents of a basin, but nevertheless this death presents an evident reworking of the first, and perhaps the most significant, death of the text: the death of Louise's baby in the bare room with the red tiles.[17] The death of the foetus is in fact only one of the multiple echoes in the text of the death of Louise's baby, a death echoed in Hélène's terse explanation that she is giving up her car seat to a woman because 'that child of hers will drop dead' (BO p. 203); in Blomart's italicised commentary, 'A child dies, his chest crushed by blows from rifle-butts' (BO p. 99); and, most distressingly of all, in the fate of Ruth and the other Jewish children, torn from their mothers and rounded up to be sent to their deaths (BO p. 229).

Blomart's guilt at the fate of the hostages is also fed by the memory of Louise's baby; when he has to face his mother's hostility over the hostage issue he recalls the scene of his childhood in which he hid beneath the piano and dug his nails into the carpet because 'Louise's baby is dead' (BO p. 224). Earlier in the evening he had come face to face with the posters announcing the death of hostages in retaliation for the bomb he had thrown — posters which were in historical fact yellow, but here transformed into a 'red notice against the white tiles' (BO p. 223), recalling the red tiles of the room in which Louise's baby lay.[18] As on the day of that death, the soup awaits Blomart, and for a second time he has literally to swallow his guilt. Guilt, disgust, childbirth and death are constantly bound together in the text. As early as the second page of the novel, Blomart refers to the 'utter rottenness hidden in the womb of all human destiny', present both 'at my birth' and in the 'odour and shadow of the death room' (BO p. 8).[19] Perhaps it is in the real-life death of Louise's baby that the origins of the link between the womb and destruction might be sought; in the text the representation of the womb as source of destruction is doubled by the association made between the womb and the sickly sweet existential void, the source of nausea and a defining characteristic of the being-for-itself (see my Chapter 1). Both sets of connections — womb and destruction, womb and the sugary existential void — come together in the striking image of the sugar almond: 'Pleasant sugary shell, full of memories and scents, calm and dark as a belly. Tomorrow it will be blown into fragments' (BO p. 157).

Hélène's sexuality, a powerful force which commands the entire action of the fourth chapter, is itself bound up with existential nausea and the void. When Paul caresses her she feels enveloped in 'some pale sickly vapour'; her flesh becomes a 'humid and spongy moss' stabbed by the 'honeyed stings' of 'a thousand buzzing insects'; paralysed and sinking, Hélène struggles to escape the viscous depths in which she has become a formless jellyfish (BO pp. 79–80). Images of sweetness and sickliness echo the 'sickly spirals' which Blomart experiences as a child, mingled with the caramel odour of the Blomart household (BO pp. 8–9); sensations of dampness and the image of the formlessness of sea creatures reincarnate the void familiar to Hélène in which her flesh becomes 'glaucous and flabby and slightly, shiveringly, sensitive. Just like an oyster' palpitating in its shell (BO p. 43). In Chapter 4 Hélène tries at first to resist this ambiguous flood of feelings, but when after refusing Paul she is in turn refused by Blomart, she deliberately subverts her desire by immolating herself in the arms of the 'dirty beast', punishing both herself and Blomart with the resulting abortion. Female sexuality and the female body, from the palpitating oyster to the womb and its foetal contents, or the sugary belly of the almond, thus are made into a source of nausea and danger, blood and guilt. His vigil by the bedside of the dying Hélène brings all these elements together for Blomart.

In later sections of the book, Hélène's sexuality appears less culpable (because mastered by Blomart?), but the fate of the other women in the novel is not encouraging, in this or most other respects. Yvonne, chained to a hypochondriac mother, pours ridicule over the bodies of her female clients, and jokes uneasily with Hélène about wedding nights; Madeleine sets the same low value on her body that she does on the rest of her life: 'Her body had no value, she gave it with indifference to anyone who asked for it; her time had no value, she spent it chiefly in sleeping or in smoking while she stared into space' (BO p. 64). Both Madeleine and Denise recall the figure of Elisabeth in *She Came to Stay*, though Madeleine is more sympathetically presented than the other two. Like Elisabeth, Denise is presented as a leech on the life of others and a profoundly irritating personality: 'Even I was frequently annoyed by her' (BO p. 123), Blomart loftily remarks. She too is seen as having a perverse relationship with language, using 'words which had no meaning for us' (BO p. 32). Her attempt at writing is presented as a failure (echoing Elisabeth's at painting); the arbiter of this judgement is Blomart, who dismisses Denise's novel as 'hopeless' (BO p. 136) despite the fact that he is not interested in literature and 'didn't know much about poetry' (BO p. 22). Denise's breakdown, resulting from this failure, and from the treatment she receives at the hands of Marcel (including, like Elisabeth, humiliating sexual experience; see pp. 126, 147), is only the first of a series of increasingly serious breakdowns which stalk women's destiny in Beauvoir's writing (Paule in *The Mandarins*, Laurence in *Les Belles Images*, Murielle in 'Monologue'), a phenomenon of which Françoise's illness in *She Came to Stay* can be seen as a forerunner. Denise's delirium in her suffocating upper-floor hotel room raises the spectre of 'the mad woman in the attic', the image of female alienation so often found at work in women's writing[20] and which is evoked in even more nightmarish terms by the chamber of Madame Kotz: 'The forbidden room, full of darkness and nightmares and the odour of madness (. . .) Madame Kotz was buried under the covers, only her head emerged, a head with cropped hair and bulging cheeks covered with soft black hair' (BO p. 228).

While Madame Kotz is subsequently consigned to the worst fate of all — the concentration camp — Denise, Madeleine and Hélène all eventually gather in the Resistance group which functions as a nurturing group for Blomart, substituting for the mother whom he has alienated but whom he wants to 'tuck me up in bed and give me a long kiss' (BO p. 225). The ambivalence of Blomart's feelings towards his mother has already been noted. It is she who teaches him that 'each of us is responsible for everything and to every human being', but she refuses to make the kind of stark choices which Blomart does. Living in perfect — but unarticulated — lucidity a life built on contradictions (she maintains an impeccably bourgeois household whilst spending her evenings darning stockings), she remains the pure voice of conscience for Blomart. Thus it is in her that are invested the moral arguments against resistance action which weigh so heavily for him. By eventually taking up the opposite view, Blomart chooses praxis over moral scrupulousness, chooses his father's way over his mother's. Reunited by his action with the 'odious' father, Blomart eventually comes to face the fact that he is not five years old, that he cannot always have the total approval of his mother, cannot be 'tucked up in bed'. In this sense the whole novel can be read as the account of how Blomart resolves his oedipal feelings towards his mother.[21] The oedipal theme also, however, reinforces the final choice of the hero, since it bolsters it with the notion that this is the 'mature' choice of a hero at last untied from his mother's apron strings.

Thus, by the end of the novel, Blomart is supported not only by Madeleine and Denise, by Paul (also a source of guilt in the past) and by Laurent and Marcel, but by his father and by other members of the social class from which he had once alienated himself. The evolution of Marcel provides yet another example of a character who gravitates towards support of Blomart during the course of the novel. In the early stages of the novel he appears autonomous, assured, even superior to Blomart in his awareness of the contradictions of Blomart's position. But his situation soon comes to echo that of Blomart. His desire to create a work of art which could exist for and by itself (a dream of pure being-in-itself existing without the complicity of the for-itself, 'protected from consciousness'; BO p. 31) fails, as Blomart had failed to construct an island for himself in which he could draw up the bridges and cut himself off from effects on others. The various solutions which Marcel tries out to solve this problem resemble Blomart's efforts; like Blomart he is loved by a woman to whom he decides to lie to make her happy (see BO p. 152), like Blomart the experience of the war is a capital one for him. He even speaks, when he discovers his solution, of the assault he makes on his audience's freedom (BO p. 220) in a parallel to Blomart's feelings towards the hostages.[22] Thus a character who initially is placed in a degree of opposition to Blomart, evolves into his shadow. It is worth noting, though, that despite all his failures Marcel's vocation as an artist is never questioned in the way that that of Denise or Elisabeth is.

By the end of the novel Blomart's stature has been raised to the point where all the remaining characters have adopted a satellite function in relation to him. The narrative structure, examined at the beginning of this discussion, itself demonstrates the point that this is Blomart's story; Hélène's story is literally enclosed in his narrative and is brought to a close by the death which functions as a liberating force for Blomart, allowing him to project forward into a future which is not for her. Though the narrative structure initially sets up an antithesis between male and female, each facing the other as the individual consciousness apprehends the other, this antithesis is dissolved as the female discourse is eventually absorbed into the male. After the woman-centredness of *She Came to Stay*, *The Blood of Others* is the novel of a male character to whom the female character is literally sacrificed. However, this man, with his constant worrying and concern for others, with his heavily foregrounded ambivalences and lack of certitude, is not built on the semi-Sartrian Don Juan model of Pierre (of *She Came to Stay*). In so far as the Blomart–Hélène relationship has an autobiographical base, it echoes the structure not of the Beauvoir–Sartre model but of the encounter which Beauvoir had during Sartre's absence in the war with Nathalie Sorokine, to whom the novel is dedicated.[23] Given that Sartre was largely absent from Paris during the period to which this novel essentially relates, and that the pattern of pursuit and flight was actually enacted between Beauvoir and another woman, it becomes apparent how Beauvoir was able for once to eject the ubiquitous Sartre-model male from her fiction and create a male figure in whom her own experience could be partly embodied.

A reading of *The Prime of Life* also suggests a relationship between some of the ambiguities of the text and Beauvoir's attitude to the discovery of history, referred to earlier. 'History took hold of me, and never let go thereafter,' writes Beauvoir (POL p. 359), an experience which is lent in a more condensed form to Hélène. But Beauvoir also describes how her strong attachment to individualism led her to refuse the facts of her own relation to history until it was absolutely impossible for her to continue closing her eyes any longer. The ambiguities and contradictions at work in the novel reflect the reluctant nature of this discovery. The choice of the Resistance, for example, can be seen not only as the choice dictated by the historical moment, but also as the choice of a situation fraught with ambiguities which in themselves reflect Beauvoir's own ambivalence. Equally, the treatment of the theme of the individual's responsibility to others through the Jean–Hélène relationship which, as I have argued, actually undermines the general thesis of intervention and commitment, can also be seen as being rooted in this ambivalence. Finally, the obsessive figure of death, the traumatic repeated experience of the death of the child, which intensifies the weight of guilt, can also be read as an effect of Beauvoir's anxiety and emotional insurgence against an intellectual and political truth which she 'used words to talk myself into accepting' (POL p. 547).

The narrative structure and the patterning of the argument of this text are clearly organised with a much more didactic intention than is to be found in Beauvoir's first novel, *She Came to Stay*. Despite this, however, the commitment made to praxis and to history in *The Blood of Others* is a highly ambiguous one, subverted from the outset by the plurality of the title. The sacrifice of the main female character on the altar of the political and moral education of the male hero means that the woman — the 'Other' — is again destroyed in this text, as Xavière is destroyed in *She Came to Stay*, this time in the interests of commitment. The struggle with history was a hard one for Beauvoir, convinced that she should be more ready to commit herself to its imperatives, and it is a struggle that continues beyond *The Blood of Others*.

Notes

1. This wordplay works slightly better in the French, where *histoire* means both 'history' and 'story'.

2. The account I have given of the narrative situation in these chapters does not solve the problem of the brief final chapter. The time sequence in this chapter, unlike all the others, is continuous and corresponds to the present of the 1940s Blomart. One would therefore expect the whole chapter to be narrated in the present tense and to represent the unmediated thoughts of Blomart. The opening of the chapter does conform to this; however, after the first paragraph, the past tense is resumed, and the narrative situation resembles strongly that of a covert external narrator focusing through Blomart. Has the external narrator of Hélène's chapters suddenly been permitted access to Blomart's narrative?

3. See *Memoirs of a Dutiful Daughter* (1958), p. 131. The event was all the more traumatic in that it concerned a woman — also named Louise — who had had total care of Beauvoir in her early years. Many of the details are the same.

4. Blomart does not therefore carry his pacifism to its logical conclusion and refuse, as many did historically, to fight. By going along with the war and accepting orders as a soldier, Blomart is already accepting the necessity of war.

5. In *The Prime of Life*, p. 548, Beauvoir describes a play which she abandoned writing, but which was to show the interrelation of personal passions and a sense of responsibility to the community.

6. Not least by Beauvoir herself who, with characteristic eagerness to accept criticism, subscribes to Blanchot's dismissal of her book in *The Prime of Life*, p. 544.

7. See Susan Suleiman, *Authoritarian Fictions*, pp. 10, 56.

8. See Maurice Blanchot, *La Part du Feu*, pp. 195–211.

9. See *The Prime of Life*, p. 498, and Henri Michel, *Paris Résistant*, p. 165. Even today the issue remains controversial. Henri Michel, one of France's leading historians on the Second World War, concludes that 'given the uncertain, even illusory benefits of this kind of action, its costs were high, no doubt too high' (p. 172; my translation).

10. One may wonder what distinction it is possible to make between a *roman à thèse* and 'committed' literature. Using Suleiman's criteria it seems possible to distinguish between commitment to a specific action in a specific situation, and an attempt to set up a system of absolute values, of 'right' and 'wrong'.

11. See *The Prime of Life*, pp. 412–21, 426–32.

12. There are evident similarities between Hélène's arguments and Sartre's analysis of the phenomenon of collaboration in 'Qu'est-ce qu'un collaborateur?' (What is a Collaborator?), where he denounces the 'intellectual malady of historicism'. See *Situations III*, pp. 43–61.

13. It has frequently been noted that Hélène is a classic example of the *amoureuse*, one of the stereotypical forms of women's flight from responsibility established by Beauvoir in *The Second Sex*. See my Chapter 1 and Jean Leighton's *Simone de Beauvoir on Woman*, pp. 125–31.

14. This behaviour nonetheless attracts almost universal horror in critics. See, for example, Leighton who describes Hélène as pursuing Blomart 'shamelessly with a fury of self-abasement' (p. 126).

15. It has often been noted that Beauvoir displays a marked distaste for female bodily functions in *The Second Sex*. See pp. 60–61 for her

description of menstruation which, for Beauvoir, makes the woman 'feel her body most painfully as an obscure, alien thing'.

16. The use of the equivalence woman/the other is particularly evident in the letters Sartre sent to Beauvoir during the war (*Lettres au Castor*, 1983). Beauvoir herself is frequently referred to by Sartre in these letters as 'vous autre'.

17. The red tiles appear only in the fictional and not in the autobiographical version of the baby's death (see *Memoirs of a Dutiful Daughter*, p. 131). It is also of interest that the absence of the father of Louise's baby is repeated in the physical absence from the text of the father of Hélène's baby, who features only as a voice on the telephone and through Yvonne and Blomart's references to him.

18. I am grateful to Margaret Atack for pointing out to me that in reality these posters were yellow.

19. The French text refers to the rottenness hidden *au sein* (literally 'in the breast'), equally an association between destruction and the maternal body.

20. See Sandra Gilbert and Susan Gubar's classic essay, *The Madwoman in the Attic*, where the image of the mad woman in women's writing is seen as an image of the female writer's 'anxiety of authorship'.

21. Blomart constantly treats his mother like a lover — see for example the shoe incident (p. 138), and his descriptions of her early in the book (p. 12).

22. Margaret Atack draws attention to the 'positive assumption of violence' by Marcel, which parallels Blomart's at the end of the novel. See Atack, 'The Occupation in Fiction: A Study of Changing Narrative Structures 1940–1945', p. 284.

23. It was Nathalie Sorokine, we learn from *The Prime of Life*, who lay in wait outside Beauvoir's building, who stole a bicycle, computed what percentage of her time Beauvoir allotted to her and marked in red on her calendar the days on which she succeeded in seeing Beauvoir. It was Beauvoir who closed her ears to Sorokine's insistent ringing on the doorbell and who was amused at the girl's jealousy of the absent Sartre, whom everyone in Beauvoir's entourage appeared to admire (POL pp. 431–33, 460–62). As in *She Came to Stay*, the text thus carries an epigraph of an abstract nature from a male writer and a dedication to a woman friend whose difficult relationship with Beauvoir is figured in the text.

4

All Men Are Mortal

All Men Are Mortal, the third novel which Beauvoir worked on during the years of the Second World War, is even more profoundly marked by the problem of the individual's relation to history than is *The Blood of Others*. 'In 1943–44 I was obsessed by History', writes Beauvoir in *Force of Circumstance* (FOC tr. adap., p. 71); in *All Men Are Mortal*, begun in 1943, she took on a broad sweep of more than 600 years of the history of Europe in an attempt to face some of the issues which she saw the historical dimension of human existence as posing. Can there be any logic in individuals sacrificing themselves for the uncertain future good of humanity? Are such terms as 'the Future', 'Mankind' or the 'Universe' meaningful? Is history gradually moving towards a better state of affairs, or is it condemned by man's natural savagery, by the narrow personal ambitions of individual rulers and by the inflexible mechanisms of economic realities to an endless series of sterile repetitions? The whole question of whether an individual can make historically meaningful sacrifices has an evident relation with the war years, and with the deaths which Beauvoir experienced amongst her close friends. By the time she completed the novel, in 1946, the cost of the Allied victory could be counted and evaluated in terms of what had been achieved. The dropping of the world's first atomic bomb had, in particular, made these costs look high. In *All Men Are Mortal* death recovers the scandalous quality in part commuted in *The Blood of Others* by the rhetoric of commitment. Death and mortality become a crucial element of the argument about the potential of individual action for historical significance.

In order to approach the theme of mortality, and its impact on individual action in relation to history, Beauvoir uses a tactic familiar to readers of her later fiction: she presents an image of the other side of the coin, in this case of the fantasy of immortality. The story of the immortal Count Fosca, with its echoes of Faust and the dilemmas of the Greek gods, takes the novel further into the realms of the imaginary and the mythical than any other of Beauvoir's works. At the same time Fosca's immortality is a device for surveying six centuries of European history from a single point of view; the sheer scope of the enterprise accelerates the opening-up process already noted in *The Blood of Others*, as the narrative ranges far beyond the confines of contemporary Paris and France to the struggles of medieval Italy and the pioneering explorers of the forests of North America. Despite the mythico-poetic aspect of the theme of immortality, therefore, the novel is grounded in historically based situations presented in careful detail and raising concrete questions about the means available and necessary to achieve political aims.

All Men Are Mortal is one of the most open of Beauvoir's texts. This is not because the principal narrator of the text, Fosca, does not produce a conclusion in favour of meaningful action — he does — rather it is due to the fact that this conclusion is itself thrown off balance by other elements of the text. One of the most obvious of these is the fact that the eventual conclusion is of no use to Fosca, and that it is also beyond the reach of Régine, the only character who is present from beginning to end of the narrative. Both these characters have considerable structural importance: Fosca narrates the five principal sections of the text, and produces its central argumentation, whilst Régine has the double role of acting both as narratee in Fosca's sections, with all that that implies in terms of weighting one particular reading of the story, and as the focus through which the narrative is produced in the prologue and epilogue which enclose Fosca's narrative. It is thus of some import that the brief epilogue, which features only these two characters, is dominated by their despair and not by the cautious optimism which Fosca's argument eventually produces.

The structure of the five sections of the story which Fosca narrates to Régine is remarkably similar to the pattern of *The Blood of Others*: in the space of a single night, the male narrator recounts his life story from his earliest years to the present. In each section a brief return to the narrative present marks out the passage of narrative time (in this case from the afternoon on which Fosca begins his narrative to the following morning when it ends). In both novels the point of the narrative is to expose the oscillations of the narrator between two antithetical points of view, and even the three-stage pattern of the oscillation is the same: Fosca's belief that he can change the course of history is first adopted in an absolute kind of way, then rejected in despair and then finally cautiously re-asserted despite all its attendant difficulties and limitations — thus following exactly the pattern of Blomart's thinking in *The Blood of Others*. However, the severity of these limitations is such that they operate in *All Men Are Mortal* as a further element throwing into question the optimism of the logical conclusion. A further important difference operates in the function of the narrative: whereas Blomart the narrator is plagued by doubts and uses his narrative to focus on his own dilemma, Fosca's mind is already firmly made up at the beginning of his narrative. Blomart the narrator constantly evaluates and interprets his past, moving from one subject to another according to the flow of consciousness; Fosca, on the other hand, rarely intervenes in his narrative, con-fining himself as far as possible to a linear account of events and of the development of his thought in relation to them. Fosca's style is much more formal, more expository than Blomart's, making use of the past historic tense (in the French text) whereas Blomart mixes this with the more personalised *passé composé*. The effect of this relative formality is to focus the narrative on events, rather than on personal interpretation, on history rather than on an individual; the impression is created that it is history that is being examined rather than an individual's story, that history is in the dock and that Fosca is simply an impartial judge.

However, what we are actually presented with is of course a careful selection of historical moments. In the first two sections of Fosca's narrative, which represent the first stage of the three-part pattern and in which Fosca believes that he can achieve meaning-ful historical action if only this or that impediment were removed, Fosca is situated first in medieval Italy, then in sixteenth century Germany. Beauvoir writes in *Force of Circumstance*: 'Stupid wars, a chaotic economy, useless rebellions, futile massacres, population increases unaccompanied by any improvement in the standard of living, everything in this period seemed to me confusion and marking time; I had chosen it for this very reason' (FOC p. 72). This is then the historical experience against which Fosca's optimism is to be measured. However, there are several steps along the way to the inevitable conclusion that all attempts to organise men's destiny are futile. As ruler of the fictional city of

Carmona in the first section, Fosca at first identifies the major obstacle to effective rule as his mortality.[1] Not only is he convinced that to be effective political policy needs to be pursued in the longer term — longer than the life span of a single individual — but he is also under considerable pressure from the knowledge that none of his immediate predecessors have ruled for more than five years before being assassinated. His immediate aim, therefore, in drinking the immortality elixir, is to ensure that he can act effectively for the good of Carmona.

His calculation appears to be correct as Fosca succeeds first in removing the military threat of the Genoese, and then in building up a strong and prosperous community in the town. His optimism about the concrete possibilities of effective political action appears justified — as is his disdain for the limits of mortal action. However, other constraints on Fosca's action eventually become apparent: natural disaster in the shape of bubonic plague wipes out his economic achievements; a whole series of victories and defeats in war which do little more than cancel each other out lead him to doubt the efficacy of military action; the achievement of prosperity for all turns out to be impossible as Fosca finds himself helpless to prevent the exploitation of the workers if he wishes to avoid bringing economic disaster down on the whole community. The final blow comes when he allows his beloved son Antoine, avid for honour in battle, to lead the town back into war; not only does his son lose his life, but the whole future of Italy as an independent country is undermined and eventually lost as the result of an individual's ambition.[2] Fosca concludes that he has taken too narrow a view of the interests of Carmona, whose political and economic situation depends not only on itself but on a much wider context. To shape history, he will have to create a world dictatorship in which he will direct everything from behind the scenes and ensure the prosperity and peace of every part of the earth. The major obstacle to effective rule is now identified as the conflict of interests between different communities.

It is as a first step towards his ideal world dictatorship that Fosca becomes, in the second part of his narrative, the personal advisor of Charles V of the Hapsburg Empire, at the beginning of the sixteenth century. The identification of Fosca's fortunes with this particular ruler is again a carefully selected one: master of a huge empire, Charles V was one of the most beleaguered rulers of history, who failed in all his major aims. His continual conflicts with the kings of France led to no definitive results, while his

dream of the triumph of religious orthodoxy ended in the Refor-
mation. In this context, Fosca's totalitarian dream is quickly dissi-
pated. The endless wars with the same enemies over the same
issues bring Fosca up against the weight which the past seems to
constantly bring to bear on the present. His renewed attempts to
initiate reforms to help the poorest sections of the community
again are frustrated, this time by the power of the financiers and
merchants on whose support Charles V is dependent for his wars.
When the peasants revolt and are put down in a bloody repression,
Fosca reflects that man's savagery towards his fellow creatures
seems only to increase with the passing of the centuries. Turning
in despair to the New World in the hope that it will have been able
to free itself from some of the old constraints, Fosca discovers that
the destruction of the Incas and the dreadful exploitation in the
South American silver mines is as savage and sorry a spectacle as
any in Europe. Even Charles V does not benefit from the precious
metals found in his new domains, whose principal effect in Europe
is to drive up prices and force down wages. When Charles V hands
over power after 27 years of rule it is clear that neither his nor
Fosca's aims are any closer to realisation than at the beginning. All
the deaths and all the repressions have served for nothing; Fosca
sees that concepts such as 'the Empire' or 'the Universe' which are
used to justify such savagery are empty.

> 'What a convenient word!' I said. What did today's sacrifices
> matter: the Universe lay ahead in the future. What did burn-
> ings at the stake and massacres matter? The Universe was
> somewhere else, always somewhere else! And it isn't any-
> where: there are only men, men eternally divided. (AMM
> p. 313)

Yet it is not so much these failures which convince Fosca that 'It
is impossible to do anything for anyone' (AMM p. 317) as the
phrase of a Lutheran monk, about to be burned as a heretic:
' "There is only one good," he said. "And that is to act according
to your conscience" ' (AMM p. 282).[3] This aspect of Luther's
thought which, in the credit it gives to the individual conscience
over the authorised teachings of the Church, neatly anticipates
existentialism, is viewed by Fosca as the essential secret of mortal
human beings. People can only value ends which they themselves
have set and which will always constitute a change of whatever
circumstances currently prevail: 'What has value in their eyes is

never what is done for them; it's what they do for themselves. And those of us who claim the right to build the world for them and lock them up in it can only be hated by them' (AMM p. 315). Fosca's plan to create a perfect world is thus doomed to failure not only by the kinds of political and economic constraints against which he has come up against time and time again, but by the very nature of human freedom and desires.

It takes Fosca over 250 years to reach these conclusions at the end of the second section of his narrative. The first stage of the three-part pattern is now completed; the idea of history as a futile merry-go-round has been established. In the subsequent stages, history is no longer presented from the point of view of the ruler. Grand plans for the universe are replaced at the opening of the second stage by Fosca's involvment in the ambition of an individual explorer in the depths of the North American forests to attain historical significance by discovering a new waterway through to the sea. Carlier is defeated not by complex political circumstances but by the constraints of his own body as he is eventually forced by lack of food into shooting himself. Despite the change of scale, this episode is thus again the account of a failure — nevertheless this new failure gives Fosca further insights into the nature of human endeavours. After Fosca saves Carlier's life and prevents his whole expedition from collapse, Carlier is far from grateful. When a second impasse is reached Carlier refuses bitterly to wait behind whilst Fosca undertakes a second rescue mission, explaining that: 'I have to feel that I'm alive (. . .) Even if it kills me' (AMM p. 352). This extension of the Lutheran monk's formula leaves Fosca more convinced than ever that it is impossible to do anything for anyone.

However, he emerges from this experience in the wilderness to return to the community in Part 4 and begin an uphill climb to the end of the second stage. Part 3 had covered only two or three years (in contrast for example to the two centuries covered in Part 1); in Part 4 the perspective again widens in the sense that it covers several decades of life in eighteenth century Paris, but it remains focused on the individual level as Fosca again simply co-operates in an individual's project without himself believing in its utility. Marianne's faith in new scientific methods, her belief that through an enlightened education human beings will become more tolerant and more free cannot convince Fosca that there is any meaning to the word 'progress'. Marianne speaks of a future reign of truth and justice as though these values were absolutes; Fosca doubts whether Marianne's 'truth' is any better than that of past ages. Despite being himself involved in experimental science he doubts even the nature of scientific progress: 'Were we really more advanced than the alchemists of Carmona? We had brought to light certain facts that they were not aware of, we had organised them into the right order; but had we advanced even a step nearer to the mysterious heart of the universe?' (AMM p. 417). In Fosca's view the scientific description of the principles at work in the universe may be becoming ever more sophisticated, but he can see no real advance in the eighteenth century over earlier attributions of the origins of the universe to God.

This intellectual pessimism is reinforced by Fosca's inability to help Marianne come to terms with her mortality, just as she cannot help him face his immortality. However, Fosca's love for Marianne is nevertheless strongly valorised in the text, and is shown to protect him from the disabling view of human beings as ants feverishly running in all directions, all giving themselves to their futile occupations 'with the same stupid intensity' (AMM p. 389). Marianne has a message for Fosca which helps him to affront the events of the final part of his narrative, and which directly prepares its more optimistic thinking: ' "Try to stay a man amongst men," she said. "There's no other hope for you" ' (AMM p. 434). Marianne is also the source of hope in the text in another sense: Armand, the character who is to embody the possibility of human achievement, is Marianne's direct descendant. He will struggle for the Republic of which Marianne's name is the symbol.

Armed with Marianne's instruction, Fosca enters the nineteenth century and the final part of his narrative, in which he tries to share in Armand's revolutionary activities in the Paris of the 1840s. He thus effects a return to the political arena after the strictly personal ambitions of Carlier, and the more philanthropic ones of Marianne. Armand does not share the absolutism of Marianne and Carlier, and is not in the least deterred by the knowledge of his own mortality or by the temporal nature of the political aims that he expects to achieve. He has already internalised the lessons of history: 'Everything that we build is eventually destroyed, I know that. And that from the hour of our birth we begin the process of dying. But between birth and death there is life' (AMM pp. 503–4). Armand wants to use that life to fight for limited and achievable results — human results:

A limited future, a limited life: that's man's lot, that's enough. If I thought that in fifty years' time it would be illegal to employ children in factories, illegal to make men work more than ten hours, that the people would be able to choose their own representatives, and that the press would be free, then I would be satisfied. (AMM p. 505)

Thus a character at last articulates aims which the reader knows that history has fulfilled, at least in some form. The success of Armand and his friends in the 1848 Revolution, described in the section, also seems to allow a greater optimism, though the choice of 1848 (as opposed to, say, 1789) is clearly intended as a reminder in itself of the temporary nature of human victory. Though the 1848 Revolution did put an end to monarchy in France and ushered in the Second Republic, it was followed only four months later by the June days in which those like Armand with socialist demands were brutally repressed.[4] Less than four years after the 1848 Revolution the Republic was hijacked once again, this time by Napoleon III.

Within these historical limitations, Armand's arguments act as the culmination of a point of view which Fosca has gradually been drawing attention to since the account of his encounter with the Lutheran monk in Part 2. The monk's formula ('There is only one good. And that is to act according to your conscience.') is the axis of the argument, not only providing Fosca in Part 2 with a partial explanation of why it is not possible to do anything for anyone, but also valorising the aspirations and achievements of the individual. This thread continued in Carlier, who, despite his failure, at least 'feels he is alive', and in Marianne with her appetite for life, leads to Armand, who believes he can move the social conditions of the workers one step forward. All embody the definition of what it is to be human, which Fosca imparts to Charles Quint: 'Sometimes a flame burns in their hearts; that's what they call being alive' (AMM p. 314). The final section of Fosca's narrative takes on an important interpretative function as Fosca constantly thinks back to the events and characters of earlier sections, re-evaluating them in the light of what one might call the mortal perspective exemplified by Armand and his friends. In this 're-reading', events such as Antoine's death, presented in Part 1 as a disaster, become a triumph of the assertion of human will and desire: 'it wasn't Rivelles that Antoine had so desired, it was his victory; he had died for it, he had died fulfilled' (AMM pp. 471–72). Dying for what you believe in or what you desire becomes in this perspective not a nonsensical gesture, but the foundation of meaning and value. Individuals give their lives, it is now argued, 'in order to make their lives human' (AMM p. 472). Antoine's story also illuminates another aspect of the mortal perspective: his immediate goal of taking the town of Rivelles for the glory of Carmona may have turned out, in the long term, to be one which prejudiced the whole future of Italy; but it is now argued that the individual can act only with regard to a limited future, to the future 'on which he has a hold,' as Armand puts it (AMM p. 504). The case of Garnier, who fights to hold his barricade in full knowledge that the struggle has been called off for political reasons, is nevertheless used as a warning against excessive exaltation of the present. Though the retrospective view of history (judging an action in terms of what historically it can be seen to have achieved) is placed in total contradiction to the situation of individuals, who for Armand must identify with their own context and live in the present, this does not remove the need to take the future we do have a hold on into account, and to try to maximise our impact on it. Garnier's act exalts the present at the cost of the immediate future.

Antoine, Béatrice, Carmona, Carlier and Marianne are invoked frequently in this section as a litany not of failure but of human aspirations; at the end of his narrative Fosca argues that the temporality and the contingency of individual action, which he had once viewed as tragic, are in fact the basis on which the individual can build freedom and value. Contemplating the activists of 1848 Fosca concludes that these men 'knew that they were not gnats, not ants, but human beings and that it was important to be alive and to be the victors; they had risked — given — their lives to make this true, and it was true: there was no other truth' (AMM p. 521). Thus the argument for action and commitment comes full circle, and the uniqueness of human life is asserted.

However, Armand's solution falls far short of Fosca's original absolutist ambitions, and the limitations of Armand's position are invoked at the end of Fosca's narrative with considerable force. Fosca himself is not a mortal being, cannot take the limited mortal perspective, and has no faith whatsover in the future. When Armand and Laure speak of the future, of progress, of humanity, Fosca can only think of all the other speeches in the same vein which he has heard over the centuries:

Blood was spilled, houses burned, shouts and songs rent the
air and fluffy white lambs grazed in the green pastures of the
future. The time will come . . . I heard their breathing heavy
with emotion. And here we were; the time had come, the
future was today, the future of all those martyrs burned at the
stake, all those peasants with their throats cut, of all those
ardent orators, the future which Marianne had hoped for was
this succession of days marked out by the hum of machinery,
by the slow torture of children, by prisons, slums, fatigue,
hunger, boredom . . . (AMM p. 501)

When Fosca sees the masses marching on the Bastille he sees in his
mind the masses marching through the ages, forever marching
with corpses in their wake towards a new future, constantly just
out of reach, forever an illusion. Despite the contention that
human action takes its value from the very facticity in which it is
grounded, the overall view of history within which this action is
inserted remains therefore resolutely pessimist.

Even Armand does not seriously challenge this overall view,
created by the juxtaposition of carefully selected periods of
European history, and designed in part to illustrate the case that
Beauvoir had argued in *Pyrrhus and Cinéas* (1944) that the
individual has to be disassociated from the universal, that it is
meaningless to carry out a project in the name of 'humanity'.
'Humanity' consists not of a totality aspiring to the same aim — as
Fosca needs to assume in order to create his world dictatorship —
but of a mass of individuals each with his or her own freedom and
aspirations. Each time Fosca tries to bring his Empire together, he
is confronted by someone like Luther who declares that 'his
conscience weighed more heavily than the interests of the Empire
or of the world' (AMM p. 255). History thus becomes a discontinuous succession of freedoms with endless departures towards
individual projects, but for which there can be no overall goal.[5]
Beauvoir was well aware that this view runs directly counter to the
Marxist view of history: 'The Communists, following Hegel,
speak of humanity and its future as of some monolithic indi-
viduality. I was attacking this illusion,' she writes of *All Men Are
Mortal* in *Force of Circumstance* (FOC p. 73).[6]

The nature of human action emerges as finite and individual;
Fosca's idea of a perfect world for all is naturally impossible in this
light, and the totalitarian methods which he tries to employ for the
collective good in both Carmona and the Hapsburg Empire must

be doomed to failure. Without ever directly refuting Fosca's political methods, Beauvoir effectively undermines them by assimilating them to the fundamentally inhuman perspective of immortality; thus when Fosca argues with Charles the Machiavellian position that a prince can 'never do good without doing harm. It is impossible to be just to all and to make everyone happy' (AMM p. 249), he is shown simultaneously to be thinking to himself: 'I could not speak to him in my own language: a life, a thousand lives are of no more consequence than a cloud of gnats' (AMM p. 249). The real thinking behind the Machiavellian type of argument is thus exposed. Even more overtly, Fosca's arguments in favour of supporting Cortez's expedition to South America in the full knowledge that this will lead to the destruction of the native Indian people, are shown, in the most lyrical pages of the text, to have appalling consequences, both in terms of human suffering and even in terms of Fosca's own long-term aims. The evident lesson is that even the best-intentioned of dictators must fail. In the essays which Beauvoir published in this period she shows why she believes that it is impossible for Fosca — or for anyone — to do things *for* others. The oppressed fight for freedom to improve their own conditions themselves; their participation in this process is crucial to the results achieved. Thus, for example, the reforms which the 1789 revolutionaries brought about she sees as the result of human belief in freedom; the reforms would have had a radically different meaning if the King had simply granted them.[6]

This philosophical position is translated into political terms in *All Men Are Mortal* by Armand's participation in the 1848 Revolution. He does not struggle *for* others but *with* others. The fraternal impulse behind Armand's action is stressed on a number of occasions, and he does gain a temporary measure of success. Another example of a possible alternative to totalitarianism is supplied by the portrait given in Part 2 of the Inca civilisation in South America. As Fosca admires the infrastructures created by the Incas and learns about their civilisation from the half-caste Filipillo, he comes to see that the Inca empire, which he has had a hand in destroying, is the model of the empire which he himself had hoped to establish:

Private property was unknown by the Incas; they owned in common the land which was shared out between them each year, a piece of public land being reserved for the upkeep of the public servants and for supplying the shops in times of shortages; it was called 'land of the Inca and of the sun'; each Indian worked on this land on certain days, and also cultivated the land of those who were ill, of the widows and the orphans; they worked lovingly, inviting their friends and entire villages to work their land: the guests were as prompt to accept the invitation as if they had been invited to a wedding. Every two years there was a distribution of wood, and in hot areas, the cotton from the royal lands went to all: everyone did all the necessary tasks in their own homes, being masons and blacksmiths at the same time as farmers. There were no poor among them. (AMM p. 306)

This idealistic vision with its emphasis on the communal ownership of land and on the co-operative nature of work, provides some idea of the type of social organisation which Beauvoir's ethical and political principles of the 1940s might permit, and which might escape through its autarkic economic organisation some of the economic fatalities which so constrain Fosca in both Carmona and the German Empire. But quite apart from the question of the accuracy of this account of Inca society (which leaves aside the repressive authority of the Inca emperors and their imposition of the religion of the sun god), the fact is that it is the destruction of this civilisation which is presented in the text. Even where harmonious forms of social and economic organisation are constructed, therefore, history is deployed to show that they are vulnerable to the greed and brutality of others.

The view that history abolishes all human endeavours, to which both author and character-narrator evidently subscribe, weighs against Armand's optimism. It is joined in the balance by the fact that Fosca's personal destiny is inevitably rendered black by Armand's solution: if mortality is to be the basis of value, Fosca is condemned by definition to endless and meaningless existence. Of course the very tragedy of Fosca's situation is an argument for Armand. From the prologue onwards, Fosca's immortality is explored to show us that without the focus of a life limited by mortality there is no virtue (How can we be generous if our resources are not limited? How can we be brave when we risk nothing irreparable?), no value, no sense of identity (Fosca changes 'character' at different points of his career and cannot identify with any single place or person), no aesthetic pleasure. It is our insertion in a particular era and a particular place, it is argued, which allows us to develop commitments to people and to values, and which gives us a sense of stability and uniqueness. When Régine takes Fosca to visit the places of her childhood she is able to evoke with happy tranquillity her early memories, the surroundings in which she grew up and which remain virtually unchanged when she revisits them. Régine has

> 'only one childhood, only one life, my life.' For her, time would one day stand still, it was already still, it was held back by the impenetrable wall of death: Régine's life was a great lake in which the world was reflected in unbroken images. (AMM p. 91)

For Fosca, however, time can never stand still; the world around him is a series of shifting images and his life as lacking in coherence and identity as the flimsy assemblages surrounding him. All this is an argument for the human lot, but the fact that the character who narrates the lion's share of the text and who sets out in good faith to help others suffers a tragic fate, inevitably contributes to the pessimistic flavour of the closing pages of the text, even if we know that Fosca's defeat is our victory.

A rather different order of limitation is signalled by Régine. After hearing the narrative, she ought logically to embrace her finitude and imitate Armand in living her life towards her own goal. Yet Fosca's whole motivation in recounting his narrative to Régine is not to help her to decide how to live her life but to convince her of the tragedy of his own situation and to prove to her that he can do nothing for her. Régine's attitude is strongly marked by Fosca's; she is the most docile of narratees, making only very brief interventions which never challenge the narrative or interrupt its flow. Still curious and interested at the end of the first part of the narrative, she becomes progressively more sombre, and by the end of the second part listens only to put off the moment when she will have to decide what to do. Like Carlier and Marianne before her, she becomes the victim of Fosca's perspective on human activities which abolishes her uniqueness, converts her into an anonymous blade of grass, a feverishly active ant with no weapon against the futility of death. 'After wars peace, after peace, another war. Every day men are born and others die' (AMM p. 526). Fosca's summary of the story of history with its meaningless figure of death precipitates Régine's desire to scream out her anguish from the depths of her physical being. The solution offered her by Armand's example flutters in her consciousness barely a split second before disappearing. 'Gnat, foam on a wave, ant until death' (AMM p. 528); when Fosca walks away Régine is left with this view of herself. The passing of time marks out only the approach of death, and so it is with the striking of the clock that Régine begins to scream out her anguish in the last line of the novel.

Fosca's immortal perspective thus nourishes Régine's primitive horror in the face of her mortality — for it is this rather than a fear of dying in itself. However, Régine's horror pre-dates her meeting with Fosca and is the very reason for her interest in him. Like Françoise of *She Came to Stay*, Régine gives enormous importance to the existence of her consciousness in the world and to her image in the consciousness of others. Her world, with its focus on the theatre, nightclubs and hotel rooms is strongly reminiscent of the closed environment of *She Came to Stay*, mirroring her preoccupation with the confines of the consciousness. If she remains present in the nightclub with Florence and Sanier, she believes, her knowledge that Florence is also involved with another man will reduce Florence and Sanier's couple to its proper proportions. But if she were to leave them alone, 'nothing would prevent their love from being an authentically great passion' (AMM p. 17). She has a great need to impose her existence onto the consciousness of others — hence her horror of sleep: 'while you were asleep, there were always other people awake, and you had lost all hold over them' (AMM p. 19). Death signals the definitive loss of this reign (Régine: regina) of the consciousness and of all trace of her existence in the world. The world will continue on in its plenitude unmarked by her passage, like the hotel room which reassumes its anonymity after the passage of each guest: 'not a ripple, not a fissure' (AMM p. 52). Her ambition to be a great actress is an attempt to mark her audience's memory and survive in them after her death, but she has few illusions about this attempt: 'You're lucky to be a writer: books remain,' she tells Sanier, whereas 'actresses are not heard for long' (AMM p. 18).

Meeting Fosca offers Régine the chance, as she sees it, to be remembered until the end of time. Her only regret is that he will necessarily remember her as a being-for-others and not as a being-for-itself, for if Régine concerns herself with her image in the consciousness of others it is only so as to be able to herself seize this image: 'If only there were two of me, she thought, one doing the talking and one listening, one living and one watching, how I would love myself!' (AMM p. 16). This is not the only drawback to her plans; before Fosca even begins his narrative she starts to count the cost: by gambling on Fosca, she loses all capacity to see things from the mortal perspective, all interest in the life which she has built up for herself. As Fosca tells his tale, she understands that she has lost her gamble: Fosca will not remember her forever, is unable even while she is still alive to differentiate her from thousands of other women. In a twist of the Faustian legend, it is here Régine who effectively sells her soul to the devil in a bid for an impossible immortality and who, as a result, loses her humanity. Régine's lesson is underlined by the experiences of Carlier and Marianne. Though they do not bring their fate upon themselves in quite the voluntary way that Régine does, they similarly pay the cost of their intimacy with immortality and become obsessed with the idea of the world continuing without them.

The attitude underlying the fear of mortality is thus a horror of the end of the reign of consciousness, a horror of the absence of any mark of the individuals' existence on a world which will continue without them, akin to Régine's dislike of sleep and of the idea of Florence and Sanier staying on in the nightclub without her. It is perhaps because this attitude is so rooted in the central importance given by Beauvoir to the individual consciousness that it carries such weight in the text. The drama of immortality, in the shape of Fosca, and the quasi-metaphysical horror of mortality experienced by Régine, both in effect undermine Armand's embrace of human finitude. Though both characters could be argued to be special cases, they are the only characters present throughout the text, and their structural roles as speaker and listener give central importance to their pessimism. Over and above the dialectic of death as a source of horror, and death as the basis of meaning to human life, there remains the vision of history as an endless process of ebb and flow: 'it was as though some stubborn god spent their time in an immutable and absurd balancing act between life and death, prosperity and poverty' (AMM p. 275). Fosca experiences history as a 'monstrous mechanism' (AMM p. 261) in which each cog is driven forward by the fatalities of economics, of the weight of the past, of individuals' narrow and conflicting ambitions. Beauvoir writes in *Force of Circumstance* that in the aftermath of the Second World War, she could not possibly believe that her own century, with its bombings, battlefields and concentration camps was in any sense better than earlier ones (FOC p. 72). Believing in the individual's capacity to create meaning through one's own struggle towards a goal, irrespective of the aims achieved, Beauvoir herself imitated Armand; yet she remained deeply pessimistic about the idea of any better collective future. *All Men Are Mortal* conveys a strong sense of the paralysis which can grip the individual who contemplates at too great a length the absolutes of history and death, and Beauvoir was only too aware of her personal need to conjure this temptation.[7]

Fosca's narrative dominates the novel in terms of themes and in terms of sheer weight of pages (constituting roughly three-quarters of the text). However, structurally speaking, Fosca is a character in a text which focuses on Régine; it is for her that Fosca's story is told. She is the first (the first presented in the text) and the last (in chronological terms) of the women who attempt to form a couple with Fosca. Like all the others, their couple fails. Most fail because the women cannot withstand the measure of their mortality against Fosca's immortality, and are destroyed in the process. Laure is the exception; in parallel to Armand she is prepared to invoke the plenitude of the present against the gulf of immortality: 'Even if you forget me, our relationship will have existed; the future can't change that' (AMM p. 501). Laure takes the view that Fosca's past and his lucidity about the future that awaits him are part of who he is, and she is prepared to accept this. This chance to be at last loved in his freedom is, however, beyond Fosca's grasp; he is too weary of human activities to begin another relationship. Régine, in contrast to Laure, wants Fosca to love her 'as he's never loved, as he'll never love again' (AMM p. 69). She regards him as her sole access to meaning: 'It's him. He's my destiny. He has come to me from the depths of time and he will carry me in his memory until the end of time' (AMM p. 67). This desire to achieve meaning through love is an extreme version of Hélène's romantic absolutism in *The Blood of Others*, and the unspoken assumption of all Beauvoir's *amoureuses*.

The failure of Régine's imperious desire clearly has implications for relations between mortal beings, as well as immortal ones; authentic relations, it is implied, are founded on the basis proposed by Laure rather than that desired by Régine. Régine belongs to the line of characters in Beauvoir's fiction (Elisabeth, Denise, Paule) who are denied reciprocity with others, and whose ambitions as artists of one kind or another are flawed. Régine's acting gradually invades her whole life as she becomes more and more deeply imbued with Fosca's perspective. The roles she plays on stage are used to suggest a comparison between the brief life of a character who, after the fall of the curtain, inevitably dies, and the life of any human being when viewed from the historical perspective. Fosca likes Régine's acting because when she is on stage she 'believes in her own existence with such passionate faith' (AMM p. 100), but under his influence she loses this faith. In the party scene, like Elisabeth of *She Came to Stay*, her whole life comes to seem to her to be nothing but a series of masquerades: 'the hostess role, the famous actress role, the seductive role, they all belonged to the same play: the play of existence' (AMM p. 105). Behind her words, her smiles, her gestures, she can find only emptiness.

Almost all the women of Fosca's narrative — Catherine, Eliane, Béatrice, Marianne, Laure — feature essentially as his actual or potential lovers, making Fosca into a somewhat unwilling Don Juan figure. In *The Second Sex*, published only three years after *All Men Are Mortal*, Beauvoir surveys history again — this time in an attempt to understand how the situation of women has been historically constituted. 'History shows us,' she concludes, 'that men have always kept in their hands all concrete powers' (TSS p. 187). The women of *All Men Are Mortal* are an almost exclusively depressing demonstration of the marginality to which history has largely confined women. Catherine and Béatrice are shown to have virtually no possibility of individual concrete action: Catherine has the humiliating dependency of her position brought home to her when she alone as Fosca's wife is exempted from the fate of the other women of Carmona, left outside the walls to die as expendable members of the community.[8] Béatrice, like many women of her era, is forced into marriage against her will; her response is to retreat into a room of the chateau where she spends her days illuminating manuscripts, cutting herself off from all emotions and desires. Although Fosca thinks of this as a tragedy, this reaction is a quite ahistorical one; such occupations were the common lot of the lady of the chateau, and Catherine appeared to have no more active occupation.[9] When Fosca eventually offers Béatrice her freedom she is incapable of taking it. Marianne, three centuries later, is considerably more independent: she is educated, takes an active role in the life of the salons, participates in scientific experiments, and works with men to achieve her dream of a new kind of university. She exemplifies the way in which women of certain social milieux found themselves able to make a mark in the cultural domain, from the Renaissance onwards, if much less easily in more prosaic — and more powerful — areas of life.[10]

Unlike Laure, Marianne cannot accept Fosca's immortality or the idea that she will be only one woman amongst many for him (an echo of Régine's insistence on uniqueness). In the post-Revolution period, Laure is even more emancipated than Marianne, working side by side with Armand and Spinelle, speaking at political meetings and touring the country in an attempt to unionise the workers. She has broken out of the yoke of the family unit; but she is also shown doing the cooking and the ironing for her male companions, and her reward for all her efforts appears to be physical exhaustion and emotional solitude.

All these women are part of Fosca's narrative and are thus perceived from Fosca's point of view. When he first meets Laure he remarks, 'A woman: a heart beating in warm flesh, their gleaming teeth, their eyes searching for life, the smell of their tears; just like the seasons, the times of day, the colours, they had stayed just the same' (AMM p. 497). The passage from the individual to the gender category, so starkly formulated here by Fosca, affects the presentation of all the women in his narrative. Only Régine is able to turn the tables on Fosca by perceiving him through her own consciousness and by trying to use him for her own ends. The vitality of the character is considerable, but her role in the text is severely limited. Though *All Men Are Mortal* mirrors *The Blood of Others* in having what amounts to two narrative strands, one narrated in the first person by a man and one narrated by an external narrator focusing through a female character, the role allotted to Régine in *All Men Are Mortal* is not even as great as that of Hélène in *The Blood of Others*. The title of the sections focusing through her — 'Prologue' and 'Epilogue' — are sufficient in themselves to signal her subsidiary function. At the end of the novel she appears to be on the verge of the madness which had already threatened her in the party scene, and into which so many of Beauvoir's women characters sink.

Human relations do not emerge well from *All Men Are Mortal*. This is partly intended as an illustration of the impossibility of relations between a mortal and an immortal being, but there is virtually no counterpart showing that human beings, conversely, *can* find reciprocity. In 600 years, Fosca seems to come across very few happy couples: Béatrice loves Antoine but he does not love her; Henriette loves neither her husband, nor her lover; Laure loves Armand, Armand loves someone else who is either far away or not interested; Spinelle loves Laure. In terms of relations between parents and children, Fosca and Marianne have two children: one appears to die and one is unhappy and embittered; the portrait of relations between Fosca and Antoine presents a classic case of a parent desperately trying to live his own life through his child, and contributing to the child's self-destruction by his obsessive protectionism. Béatrice tells Fosca that he had left Antoine nothing to achieve for himself except death; Fosca is not the last of Beauvoir's parents to drive their children to their deaths. Fosca also actually murders one of his earlier sons, Tancrède, without apparently a moment of remorse. The status of Armand has to be considered carefully in this context: at one and the same time he is Fosca's descendant and physical double, yet sufficiently removed from him in generational terms to imply any necessary relationship between them. It seems that it is this lack of a pre-determined element and of any power relationship (compare with Tancrède and Antoine, who both seek to replace Fosca as ruler) which permits Armand to be Fosca's alter-ego.

The figure of Armand has to bear almost the full weight of the text's option in favour of human struggle and commitment; behind Armand there is a line of figures who incarnate a faith in human desire to act and bring about change, even when it takes the form of the violence of the Anabaptists, but there is a much greater pessimism about results. 'Sometimes a flame burns in their hearts; that's what they call being alive' (AMM p. 314). The image suggests heat and passion, but which is destined to burn out without constructing anything. ' "Don't you know what a desire is?" ' Armand asks Fosca (AMM p. 503). Desire, it is suggested, has to be valued for itself, since its results, whether counted in terms of human relations or the achievements of history, are at best precarious.

It is often said that Beauvoir's political thinking is basically ethical in its impulse.[11] In *All Men Are Mortal* nevertheless, the ethical dimension, although undoubtedly present, is remarkably understated. The fundamental question posed in the text is not, what *should* we do, but, what *can* we do; not, what is the relation between means and ends, but, what ends can we set. The conclusion given to this question has ethical and ideological implications, since it is weighted in favour of the character who opts for freedom and fraternity, and in favour of the struggle of revolutionaries, but it is argued largely in pragmatic terms. *All Men Are Mortal* marks the end of an era in Beauvoir's struggle with history. Having achieved, through the immortal and ahistorical Fosca, a negative demonstration of the value lent to human action by the individual's mortality and consequent historicity, her fiction henceforth takes on strictly limited time spans and political contexts. There is an assumption, from this point on, that the significance of human action is necessarily tightly circumscribed — for Beauvoir, as *All Men Are Mortal* amply demonstrates, history is not going anywhere.

Notes

1. Carmona is an imaginary city, set in the Po valley in Tuscany. It has some parallels with the town of Cremona, especially in its reliance on the textile industry and on agriculture, but other elements are drawn from the history of the other great Italian cities of the period.

2. This episode shows the influence of Simonde de Sismondi's 12-volume history of medieval Italy (published 1807–1818) which Beauvoir read as a preparation for her novel. Sismondi presents the fourteenth and fifteenth centuries as a period of tragic tyranny in which the failure of the Italian communities to unite led to foreign domination.

3. Spiritual figures are invested with considerable significance in this text. In addition to the Lutheran monk, whose phrase recurs throughout the text, Fosca is haunted by the dark-faced monk who tells him in Carmona that he can achieve nothing (see AMM pp. 155, 161). Luther himself is seen as someone whose passion *has* marked the world (AMM p. 290), and even the destructions of the Anabaptists are treated as evidence of human desire (AMM p. 280). However, the sympathy for these (essentially nonconformist) figures does not extend to God himself. Fosca's impossible desire to create a paradise for mankind has evident implications for the notion of a Christian God, and these implications are sometimes explicitly alluded to in the text (see for example AMM pp. 246, 256–57, 268–69).

4. It is made explicit that Armand refuses bourgeois demands for reform on the grounds that 'freedom could not be the apanage of one class and that only the advent of socialism would permit the workers to gain access to it' (AMM p. 487).

5. See *Pyrrhus et Cinéas*, pp. 279–88.

6. See 'Idéalisme morale et politique', p. 80 in *L'Existentialisme et la sagesse des nations*, first published in *Les Temps Modernes* in 1945. Anne Whitmarsh, in *Simone de Beauvoir and The Limits of Commitment*, p. 64, gives a useful summary of this point.

7. In the wake of Geniève Gennari, a number of critics have called this aspect of Beauvoir's writing 'the temptation of indifference'. See Gennari, *Simone de Beauvoir* (1958). Laurent Gagnebin specifically takes up this theme in his *Simone de Beauvoir ou le refus de l'indifférence* (1968). See pp. 79–84 for his section on *All Men Are Mortal*.

8. It is worth noting that Beauvoir's only play, *Les Bouches Inutiles* (translated by Francis and Gontier as *Who Shall Die?*) was composed and performed during the period she was writing *All Men Are Mortal*. It

functions as a kind of *mise en abyme* of *All Men Are Mortal* since it duplicates the situation of a town under siege which decides to cast out of its walls all the members of the community judged not necessary to its immediate survival. However, whereas Fosca's carries out this plan to the letter and leaves the victims to die, the inhabitants of this republic eventually conclude that such an action would compromise the very meaning of the community whose existence they are fighting to preserve. Fosca doubts expressed in Part 4 of the novel about whether he ought to have kept the gates of Carmona closed are thus emphatically underlined by this play.

9. Somewhat ironically for a text focusing on history, Fosca is in fact constituted as a quite ahistorical figure — in the eighteenth century, for example, he doubts the nature of scientific progress. Throughout the text, despite the careful reconstruction of the political realities of each period, there is little attempt to show the shaping of mentalities by historical context. This is particularly true of the epilogue and prologue, which are difficult to tie down to any specific decade of the twentieth century.

10. See *The Second Sex*, pp. 136–39.

11. This is the central argument of Anne Whitmarsh's *Simone de Beauvoir and the Limits of Commitment*.

5

The Mandarins

The Mandarins, the novel for which Beauvoir was awarded the 1954 Goncourt Prize, was also Beauvoir's own personal favourite.[1] The longest and perhaps the richest and most complex of her novels, it was the fruit of her experience and reflections in the postwar period on a number of fronts. Politically, her interest in the broad consequences of her discovery of the individual's historicity, the dominating subject of *All Men Are Mortal*, gave way, in the postwar period, to a concern with the role of the intellectual in politics, with the problem of co-operation with the French Communist Party and the problem of the interrelation between morality and political action. The late 1940s and early 1950s were rich with issues which act in the novel as a focus for this reflection — the dropping of the first nuclear bomb, the Cold War, the emergence in the West of details of the Soviet labour camps, the issue of the *épuration* (the 'purge' or meting out of justice to those who had collaborated with the Germans during the war).

But Beauvoir's thinking had also undergone a quite different kind of transformation and radicalisation in between the writing of *All Men Are Mortal* and *The Mandarins*; in between the two she had written — and discovered — *The Second Sex*.[2] Sexual politics, hitherto virtually invisible to Beauvoir, opened up a new way of looking at the world. In *Force of Circumstance* Beauvoir describes how she began to

> look at women with new eyes and found surprise after surprise lying in wait for me. It is both strange and stimulating to discover suddenly, at forty, an aspect of the world that has been staring you in the face all the time which

somehow you have never noticed. (FOC p. 195)

Gender role construction, the question of the ways in which men and women can construct relationships with each other, the problems of the mother–child relationship — all these issues which had already figured in Beauvoir's fiction reappear in *The Mandarins* in a more consciously organised way.[3]

As in the *The Blood of Others* (1945), the problems which the characters encounter in the construction of different types of heterosexual couples are posed in parallel to the characters' problems of political commitment. Both political and sexual choice come to be governed by the notion of 'preference', the key value around which the text is organised, and the enunciation of which is entrusted to the novel's sage figure, Robert Dubreuilh. 'Commitment is nothing other than a choice, love is nothing other than a preference. If you wait until you meet absolute perfection before committing yourself, you'll never love anyone and never achieve anything' (MND tr. adap. p. 729), he claims. In the climate of black-and-white choices produced and thematised by the Cold War, Dubreuilh's conviction eventually prevails, if only precariously: politically, he and Henri decide to swallow their doubts and moral preoccupations in favour of action in tandem with the Communists, whilst on the interpersonal level first Henri and then Anne abandon romance and sexuality with politically or geographically remote partners, in favour of a 'preferred' companion.

The notion of 'preference' is underpinned by — and develops out of — the basic structure of repetition, already employed in *The Blood of Others* and *All Men Are Mortal*. In both their personal and political lives the characters have, or take on, commitments which are abandoned or thrown into question in the course of the novel, only to be eventually 'preferred' despite all their drawbacks and difficulties. This structure of meaning becomes insistent in *The Mandarins*, and is underlined both at the level of the characters' discourse, and in the author's exegesis of the novel in *Force of Circumstance*:

One of the principal themes that emerges from my story is that of *repetition* in the sense in which Kierkegaard uses that word; truly to possess something one must have lost it and found it again. At the end of the novel, Henri and Dubreuilh (. . .) return to the point they started from, but (. . .) instead of being content with a facile optimism, they take upon themselves all the difficulties, the failures, the scandal implied in any undertaking. Their old enthusiastic adherences are replaced by preferences. (FOC p. 282)

The preferences of the wider political stage and those of the characters' interpersonal relations are bound together in the double narrative structure alternating between male and female focus, which is equally familiar from the two previous novels. However, in *The Mandarins* the female narrative attains parity with the male in terms of length, and has the concluding chapter of the narrative within its remit. Even more importantly, the female narrative focus becomes, for the first time in Beauvoir's novels, a narrative voice. In a reversal of the narrative situation of *The Blood of Others*, the female character (Anne) narrates her sections in the first person as a homodiegetic (internal) narrator, whilst the male character acting as narrative focus (Henri) is deprived of a voice and is subjected to the discreet authority of an external narrator. However, neither of the characters through whom the narrative is focused is entrusted with an authoritative interpretation of events which the reader is invited to accept. Anne therefore does not inherit the authority of Blomart in *The Blood of Others* and of Fosca in *All Men Are Mortal*.

Accompanying this change is the abandonment of the retrospective time structure. Instead of being recapitulated from a single fixed point in time, story and narrative time roughly coincide, moving forward together and giving a greater sense of the open nature of the characters' future. The historical period with which the characters engage is at the same time compressed to the four-year span of 1944–48. The novel's construction of the era is extremely detailed and depends heavily on autobiographical material, on Beauvoir's perceptions of the intellectual, political and literary dimensions of the four or five years preceding the writing of the novel (1944–49), as well as on emotional experience. The dilemmas of Henri and Robert are alimented by the twists and turns which marked Sartre and Beauvoir's relationship with the Communist Party after the War, by the bid to redefine the values of traditional humanism in which Sartre engaged, and by his attempt in 1948–49 to work within an independent left-wing grouping — the RDR, transmuted in the novel into the SRL.[4] The pleasure which Beauvoir took in the running of *Les Temps Modernes*, the review which she and Sartre launched in 1945 as a forum for writers of the left, is clearly reflected in the

characters' enthusiasm for *L'Espoir* and *Vigilance*. Beauvoir's visits
to the States and her relationship with the American writer Nelson
Algren (which began in the spring of 1947) are recounted with a
minimum of fictionalisation in Anne Dubreuilh's relationship with
Lewis Brogan.

But the text does not simply draw on events which took place
before Beauvoir began writing in the autumn of 1949 — it also
reflects events and changes taking place during the four-year
writing process. The news of the existence of the Soviet labour
camps, for example, broke at the end of 1949. Beauvoir's relationship with Algren was still in full swing as she began writing (she
had spent part of the summer travelling in Europe with him); the
painful summer in the house on Lake Michigan which began with
Algren's announcement that he no longer loved her and which
Anne lives through with Lewis in Chapter 10 did not take place
until the summer of 1950, when the writing had been going for
almost a year.[5] Beauvoir completed her first version of the novel in
June 1951, but it was only in October of that year, after a return
visit to Lake Michigan, that she found herself faced with the fact
that her relationship with Algren was definitively over.[6] Did Anne
abandon Lewis in this version of the novel? The use of the writing
process to work through immediate and painful personal experience is abundantly clear, as is its effect on the final shape of the
work.

Sartre read the first version during a trip to Norway with
Beauvoir in the summer of 1951, and was, according to Beauvoir's
account in *Force of Circumstance*, severe in his criticisms — largely,
we are told, of the structure of the book (see FOC p. 260). Beauvoir
worked on revising it until the autumn of 1952, and was for much
of the period in a depression which finds an evident expression in
Anne's distress. However, 1952 was also a political turning point,
the year in which Sartre emerged from the political wilderness into
which his break with the RDR had precipitated him, and in which
he began his rapprochement with the Communist Party, with
which he worked closely until 1956. The Henri Martin affair
which led him into renewed contact with the Communists from
December 1951 onwards, played the same role for him as the
Madagascar affair plays for Henri in the novel.[7] Even at this stage,
therefore, events contemporary with the writing were shaping the
text — again, one wonders how the novel ended in the first 1951
version, completed before Sartre's return to the political arena,
and at what stage of the writing Beauvoir decided on the structure

of repetition and 'preference' which supports the characters' return to action.

It seems clear that the numerous rewritings of the novel over two years were in fact occasioned as much — if not more — by changes in the couple's political thinking as by attempts to remedy the 'technical faults' to which Beauvoir rather airily refers in her autobiography. It is evident, for example, that Sartre's rapprochement with the Communist Party in 1952, together with the influence of Claude Lanzmann who read and discussed the novel with Beauvoir in March 1953, must have affected the portrayal of the Communist Party.[8] The final revision of the manuscript took place after Lanzmann's (and Bost's) reading, and it was eventually completed in the autumn of 1953, four years after its inception and more than two years after completion of the first version. The history of the text's genesis makes it clear that the text is caught up in the circumstances of its production to an extent which even *The Blood of Others*, written during the German occupation, does not really match.

It was not until the completion of the manuscript that Beauvoir chose its title. Deciding against *Les Suspects* ('The Suspects') and *Les Survivants* ('The Survivors'), she eventually selected Lanzmann's suggestion, *Les Mandarins*. The choice of this routine metaphor, with its semi-ironic distancing effect, is a tactic which Beauvoir was to repeat in later work. Through its potentially pejorative implication (milder, however, than *Les Suspects* would have been), doubts are raised about the status of the intellectual and about his or her actual influence on the centres of power. The reader is left uneasy, unclear about the author's relation to her text. Questioned about this in a 1954 interview with J. F. Rolland, Beauvoir said that though the title was intended to convey a mild and sympathetic irony, she was in total sympathy with her characters' political positions. The question itself, however, is evidence of the unease which this irony produces in the reader.[9] Nevertheless, the title does point clearly to the whole problem of the conciliation of the role of the intellectual with that of political activist — one of the two principal spheres of choice in which the structure of preference is enacted.

The problematic of this conciliation is dealt with in both of the text's narratives, but largely in terms of the dilemmas of the two principal male characters, Robert Dubreuilh and Henri Perron; since both are writers, the question of the intellectual's role in politics often becomes that of the relationship between literature and politics (thus the problem of defining what is meant by an intellectual, a problematic area in Anglo-Saxon thinking at least, does not really arise). The question is raised in the opening scene of the novel, where Scriassine warns Anne that Henri and Robert will have to choose between sacrificing all their time and energy to political activities, or withdrawing into writing and risking cutting themselves off from the realities of their era. Though she does not write herself, Anne has an absolute belief in the power and value of literature.[10] For her, it is impossible that Robert should give up writing. The two men, however, have acclimatised themselves to the rigours (and rewards) of political action in the Resistance struggle. Robert is ready to concede that, in the period of rapid social transformation which he hopes the world is about to traverse, literature may not be on the agenda (MND p. 54). Henri has experienced a sense of solidarity in the War which he needs to feel he can go on earning. On his trip to Portugal in the third chapter he is abruptly faced with the opposition between this duty — this need — and literature: the novel celebrating the pleasures of peace and the beauties of the world which he had planned to write seems impossible in the face of the poverty and the hardships which he meets. How can he celebrate the pretty little lights on the Tagus river when he is fully aware of the misery and poverty which the lights conceal? (MND p. 212). For a period, both Henri and Robert stop writing, and Robert begins the process of rethinking their prewar values. He decides that it had been too optimistic to look for a conciliation between the revolution and the old humanist values; the concepts of literature, truth, freedom, individual morality and judgement would have to be 're-invented' to avoid jettisoning them entirely (see MND p. 226).

In the early chapters of the novel, discussion along these lines remains largely theoretical. However, it is brought into sharp focus by the issue which dominates the seventh chapter, of whether to publish documentation on the Soviet labour camps. For Anne, again, the issue is clear: 'As an intellectual, you've taken on certain commitments — to tell the truth, among others,' she tells Robert (MND p. 443). Henri's reaction appears hardly less certain in its moral absolutism: 'In what measure had George told the truth? — that was the only question' (MND p. 399). The consequences of this attitude do, however, disturb him; in the past he has felt able to affirm that his duty as a journalist is to tell the truth without regard for what uses might he made of it (see MND p. 170). Now, he faces the fact that he believes that the truth he has to tell may damage the hopes of a thousand million people living in subhuman conditions whose only hope for the future is the Soviet Union (MND p. 400). Can 15,000 people in labour camps be sacrificed for the sake of a thousand million other people? Neither Henri or Anne can bring themselves to make this calculation. Their fundamental belief in individualism leads them to the position which Anne argues, that such calculations are false: 'One individual plus another individual doesn't make two; it will always make one plus one' (MND p. 445, trl. adap.). Despite his fear of the political consequences, Henri, like Anne, opts for individualism and the primacy of moral value: ' "It has to be brought out into the open," Henri concluded. "If not I'll be an accessory" ' (MND p. 473).

This decision leads the character into the second term of the structure of preference, as he rejects his initial commitment in the light of an absolute, and finds himself as a result in an impasse. Robert ends up at the same destination by a different route. When Anne tells him that it is his duty as an intellectual to tell the truth he invokes in the balance against the truth the fate of all the starving millions in the world, the fate of all those ravaged by disease and epidemics, all those enslaved by exploitative political regimes before declaring, '. . . my duties as an intellectual, my respect for the truth — that's all twaddle! The only question is to know whether, in denouncing the camps, you're working for mankind or against it' (MND trl. adap. p. 444). He is even more dismissive of moral considerations in discussion with Henri: ' "Those are moral considerations; they don't touch me," he said. "I'm interested in the results of my actions, not in what they make me appear to be" ' (MND p. 498).[11]

Unlike Henri, therefore, Dubreuilh thus deliberately breaks the connection between the intellectual on the one hand and individual morality and truth on the other. But he still joins Henri in the wilderness because he cannot bring himself to *act* on his conviction. In the book which pushes his line of argument to its limits Robert writes, 'Today a French intellectual can do nothing' (MND p. 619), and he goes on to condemn the 'old humanism' in favour of a new one 'in which force figured large and the concepts of justice, freedom, truth, hardly at all' (MND p. 619). This is the only set of moral values viable in today's situation, he claims — but at the same time he admits that he personally could never adopt them. The years of struggle for the triumph of values which he himself now judges to be inappropriate, constitute an

impossible barrier for him to cross. He thus declares himself condemned to inaction and silence. Even the writing of literature is
impossible for him; he had thought that literature could avoid
doing harm, even when it did no good. But, he tells Anne, 'At the
moment all literature that aspires to give man something besides
bread is exploited to prove that he can very well do without bread
(MND p. 541).

Both Anne and Henri are quick to grasp that Robert's disassociation between what he feels personally capable of and what
ought to be done is suspect — and one could add that his description of the 'new humanism' remains very vague. Robert does not
maintain for long the absolutism of this position, which is above all
a cry of frustration. Henri's position of absolute morality fares no
better. Even when making the choice over the labour camps he is
aware that he is choosing not between right and wrong but
between two evils: 'if evil were everywhere, innocence didn't exist.
Whatever he did he'd be wrong,' he tells himself in an echo of
Blomart in *The Blood of Others* (MND p. 401). Two issues bring
him up against the limits of moralism. In the Mercier affair, Henri
is faced with the choice of inventing evidence to get an ex-Nazi
collaborator acquitted, or allowing the fragile Josette to face
investigation of her love affair with a German officer during the
war.

> On the one side, there was Josette, on the other, qualms of
> conscience (. . .) At any rate, there was damned little to be
> gained from having a clear conscience. The thought wasn't
> new to him: you were just as well off being frankly in the
> wrong. Now he was being offered a fine opportunity to say to
> hell with morality; he wasn't going to let it go by. (MND
> p. 628)

But this cynicism is far from natural to Henri; he finds it sickening
to have to throw doubt on the evidence of the two women sent to
Dachau as a result of Mercier's treachery. He remains uneasy
despite Dubreuilh's assertion that the incident is an illustration of
the impossibility of individual morality. Dubreuilh's argument
that 'personal morality just doesn't exist' because 'you can't lead a
proper life in a society which isn't proper' (MND p. 646) is too
generalised for Henri; the key question for him is to know what
Dubreuilh — as an individual — would have done in his place.
The second event which strains Henri's faith in moral principles

is the issue of what to do with Sézénac: 'Four years earlier everything would have been simple. When action means something, when you believe in certain objectives, then the word justice has a meaning: you execute traitors. But what do you do with a traitor from the past when you've lost all hope? (MND tr. adap. p. 737). The issue is settled by the abrupt intervention of Vincent, who has no hesitation in killing Sézénac; 'you've got to know what side you're on (. . .). You've got to get your feet wet,' he argues succinctly (MND p. 744). Without approving Vincent, both Henri and Robert are struck by the fact that their moral uncertainty stems from their lack of situation and commitment: 'If we were still active, there would be no problem. Only now we're on the outside, so our decision will necessarily be arbitrary' (MND p. 739).

When the situation which Henri is lacking presents itself in the form of the Tanarive trials, his whole perspective changes; even the smell of the flowers in the garden 'didn't have the same savour as before' (MND p. 719). He moves into the final term of the structure of preference when he takes the decision not to retire into exile in a sunny corner of Italy, but to work instead with Dubreuilh on a new left-wing journal. However, this return to commitment does not mean that Henri really abandons his individualism and his moralism. 'You don't prevent a war with words,' he admits — but for him words are not simply 'a way of changing history', they are 'also a certain way of living it' (MND p. 752). How he feels about his own stance is thus valued just as highly as the effects of his action. In *L'Espoir* he had always aimed to educate his readers into making informed judgements — there is no indication that he will do anything other than this in his new venture. The idea of moral principles is not abandoned, even if he now sees morality as inseparable from a commitment and a situation rather than deriving from an absolute. Dubreuilh, in apparent contrast, emerges from his blind alley declaring that he is after all prepared to drop the old values and personally assume the 'new humanism': 'You can no more reject it than you can reject the world' (MND p. 728). The world political situation has deteriorated in his view to a point where he has to prefer the Soviet Union over the United States without concerning himself with what the Soviet Union *ought* to be like: 'on the one hand there's reality, and on the other, nothing. And I know of no worse error than preferring nothing to something' (MND tr. adap. p. 730). He thus appears to be essentially using his 'preference' theory to divest himself of moral considerations and choose the Soviet Union. However, Dubreuilh's jettisoning of the 'old' values is also more apparent than real. He overcomes a specific moral scruple — accepting the existence of the labour camps in the Soviet Union — but it takes him months to arrive at this position. It is clear that moral or intellectual scruples could interrupt his co-operation with the Communists at any moment — as indeed the Soviet invasion of Hungary did for Sartre only two years after the novel's publication, in 1956.

The humanistic aspect of Dubreuilh's projects for the future also emerges in the salvaging of literature, which both men ultimately agree on. For Henri, the problem of a 'pure' versus a 'political' literature, symbolised by the lights-on-the-river dilemma, is compounded by the problem of individualism. Dubreuilh settles the lights problem by cutting through the dichotomy:

> 'if you make a thing of beauty out of those lights and forget what lies behind them, you're a bastard. But that's just it: you've got to find a way to write about them which differs from the way right-wing aesthetes write; you've got to bring out at one and the same time the fact that they are pretty and that they shed light on misery. That's exactly the task that writers on the left should set themselves,' he said excitedly. 'Making us see things in a new perspective by setting them in their true place. But let's not impoverish the world. Personal experiences — what you call mirages — do exist.' (MND tr. adap. pp. 302–3)

Literature and individual experience need not be abandoned, as long as the individual is not seen in isolation from a wider context. The novel which Henri had begun and then abandoned immediately after the war is now seen to be located within this problematic; he had tried to 'talk about himself without setting himself in either the past or the present. But the truth of one's life is outside oneself, in events, in other people, in things; to talk about oneself, one must talk about everything else' (MND p. 341). His play, in contrast, is a play 'set in a definite place, at a definite time, a play that meant something' (MND p. 342).

Thus the ethos of preference, the rejection of idealism in name of a modest praxis, by no means prevents the redempt' the individual, the beautiful and the literary. Although ' humanism' of the intellectual is severely strained in ' many of its values survive, though not as absolutes. Morality becomes a function of a situation, and a specific role is defined for literature. Sartre had come round by the early 1950s to the view that morality 'is a collection of idealistic tricks' (FOC p. 210), and Beauvoir writes of herself under Lanzmann's influence 'gradually liquidat[ing] my ethical idealism' (FOC p. 302). The attitudes of the characters of *The Mandarins* lag well behind this position. On the question of the role of literature, however, Henri's stance is very close to Beauvoir's; she frequently feels the need to justify the practice of taking her own experience as a starting point for writing, in terms which are virtually identical to those of Henri and Robert.[12] Henri's novel is clearly the mirror image of Beauvoir's intentions for *The Mandarins* itself: 'a story of today in which the readers would find their own worries, their own problems' (MND p. 342) and for which he draws heavily, like Beauvoir, on autobiographical material. In an evident desire to ward off any attempt to treat her novel as a *roman à clef*, Beauvoir has Henri explain to Nadine that his book is nothing of the sort:

> I didn't write about us. You know very well that all the characters are made up . . . Of course, I tried to depict present-day people, men and women who are in somewhat the same situation as ours. But there are thousands of people like that; neither your father nor I is specifically portrayed. On the contrary, in most respects my characters don't resemble us at all. (MND p. 732)[13]

Whilst Beauvoir's situation may not have been so easily identifiable as identical to that of 'thousands' of people, the concept put forward here of a novel which would be a portrait of the times is central to *The Mandarins* itself, so that the very concept of the work and its construction echo the characters' conclusions. The issues of the postwar era, as Beauvoir saw them, are employed as a defining context for the characters and their struggles — Anne, depressed by the deaths in the War of those close to her; Henri and Robert, full of the optimism and idealism which the successful struggle of the Resistance has instilled in them; Nadine, Vincent and Sézénac, destabilised by the brutalities with which they had come into contact at a very young age. The heritage of the War thus continues to be a defining factor for the characters, but, as the novel develops, the situation which increasingly dominates and structures their lives is the climate of the Cold War, forcing the characters out of neutrality in areas of their lives extending well beyond the political.

The two power blocks centering on the United States and the Soviet Union, which constitute the binary political universe of *The Mandarins*, both figure powerfully in the novel, embodying at different moments political, cultural and emotional options. Although Henri and Robert attempt to forge a path between the two blocks in the early chapters of the novel, they are clear from the beginning that in the case of a choice they will unhesitatingly choose the Soviet Union. However, they have extremely limited information about it, and the Soviet Union retains above all in their minds a mythical status, a symbol of a country attempting to put a political ideal into practice. 'I don't doubt the fact that everything in the Soviet Union isn't perfect. I'd be surprised if it was. But, anyhow, they're the ones who are on the right road,' declares Henri (MND tr. adap. pp. 339–40). The camps issue brutally reveals this apparently tough realism to be a sheep in wolves' clothing. When Henri is faced with the documentary evidence that the Soviet labour camps exist in an institutionalised form, and for the economic purpose of creating a sub-proletariat, the extent to which he had made the Soviet Union into a myth becomes evident: 'It was impossible to deny: in the USSR, too, men were working other men to death!' he exclaims in despair (MND tr. adap. p. 396). He has, in fact, such difficulty in accepting that 'everything in the Soviet Union isn't perfect' that he is driven to publish the facts about the camps on a wave of moral absolutism which subsequently he is unable to maintain; his moral absolutes collapse about him and he is left in a void until the very end of the novel.

Dubreuilh withstands the discovery of the camps with more determination, arguing that since they have no means of influencing the Soviet Union all they can affect by publishing the evidence is the idea of the Soviet Union that the French have. However, after the collapse of the SRL, he refuses Communist overtures to merge with para-communist groups, evidently unable to accept in private what he argues in public. In both men's case the commitment to the Soviet Union is essentially moral, and if they eventually revert to supporting it it is because Dubreuilh's 'preference' theory leads them to accepting the Soviet Union as preferable to the United States, whatever the former's faults. The characters never visit the Soviet Union (neither Beauvoir nor Sartre did so until after the completion of *The Mandarins*), and the few Russian characters that do appear in the book are opposed to the Soviet system (most notably Scriassine, and Peltov). The view of the Soviet Union that the characters have is thus, *faute de mieux*, bound up with the French Communist Party, which had emerged from the war with a greatly strengthened organisation and support, and which receives a considerable profile in the novel. Neither Henri nor Robert ever considers joining the Party, though their attitudes are sometimes so indistinguishable from Party thinking that Henri himself is easily duped into thinking that Robert has become a member. They are called upon several times in the novel to explain their differences with the Communists; over and above minor divergences, their antipathy essentially relates to the high value they place on intellectual independence (belonging to the Party is seen as synonymous with intellectual facility) and their moral scruples. Beauvoir does not attribute to the characters the kind of philosophical divergences with Marxism with which Sartre was struggling in the late 1940s. Indeed, there is very little discussion of political ideologies — Robert's idea of socialism seems to approximate that of Jaurès (cited several times in the novel), for whom socialism and individualism went hand in hand, but this information is disclosed by Anne rather than emerging from the character's remarks (see MND p. 63). The result of this silencing of ideological debate is that the characters' reluctance to work within the Communist Party is not made to derive from any quarrel with Marxism, but rather from an objection to the practices of the Party itself, and to a generalised rejection of any form of intellectual conformism.

Beauvoir was well aware that the portrayal of the Party in the novel might appear hostile, and it was in an attempt to counter this that she broke her embargo on press interviews in connection with the Goncourt Prize and gave an interview to J.-F. Rolland in the communist *Humanité-Dimanche*.[14] Despite a suggestion by Rolland that the reality of the Communist Party might be more complex than Beauvoir's portrayal, the interview is cordial and Beauvoir stresses the fact that her characters do eventually decide to work again in tandem with the Communists. What is carefully avoided in the interview is any reference to the polemic engaged in by existentialists and Communists in the 1940s, and the personal attacks to which both Beauvoir and Sartre had been subjected. Between 1945 and 1950 several studies were published by Communist Party members attacking existentialism as the latest form of bourgeois ideology. Some, like that of Jean Kanapa, a former student of Sartre's, were highly personal in tone; others, like that of Georg Lukacs's *Existentialisme ou Marxisme?* (1948) showed, as Mark Poster writes, that the writings of the French existentialists had 'become important and dangerous enough to the communists for them to have their foremost theorist write against them'.[15]

This polemic is nevertheless reflected in the novel in the attacks made on Dubreuilh and Perron, and in the Communist accusation that the two men's writing is reactionary. Even the most sympathetic Communist character, Lachaume, writes an article accusing Henri of 'fascism' and 'reactionaryism', and of insulting the Resistance in his play. However, Lachaume is also presented as intelligent, disinterested and above all determined to serve in the Party what he sees as the only effective means of bringing about the revolution. Henri respects Lachaume's sentiment that 'there's one thing I'm sure of: the communists are the only ones who are doing useful work. So look down on me if you like, but I'd swallow anything rather than quit' (MND p. 382). Lachaume's concern with effectiveness and disregard for 'little personal problems' (MND p. 382) contrasts strongly with Henri's preoccupation with his own position, as the latter is well aware. The other Party members portrayed are considerably less sympathetic than Lachaume: the servile fanaticism of Lenoir, the self-important *arrivisme* of Marie-Ange Bizet, the converts who join the Party after its successes in the elections 'out of opportunism, or fear, or moral comfort' (MND p. 610). The episode of Lenoir's playreading permits a satirical account of the Party's expectations of literature. In *The Prime of Life* Beauvoir remarks that on the publication of *The Mandarins* the bourgeois papers found that the novel 'had a pleasing odour of anti-Communism' (FOC p. 326) — and it is not difficult to see why they thought so. Given the atmosphere of the Cold War, it is legitimate to speculate whether the novel would in fact have received the Goncourt Prize at all had it been seen in a different light.[16] Beauvoir had clearly been worried by potential Communist hostility to the novel, and its sympathetic reception by the Party probably says more about the close working relationship with the Communists which Sartre and *Les Temps Modernes* had in 1954 than about the portrayal of the Party in the book. In fact, *The Blood of Others* has a more sympathetic, if wooden, portrayal of a Communist in the personage of Paul; it is also worth noting that Blomart, the hero of the same text, is actually a Party member for a period, whereas Henri and Robert are not.

M.-A. Burnier describes Party membership as something of a 'forbidden paradise' in *The Blood of Others* — a phenomenon which he attributes to the unease of the bourgeois intellecual who has the possibility of choosing a party which, to the worker, represents his only chance of liberation.[17] This element virtually disappears in *The Mandarins*, where the Party is perceived more as a place of enforced intellectual conformity than as a place of forbidden felicity. However, there remains a strong paradisaical element in the portrayal of the Soviet Union itself, represented as a symbol of the hopes of the world's starving millions, a country to which the characters have a strong moral and political commitment, despite or even because of the fact that it remains for them a mysterious and inviolate place.

The presentation of the United States, though not without its mythical elements, is, in contrast, strongly rooted in Beauvoir's experience of the country. The four-month visit which she made there in the spring of 1947 is described in *America Day by Day*, an essay written immediately on her return and published in 1948. One of the principal events of the visit was Beauvoir's encounter with Nelson Algren; in *America Day by Day*, Algren (here 'N.-A.') is presented as a friend amongs others, but the full intensity of Beauvoir's emotional experience with Algren feeds into the relationship of Anne and Lewis in *The Mandarins*. This factor weights the difference between the two texts' representation of the States, though both begin by describing high expectations and become increasingly more hostile. The opening of the novel reflects French enthusiasm for their liberators: Henri recalls having shouted 'Long live America' at Paule's party (MND p. 739). America is the country of the future, the land of plenty, the home of jazz and the best in the cinema. By the time of Anne's first visit to the States (halfway through the novel in Chapter 6), political doubts have begun to cast a shadow: why have the Americans not gone on to remove Franco and Salazar, after Hitler? How are the American liberators treating the inmates of the German camps? Is American aid not a form of colonisation? The dropping of the first atomic bomb by the United States, recounted in the fifth chapter, blackens the picture still further (see MND p. 369).

In the first half of the novel the character most associated with America is Scriassine — not an American himself but a character who has made a political option in favour of the States. Despite his excesses, the character is at first portrayed fairly favourably — but, significantly, Anne's brief sexual encounter with him is a failure, and he rapidly becomes alienated from the central group.

The other American characters in France — Preston, Bennet —
are insignificant, so that Anne's visit is the first real encounter in
the novel with Americans themselves. The meeting with Lewis
Brogan takes place on the second page, indicating the dominating
role which the encounter with the man is to play over the encounter with the country. Even at this stage Anne does note what she
sees as the conformism and false optimism of Americans, does
contrast the fundamental solitude of many individuals with the
myths of togetherness propagated by the billboards, and expresses
surprise at the political passivity of most of the intellectuals she
meets. But her American experiences are largely refracted through
her relationship with Lewis, so that America means the romantic
appeal of the Mississippi, and the exotic underworld and urban
landscape of Chicago to which Lewis introduces her.

By the time of Anne's last visit, however, the political climate
has deteriorated sharply. Henri refuses the politically loaded offer
of paper for *L'Espoir* made to him by the American Bennet, telling
him that America is

> the country which everywhere and always systematically takes
> the side of the privileged. In China, in Greece, in Turkey, in
> Korea, what are they defending? It isn't the people is it? It's
> capital, it's the big land holdings. When I think that they're
> supporting Franco and Salazar . . . (MND p.508)

Anne, on her last visit in Chapter 10, is increasingly able to
separate America from Lewis, and experiences the country as
more and more hostile: 'things had changed in two years, and
Lewis's love no longer protected me. Now, America meant atomic
bomb, threat of war, nascent fascism. Most of the people I passed
were enemies' (MND p. 679). She reacts strongly to the patronising attitudes of their neighbours at Lake Michigan, whose
'scruples concerning us were like those a man could feel towards a
weak woman or a passive animal' (MND p. 689). At the local fair
the history of Europe is reduced to a row of wax figures (MND
p. 687).

Anne's strongest criticism of Americans, however, is the complicity which she accuses the intellectuals of maintaining with the
system. Lewis himself, as he jokes about American 'aid', strikes
Anne as too unprepared to act for change (see MND p. 690),
but the situation is really brought home to her when she has a
reunion with Myriam and Philipp in New York. Anne dislikes the

pretentiousness of the restaurant which her friends choose, and their insistence on seeing poetry in the Mexican villages where Anne sees poverty and disease. The couple are further invalidated by being caught up in a mother–son symbiosis which the mother protects when she effectively places an embargo on a sexual relationship between her son and Anne. Philipp argues that the intellectual is politically powerless, and sees the desire of the French intellectual to engage in action as an obsession.[18] Philipp and Myriam's desire to withdraw from 'this distressing age' into 'some remote corner' (MND p. 704) strikes Anne as the height of egoism; it is no coincidence that this couple also support American foreign policy — thus the point which Henri makes to Lambert, that political abstentionism equals defence of the status quo, is made on both sides of the ocean.

By the end of Anne's visit, 'Lewis's country' has become the United States; by the end of the novel the characters set their faces firmly against a country 'which was preparing to subjugate Europe' (MND p. 739). The choice which they had hoped not to have to make at the beginning of the novel becomes inevitable by the end. Yet the novel remains less anti-American than *America Day by Day*, and than one might expect from the editorials of *Les Temps Modernes* which accused America of racism and incipient fascism from July 1948 onwards.[19] This has largely to be attributed to the fact that, unlike the Soviet Union, which functions principally as an abstract ideal in the novel, the United States represents an emotional and sexual option, as well as an increasingly negatively coded political pole; eventually, the emotional rejection and the political rejection of the States run hand in hand. In broader terms, the opposition between the two blocks which structures the entire novel is a strong factor not only in creating the mood of stark choices which is the novel's ambience, and the stumbling block of intellectuals bent on perceiving nuances, but also in the characters' feeling that, politically speaking, France — even Europe — is no longer on the world stage. 'Admitting that you belong to a fifth-rate nation and to an outmoded era isn't something you can do overnight' Dubreuilh reasons (MND p. 643); for him 'the game was between Russia and the United States from the start. We were completely out of it' (MND p. 641). Though Dubreuilh and Henri decide to return to action at the end of the novel, it is still within this perspective of the two blocks, so that the idea that they are 'out of it' because they are intellectuals is reinforced by the notion that they are 'out of it' because France has no significant role to play.

The choices to be made in the novel in world politics are played out with equal starkness in the personal choices of sexual relationships. The use of the United States as the location of a pole of choice in both political and sexual terms underlines the parallelism between the two sets of options. The account of the relationship between Lewis and Anne, and the choice which Anne has to make between what Lewis and Robert represent which dominates the second half of Anne's narrative, is often taken as a marginal episode of the novel. To take this view is to ignore both the central role which the exploration of types of male – female couples occupies in the text, and the way in which sexual choice in the novel is just as governed by the structure of preference as is political choice. Anne's eventual choice of Robert is echoed by Henri's choice of Nadine; in a sense both choose Dubreuilh, but in broader terms both follow the pattern of preference.

Of the two, the Anne – Robert couple is the dominant model, and is characterised from the point of view of Anne in her first section of narrative. For Anne, Robert represents security ('I had only to speak his name and I would feel safe and secure'; MND p. 33), and total identification with herself ('I've lived with him as if from the inside, with no distance between us'; MND p. 57 tr. adap.). More than 20 years older than Anne, Robert is literally her teacher when she meets him, and he soon assumes a Pygmalion role in other areas of her life, assigning moral and political meaning to the world about her through their conversations and his writing (see MND pp. 58 – 61). After revealing to her that she loves him (MND p. 59), he goes on to teach her the pleasures of sexuality: 'It seemed a simple and joyous thing to me to become a woman in his arms; when the pleasure was frightening, his smile would reassure me' (MND p. 60). But he also teaches her that desire wanes and that in giving up the sexual aspect of their relationship they have 'so to speak lost nothing' (MND p. 62). For him, sexuality and love are naturally separable: 'Picking up a good-looking girl in a bar and spending an hour with her seemed perfectly natural to him' (MND p. 95).

Anne takes up the career that Robert encourages because he 'believes that psychoanalysis can play a useful role in bourgeois society and that it might still be of use even in a classless society' (MND p. 61); she also has the baby that Robert wants. But Anne has great difficulty in assuming caring roles; she is unable to love her daughter, resents her couple with Robert being turned into a trio by Nadine, and feels increasingly hostile towards her patients. To these difficulties are added her problems in coping with Robert's lack of need of her: despite her pupil status Anne does not in fact share all Robert's values, and is a romantic and an absolutist. The tale of the mermaid who sells her immortal soul for love and who becomes, after death, 'a bit of white foam without memory and without voice' (MND p. 33) recurs in Anne's imagination; on the one hand it represents Anne's fear of death as a void — a fear against which Robert partially secures her — but it also represents Anne's identification with a symbol of absolute love: 'I was the mermaid' (MND p. 33). Anne often evokes what she thinks of as ideal couples — Nadine and Diego, Lambert and Rosa — and for her the thought that Robert might not have loved her had he met her in different circumstances or that he might have met someone else is a terrifying notion which she dispels from her mind with speed (MND p. 60).

Anne's meeting with Lewis Brogan throws her couple with Robert into sharp relief. The most evident difference is the intensely sexual relationship which she sets up with him, reviving a part of her life which she has repressed for years. Other contrasts also emerge, however: Lewis needs security, permanence, fidelity. He likes having dinner with Anne at home, tries to create the illusion that they are married, slips a ring on her finger, is distressed by the infidelities which occur during the long months of Anne's absence.[20] Anne compares her image of the two men: Lewis, waking in bed to a room 'destroyed' by her absence (MND p. 649), Robert working in his study in which there is 'no place' for Anne (MND p. 647). Robert and Anne's relationship maintains a constant even keel; Anne and Lewis hurt each other and suffer deeply. Language and rationality are of no help to them: 'We only get things in a muddle when we talk about them,' says Lewis as one of their conversations leads nowhere (MND p. 591 tr. adap.). The contrast with Robert, who uses language to make the world for Anne 'coherent, like a book' (MND p. 60) is striking and, in the end, decisive.[21] When Anne finds that she will not be able to maintain both options, and that choice is inevitable, she consults Robert — effectively seeks his permission to choose Lewis. Robert makes no appeal on his own behalf, confirming Anne's feeling that he has no need of her, but argues, in an echo of Anne's own twice-repeated statement that 'love isn't everything' (MND pp. 574, 656), that the other aspects of her life which France represents are more important than love. However, it is not this argument which in the end holds Anne back; she *is* prepared to view love as an absolute and does eventually decide to go to Lewis if he summons her. It is in the absence of this summons that her confidence that Lewis has an absolute need of her deserts her, and she finds herself unable to abandon the security of Robert, the security and power of the *logos*. Discourse and reason, not the body and emotion, prevail.

Anne's choice is heavily supported by the development of the other couples in the novel. The pattern of commitment interrupted by an interlude with a third party and ending in reunion is echoed by the Henri – Nadine couple, but this time the pattern is viewed from the male partner's point of view. The Henri – Nadine couple echoes the Robert – Anne structure in the age gap between the two, in the strong Pygmalion element ('He had wanted to help her. He had told himself that if he could make her happy he would free her of that confused resentment which was poisoning her life'; MND p. 710), and in the move from sexuality to verbality. In the first stage of their relationship, the sexual element is uppermost for Henri: 'Nadine would have been astonished had she known just how indifferent he was to her problems' (MND p. 208); 'all he wanted was to get into bed with her' (MND p. 209). In one of the last scenes of the novel between them, when they are already married, Henri effects his 'preference' for Nadine: 'Yes, the thing you prefer to all others, you love, and he was fonder of her than anything else in the world. He loved her, and he had to convince her of it' (MND p. 746). He employs all his verbal skills to convince her, and then, with this achieved, 'he helped put her to bed, tucked her in, and went back to his room. Never had he talked so frankly with Nadine, and it seemed to him as if something had given way in her. He had to persevere' (MND p. 750). Two points emerge from this: firstly, the entire relationship is now conceived in terms of Nadine's needs (as perceived by Henri) and of Henri's strength. Secondly, and most strikingly, the terms of preference again operate emphatically on the verbal level as a preferred alternative to the sexual. 'Talking frankly' appears to automatically preclude the sexual. Thus Nadine, who 'has to put her life into words' (MND p. 467), learns to depend on Henri's word, just as Anne does on Robert's.

The choice between the verbal and the sexual is in fact heavily loaded against the sexual. There are of course some lyrical scenes between Anne and Lewis, in which Anne describes a sense of transfiguation, of recovery of the body in its most elemental form, and in which desire, happiness and love mingle. 'Between us, desire had always been love,' says Anne (MND p. 683) — but this paradise contains a serpent. As Lewis begins to resent Anne's refusal to commit herself to him, their lovemaking is perceived by Anne as first bizarre and incongruous (MND p. 579), and later brutally divorced from all tenderness as she feels treated 'as a pleasure machine' (MND p. 683). Anne is surprised and distressed by this development, yet the presentation of sexual relations earlier in the novel clearly prepares this fall. In the scene between Anne and Scriassine, in Chapter 2, the grotesque aspect of sexual relations is doubled by an aggressivity which anticipates later scenes with Lewis. This scene is positively pleasant, however, in comparison with the one which takes place in the first chapter between Henri and Paule, and which is truncated in the published English translation. Henri's lack of desire for Paule shifts female sexuality into a grotesque and obscene mode: Paule is metamorphosed into 'a corpse or a madwoman' (omitted in the translation), 'a woman beside herself mouthing obscene words and clawing him painfully' (omitted in the translation). When Henri enters her, 'to get it over with as quickly as possible' (MND p. 32), he finds that 'inside her it was red just as her studio was red' (omitted in the translation). Dubreuilh calls Paule's red studio her 'brothel'; thus the red room — the place of the death of the child, of the abortion of the foetus and of Denise's madness in *The Blood of Others* — re-emerges here as a figure of female sexuality viewed as an obscene phenomenon.

In *The Blood of Others* the perception of the female body as obscene is specifically connected with woman's reproductive functions; in *The Mandarins*, it focuses on a fear of women being viewed by men as sexual predators, of women desiring and not being desired in return. Just as Elisabeth is used in *She Came to Stay* as the embodiment of everything that Françoise fears becoming (and as Denise functions to a lesser extent for Hélène in *The Blood of Others*), so Paule functions as a warning, as an image of what Anne might become. 'If ever I lost Lewis, when I lost Lewis, I would immediately and forever stop believing myself a woman,' Anne swears to herself (MND p. 668), as she witnesses Paule and Claudie making seduction attempts on handsome young men. This negative image of woman is not confined, however, to Paule: Nadine also plays the role of woman as sexual aggressor, crudely manoeuvring Henri into bed with her and taking control of the sexual situation whenever possible (see for example MND pp. 114,

125–26). In *Force of Circumstance* Beauvoir states openly that she had intended to 'avenge myself on Nadine for certain traits that had offended me in Lise [i.e. Nathalie Sorokine] and some of my other younger women friends — a sexual coarseness that revealed rather nastily their underlying frigidity, an aggressiveness that was a poor compensation for their feeling of inferiority' (FOC p. 277). This view of sexual assertiveness as related to a basic frigidity is clearly at work in the presentation of Nadine. Despite her apparently liberated attitudes to sex, she is shown to regard it as 'a tedious occupation' (MND p. 104), and she is subjected to the male criticism that she should be content to allow herself to be 'gently lulled by pleasure instead of romping about in bed with determined shamelessness' (MND p. 126). This kind of judgement, like Henri's horror of Paule, implicitly shores up Anne's sexual passivity, and her need to be the object of desire.

The function of other women characters as a negative pole to Anne operates not only in loading her choice against sexuality, but also as a pressure against the romantic absolute which, for Anne and Lewis, accompanies sexuality. Paule is the complete example of *The Second Sex*'s analysis of the *amoureuse* (the woman who makes a cult of love) who tries to attain her own being vicariously through that of the loved one.[22] In the sections of narrative focused through Henri, the weight of the burden that Paule's refusal to make her own life places on the object of her attention is fully apparent. Her refusal to relate directly to the outside world entraps her in myths and rituals which at first entrance and later infuriate Henri; both he and Anne react strongly against Paule's mythmaking use of language, which converts Henri's ambitions into his 'mission' (MND p. 238) and her life with Henri into 'a kind of experience that's simply incommunicable' (MND p. 240). Anne is not tempted to follow Paule down the road of mythifying discourse, or to imitate her refusal of the passage of time. But other aspects of Paule's behaviour are echoed as danger signals in Anne's relation to Lewis: Paule's narcissism and belief in the illusion of clothes occasionally tempt Anne, and Paule's bizarre interpretations of Henri's behaviour are echoed in Anne's misunderstandings of Lewis's increasingly desperate signals that he cannot cope with her double life.

The connections between Paule and Anne become most insistent in the eighth chapter, where Paule's descent into folly is interspersed with Anne's reflections on her own situation with Lewis. Faced with Paule's distress she searches for 'meaningless' words of comfort: 'You'll get well, you've got to get well. Love isn't everything' (MND p. 546). Anne repeats these 'meaningless' words to Lewis later in the chapter: ' "If you love me the way I love you, why waste three-fourths of our life waiting?" Lewis said. I hesitated. "Because love isn't everything," I said' (MND p. 574). But, before she even pronounces these words to Lewis, Anne knows that she does not believe them. Though Anne herself is frightened by Paule's delusions she knows that 'in her place I would never want to get well and bury my love with my own hands' (MND p. 546). She values feeling and suffering more highly than the triumph of 'reason and routine' (MND p. 650), which she feels Paule's psychiatric treatment will bring about. She regards with hostility the bovine and resigned person which Paule becomes and revolts against sanity, against the sanitisation of feeling: 'I had less and less stomach for my work; often I felt like saying to my patients, "Don't bother trying to get better, you'll soon get better enough" ' (MND tr. adap. p. 375).[23] As she herself sinks to the edge of suicide, the idea of explaining away her feelings as 'a depression' revolts her; she determines to 'make truth triumph' (MND p. 760), and her means will be Paule's little brown vial. She will do what Paule should have done and carry out the suicide which will represent the truth of her feeling.

Of course Anne does not in the end act on her belief in the truth of suffering, of folly, of death. She is wrested from this position by the sound of voices; the power of language again triumphs, bringing with it the sense of guilt which almost permanently accompanies Anne. However, in *Force of Circumstance* Beauvoir remarks that Anne's return from the edge of suicide 'seems more like a defeat than a triumph' (FOC p. 283). Anne is 'betraying something' (FOC p. 283) — something which Anne sees expressed in the delusions of Paule, and perhaps in the more permanent folly of Maria who, like Paule, struggles to express her feelings through writing (see MND p. 430). Although Anne chooses to return to life, and acts within the structures of preference by renouncing the absolutes of death and sexuality, by preferring Robert to Lewis, life to death, she does so with little conviction. She does not share Robert's credo that love is nothing but a preference. When one remarks that Henri does not explain to Nadine that he is 'preferring' her — for the evident reason that Nadine would be unlikely to be satisfied with this — it becomes apparent that the novel's structure of preference is essentially a male structure, against which a female aspiration to absolutes occasionally breaks into revolt.

The playing out of the structure of preference on the level of the couple creates tensions in the text between certain types of femininity and, in particular, masculinity. In the wake of *The Second Sex*, the novel shows a much greater awareness than the earlier fiction of questions of gender role construction. Lambert and Nadine are both examined specifically in the text from this point of view. Nadine, the unloved daughter who, in her turn, becomes a punctiliously cold mother to her own daughter, bitterly resents any identification with the feminine. Her fury as an adolescent over the onset of menstruation (MND p. 82) is later translated into an attitude of contemptuousness towards the female body — an attitude which she parades with ostentation at the strip show which she presses Henri into taking her to. The beautiful Josette — equally unfortunate in her mother — has almost as many problems as Nadine in coming to terms with her body, experiencing her beauty as a humiliation and tortured by problems of what to wear. 'Girls are weighed down with restrictions, boys with demands — two equally harmful disciplines,' comments Anne (MND p. 470). Despite this, the difficulties of becoming a woman are presented with more sympathy than those of becoming a man. Anne appreciates that Lambert is becoming adult in a period where 'being a man' means knowing how to kill, how to make others suffer and how to take suffering himself (see MND p. 470), but the character is nevertheless discredited through Anne's detailing of physical traits such as 'his grimaces, his comical voice, the sweat which streamed down his cheeks' (MND p. 289) and by his inability to cope with drinking alcohol (MND p. 288). Lambert turns at first to the strongly masculine Henri as role model, but eventually replaces Henri by Volange, so that the character who has experienced difficulties 'becoming a man' is devalued and made to take a political wrong-turning.

If Robert and Henri play strong masculine roles, the non-Latin softly named Lewis with his attachment to security and fidelity is considerably more feminised. It is tempting to point to this feminisation as an unspoken element of the character's rejection, given the positive coding attributed in the text to the kind of stereotypical masculine role played by Henri. Combining commitment to political action with a strong moral concern, Henri is the undisputed hero of the novel, whose masculine credentials are firmly established from the beginning of the text by his image as Resistance leader. His automatic response to meeting women is to appraise them sexually: 'for him, there were desirable women and others who weren't. This one wasn't' (MND p. 359). He frequently generalises about women in authoritative terms, and adopts a possessive attitude towards the women in his life, assuming that his role is to help and support them. The morning following the first night that he spends with Josette he feels 'wonderfully happy to have this woman for himself, and to be a man'. He asks himself, 'What can I do for her?' and concludes that what would be needed would be for him 'to be in love with her; all women are like that; they need loving with an exclusive love' (MND p. 375 tr. adap.). His plans for Nadine are very similar. However, when women step outside the boundaries he defines for them, his impulse is often towards violence; when he learns that Josette had loved a German officer, Henri 'felt like reviling her, beating her' (MND p. 623). With Paule, he grabs her wrists in a fury (MND p. 353), imagines shaking her and ripping her cigarette holder from her mouth (MND p. 475), and feels 'like beating her' (MND p. 504) when she takes up his time in his office.

The relationship with Paule places Henri in a particularly unsympathetic light. Although he spends a great deal of energy on the moral problem of whether to publish details of the Soviet labour camps, he generally avoids considering the problem of his responsibilities towards Paule in moral terms. He misleads Paule, lies to her, even makes reluctant love with her, reasoning that 'it would take a lot less time to satisfy her than to have it out with her' (omitted in the English translation). He accepts that he ought to make the situation clear to Paule, but his honesty disappears when Paule senses danger and offers concessions. ' "I'm blackmailing her, that's just what it amounts to," Henri thought. "It's rather disgraceful," ' he indulgently concludes (MND p. 110), before excusing himself with an ease and rapidity that he would never permit himself over an issue that did not concern his personal relations with a woman.[24] Eventually, his relationship with Josette drives him into the open: 'it's impossible for a man to desire the same body indefinitely,' he explains (MND p. 379), echoing Robert in this definition of male sexual needs as essentially promiscuous in nature and divorced from all emotional needs. Since Anne's narrative tends to reinforce the negative perception of Paule's attitudes (though not of her suffering) which Henri's narrative offers, the text suggests clearly that Henri is simply trapped in a situation for which he bears minimal responsibility.

With Josette, Henri goes through the period of sexual temptation that Anne also passes through, in this instance clearly damned through the moral and political guilt associated with it. His return to Nadine signals a return to probity, as well as a move away from the primacy of sexuality. Nadine is a much less strongly feminine character than either Paule or Josette: 'Nadine was not pretty. She looked too much like her father, and it was disturbing to see that truculent face on the body of a young girl' (MND tr. adap. p. 22). The extent to which this relationship is caught up with Henri's attitude to Dubreuilh is clear from the beginning: 'What would Dubreuilh's head on a pillow look like?' Henri wonders (MND p. 23). The friendship between the two men is one of the strongest relationships of the novel, and echoes the pattern of commitment, withdrawal and recommitment of the other central relationships. It is quite unmatched by any relationship between women in the novel; neither Nadine nor Josette has any women friends, Anne and Paule's friendship seems to have come to an end and the mother–daughter relationship offers little but guilt and hostility. Anne's glacial attitude towards her daughter, combined with her interventions in Nadine's life behind her back, even to the extent of discussing Nadine's sexual needs with her daughter's current lover Lambert, bring the mother–daughter relationship to a nadir. It is little wonder that the indulgence which, in contrast, Anne is able to demonstrate towards the penitent Marie-Ange drives Nadine into a fury of jealousy (see MND pp. 224–25).

Anne does castigate herself for her lack of feeling towards Nadine, Henri accepts an element of guilt towards Paule — but these traits are marked as marginal, almost natural errors. Maternal frigidity (or alternatively over-possessiveness) is an almost inevitable result for Beauvoir of the immense difficulties which she describes in *The Second Sex* as embroiling mother–child relations. The question of Henri's sexism is more difficult, but it seems quite likely that Beauvoir was simply endowing her character with traits she perceived in her male entourage, and which she did not identify at the time of writing as sexist. The fundamental thesis of *The Second Sex* that femininity is a social construct naturally implies that the same is true of masculinity, and Anne's remarks show that Beauvoir had taken this idea on board. However *The Second Sex*, whilst devoting a series of chapters to the socialisation of women, did not engage in an investigation of the construction of masculinity, and it is not really surprising to note Beauvoir's uncritical portrayal of sexist and stereotypical masculine traits in a positively coded male character.

The male – female counterpoint which emerges from this analysis is foregrounded in the novel's narrative organisation. The balance between male and female points of view, more nearly attained here than in any of Beauvoir's other novels, mimics the essentially verbal relationship between the sexes set up by the structure of preference. In *Force of Circumstance*, Beauvoir draws attention to the dual narrative structure of *The Mandarins* and describes the two narratives as 'establish[ing] between them a sort of counterpoint, each reinforcing, diversifying, destroying the other' (FOC p. 277). In order to unfix meaning Beauvoir needed Anne to 'provide me with the negative of the objects that were shown through Henri's eyes in their positive aspects' (FOC p. 276). In fact this 'counterpoint' does not effectively undermine the ethos of choice, responsibility and action which prevails in the novel. Anne herself does eventually enact the structure of preference — albeit with extreme reluctance, and when she reflects on the choices which Henri and Robert are faced with, her views often support those of Henri. Indeed, it is the coincidence of these two characters' views on matters such as Paule's mystifications, on Robert's godlike status, on the moral imperatives of the intellectual's function which largely establishes the text's system of values.

However, when Anne's narrative is examined in detail, it can be seen to consist of two rather different elements. The element which dominates in terms of numbers of pages is the one which consists of first-person narrative of events in the past (*récit*), in which Anne uses the past tense (frequently the past historic). However, this account, in which the disassociation between narrating and experiencing self is visible, is accompanied by a monologue in the present tense in which narrative time and story time coincide, and in which experiencing and narrating selves come together.[24] It is this monologue which opens Anne's narrative as she lies in bed at night reflecting on death and on her anxieties about Robert, and which closes it in the final chapter of the novel where she comes to the brink of suicide: 'Who knows? Perhaps one day I'll be happy again. Who knows?' (MND p. 763). Anne's monologue, with its accent on suffering, folly and death, is the predecessor of the monologues of the women of Beauvoir's last two fictional works. The narratives of Anne and Henri, despite their similarities in some areas, thus remain differentiated by their gender marking. In *Force of Circumstance*, Beauvoir describes how she divided autobiographical traits between the two characters acting as narrative focus, one male, one female — and they are distributed strictly according to gender role. Henri has her optimism, her appetites, her taste for activity — and, of course, the pen. Anne has fear and shame, and the 'negative aspects of my experience' (FOC p. 280). In *The Mandarins* these 'negative aspects' are thus labelled female and more or less vanquished by the masculine structure of preference which, in political terms, means action not idealism, and within the couple means shared values and companionship, not sexuality and romanticism.

Henri is the only male character in Beauvoir's novels with a substantial role to play who acts as narrative focus for an external narrator (the other very minor example is Gerbert in *She Came to Stay*). Anne is the first female character to voice her own narrative through the 'I'. What these developments seem to signal is a shift of anxiety about the 'I'. Whereas Blomart and Fosca used the 'I' to examine the problem of the individual's relation to others and to history, these problems are thrown in *The Mandarins* into the more public arena of Henri's externally voiced narrative. The 'I' examines the 'negative aspects' of experience — it becomes the voice of suffering and of the temptation of folly and death which Anne shares with Paule, the fears of a 'secondary being', as Beauvoir calls her character (FOC p. 280).

In the last two works of fiction which follow *The Mandarins* this female narrative voice of suffering and folly is the only voice to be heard. Male characters neither voice the narrative nor act as its focus. The shift of the male voice from first-person narrative to third-person focus of the narrative is thus the prelude to its disappearance. However, it still has a role to play in *The Mandarins*, and is supported by the power of language on which the choices of the novel so heavily depend; writing itself also remains a male preserve. Women's writing in *The Mandarins* is an expression of suffering and madness (Paule's writing before her cure, and the mad woman Maria's), and if the suffering is removed, it becomes 'as empty, as flat as a story in *Confidences*' (MND p. 669), in other words becomes a writing fit only for other women's consumption. In Anne, a female character does achieve a narrative voice, a voice posited as reliable and which delivers judgements on many of the other characters. However, the emergence of the female voice brings with it in Beauvoir's fiction a growing focus on the illusory, the delusionary — held in check in *The Mandarins* by the structure of preference, but which reigns in the final period of her fiction writing.

Notes

1. See Pierre Viansson-Porté's interview with Beauvoir (1978), p. 592 in Francis and Gontier (1979), and confirmed to me by Beauvoir in 1985.

2. See my Chapter 1.

3. In *Force of Circumstance* Beauvoir writes of the text that 'a great many of the things I wanted to say were directly linked to my condition as a woman' (p. 276).

4. See M.-A. Burnier, *Les Existentialistes et la politique*, for an account of Sartre's involvement with the RDR and of his political development in the postwar period.

5. The visit to the 'Murrays' which took place the same summer and during which Beauvoir almost drowned, is used in the novel as part of Anne's second trip to the States in Chapter 8.

6. See *Force of Circumstance*, p. 262.

7. See Burnier, pp. 83, 105–6, for an account of Sartre's involvement in this.

8. See *Force of Circumstance*, p. 302, where Beauvoir notes Lanzmann's influence in this respect.

9. 'Interview de Simone de Beauvoir par J. F. Rolland', *L'Humanité Dimanche*, 19 December 1954. Reprinted in Francis and Gontier (1979), pp. 358–62.

10. Anne is in fact writing a book about psychoanalysis, and is said to have published other work in the field, but it scarcely figures in her preoccupations and little status is afforded to it.

11. Cf. Beauvoir's description of her growing feeling in the late 1940s and early 1950s that 'moralism — although we were not yet free of it ourselves — was the last bastion of bourgeois idealism' (FOC p. 115).

12. For example in the preface to *America Day by Day* (ADD pp. 7–8), and in 'Mon expérience d'écrivain' in Francis and Gontier (1979), pp. 439–57. Not only the conclusions, even the texts which Henri produces appear to be Beauvoir's own; the production of his first play echoes the production of Beauvoir's in 1945, and has the title 'Les Survivants', which Beauvoir considered for *The Mandarins*.

13. Beauvoir reacts strongly in *Force of Circumstance* to the 'aberrant' connections which reviewers made between Henri and Camus, Dubreuilh and Sartre. Keefe suggests that this connection could be turned on its head and that a reading of *The Mandarins* may have influenced Camus in 'Jonas ou l'artiste au travail' and in *La Chute*. See Keefe's 'Heroes of our Time in three of the stories of Camus and Simone de Beauvoir'.

14. 19 December 1954. Interview reprinted in Francis and Gontier (1979), pp. 358–62.

15. Poster, *Existential Marxism in Postwar France*, p. 122. Lukacs devotes 30 pages to Beauvoir's essays, whose conclusions he describes as 'abstract and perfectly sterile' (*Existentialisme ou Marxisme?*, p. 186). Kanapa's polemical treatise quotes frequently from Beauvoir's essays in order to attack them, and uses his reading of *She Came to Stay* as evidence that Beauvoir is 'an enemy of mankind' (*L'Existentialisme n'est pas un humanisme*, p. 117).

16. Beauvoir was awarded the prize by a comfortable majority of seven votes to two. See J. Robichon, *Le Défi des Goncourt*, p. 218. She was the

third woman to receive the prize out of the 52 writers to whom it had been awarded, after Elsa Triolet in 1944, and Béatrice Beck in 1952. Robichon describes Beauvoir as being perceived at the time as the 'semi-scandalous author of *The Second Sex*' and notes that the novel sold 4,000 copies in the first few weeks of its release (Robichon, p. 217).

17. Burnier, p. 49.

18. Cf. the reaction to *The Mandarins* of the American G. J. Joyaux in 1956, who writes of the problem of the political commitment of intellectuals as a peculiarly French problem. See G. J. Joyaux, 'Le problème de la gauche intellectuelle et *Les Mandarins* de Simone de Beauvoir'.

19. See Burnier, p. 41.

20. In her chapter on the relations between men and women in Beauvoir's fiction, Mary Evans describes the relationship between Lewis and Anne as 'astonishingly romantic' and expresses her disappointment that 'the exclusivity and commitment which western culture expects in sexual relations between men and women are reaffirmed' by the 'conventional patterns' of Anne and Lewis's affair (Evans, *Simone de Beauvoir: A Feminist Mandarin*, p. 83). Without disagreeing with her conclusion that sexuality is regarded in the book as basically dangerous, it is worth stressing that the need for commitment and fidelity is attributed more strongly in the text to Lewis than to Anne, and that it is contrasted to Robert's mode of conducting relationships.

21. There is an evident parallel with the role Pierre plays for Françoise in *She Came to Stay* (see my Chapter 1).

22. See *The Second Sex*, pp. 652–79, and the section of Jean Leighton's *Simone de Beauvoir on Woman* which relates Paule to Beauvoir's essays, pp. 119–25.

23. In *America Day by Day* Beauvoir expresses strongly her reservations about the way she sees psychoanalysis and psychiatric treatment used in the United States, not as a way of helping patients to come to terms with themselves but as a way of readapting the individual to socially useful norms (AJJ pp. 68–69).

24. Carol Ascher sees Henri's decision to perjure himself to save Josette as 'also the story of sexism, for Henri would never have spent a minute with a male collaborator; he simply hasn't the same moral standards for women' (Ascher, p. 96).

25. The opening of Anne's narrative in the second part of Chapter 1 (p. 33) is a good example of the use of monologue; in contrast, the opening of Chapter 6 (p. 402) shows the use of the narrative of the past in which the narrating character is virtually addressing the reader, organising the narrative and even offering time summaries ('I spent the following week . . .'). I explore these different elements of the narrative in more detail in my 'Narrative structure in *Les Mandarins*' (1980).

6

Les Belles Images

/

'From the point of view of style, your best books are definitely your last ones,' remarked Jean-Paul Sartre to Simone de Beauvoir in a film interview in 1978.[1] *Les Belles Images* (1966), published 12 years after *The Mandarins* and about a fifth of its length, is without doubt the most writerly of Beauvoir's novels and the most ambitious in literary terms. 'I have rarely had the impression of producing a work as literary as this one,' Beauvoir told *Le Monde*.[2] It was received as a radical departure from her earlier fiction: 'This is not real Simone de Beauvoir,' lamented some of her readers, whilst critics saw the novel as an incursion into the stamping ground of Françoise Sagan.[3]

The 12 years since the publication of Beauvoir's previous novel had indeed resulted in a considerable evolution in her attitude to the novel form. In November 1965, just as she was beginning work on *Les Belles Images*, Beauvoir gave two interviews to friend and critic Francis Jeanson. 'The problems of the novel have to be re-thought,' she said. Any new novel which she wrote would 'not be of the same kind and would pose me with new technical problems (type of narration, distance between the narrator and the charac-ters, etc.); and it would concern people in very different situations from my own'.[4] In the gap since *The Mandarins* Beauvoir had not so much abandoned writing as temporarily substituted autobio-graphy for the novel, producing in these years three volumes of autobiography (in 1958, 1960 and 1963) and an autobiographical account of her mother's death (1964). It seems clear that the writing of these texts had in part palliated her desire to write about her own situation, and allowed her to conceive of the radically different situation of *Les Belles Images*. In September 1966, just before the publication of the novel, Beauvoir told a Japanese audience that 'I was led to autobiography not as a result of the criticisms [of the traditional novel] of the *Tel Quel* group or of the New Novelists, but as a result of a personal reflection on the insufficiencies of the novel.'[5] The link between an unease about the novel form and the substitution of autobiography is here made plain. But the reference to the *Tel Quel* group and to the New Novelists also points up the fact that Beauvoir's change of tactic in the last phase of her fiction writing took place against the background of the attack which a new generation of writers and critics had launched on the traditional novel in the 1950s and 1960s, and of the formal experimentation in which writers like Nathalie Sarraute, Alain Robbe-Grillet, Michel Butor and others were engaged.

Beauvoir was perceived as an opponent of the New Novel, and she criticised it persistently in interviews throughout the 1960s. In December 1964 she took part in a debate opposing partisans of committed literature to supporters of the *Tel Quel* tendency.[6] But Beauvoir had known Nathalie Sarraute since the late 1940s and had admired her first novel, *Portrait d'un inconnu*, to which Sartre had written a preface.[7] Her later differences of opinion with Sarraute by no means indicated a wholesale rejection of the latter's methods. Beauvoir told Jeanson in 1965 that 'I am not at all a partisan of the New Novel, but I agree with a good number of criticisms that have been formulated from that point of view (and that I was already more or less addressing to myself when I wrote *The Mandarins*).'[8] Given this position, what changes does the reader discover on opening *Les Belles Images*?

One of the most immediately apparent new strategies is the use of humour. Though Beauvoir had often used irony and wit to considerable effect in her essays and autobiographies, the corrosive parody and wordplay which undermine the characters' discourse from the first sentence of the novel onwards are startlingly new in her fiction. As the characters gaze admiringly at the farmhouse 'bought for a song — or a least shall we say for an aria — and done up by Jean-Charles at the cost of a grand opera' (LBI p. 7), the reader familiar with Beauvoir's earlier novels might be forgiven for casting around in some alarm for the source of these malicious remarks. However, this source is not easily discovered. The narrative slides from external narrative statement to free indirect speech and interior monologue, incorporating judgements on the daring juxtaposition of colours in the chairs and opinions on how old

Dominique looks from behind without any formal indication of their origin or any consistent use of typographical clues. Gradually the identification of the first-person voice, with its doubts and questions, settles on the character of Laurence — but the relationship between Laurence's voice and the external narrating voice remains highly ambiguous. To the extent that the first-person remarks often qualify and question the main narrating voice, it is evident that Laurence's point of view invades the entire narrative, and that the elements drawn from other characters are restricted to their speech or to echoes in Laurence's mind of their habitual remarks and formula judgements. But it is important to distinguish between 'voice' and 'point of view'. The covert narrator of Beauvoir's earlier fiction has not become a source of judgement and comment. It is to Laurence, with hindsight, that we can attribute the caustic view of the doing-up of the farmhouse and the intimation that Jean-Charles has not failed to take advantage of Gilbert's spare millions. But though Laurence's is the *consciousness* which the narrative draws on, her *voice* is intermittent, fading for long stretches of narrative in which the character apparently retrenches behind her social persona, and re-asserting itself at moments where the character seems to approach something resembling self-awareness.[9]

The external narrating voice captures Laurence in her exteriority, presents her not just as an individual consciousness but as a socially constructed being. The fluidity of movement between Laurence's voice and that of the external narrator, the constant elision of the differences between the two, is used to underline the fact that much of what Laurence thinks or has to say does not so much originate with the character as simply echo her immediate milieu. This movement between subjective and external voice is considerably facilitated by the adoption of the present tense as the principal narrative tense. When monologue slides into external report of Laurence's thoughts, only the pronouns change; the shift of tenses which would occur if the narrative tense and the tense of Laurence's monologue were different and which would normally heavily signal a change of narrative mode is averted. The impact of the present narrative tense can be seen by comparing examples from Patrick O'Brian's published translation, which substitutes English past tense for French present as the principal narrative tense, and my own translations reproducing the French tense sequence:

'This really is an astonishing October,' said Gisèle Dufrène: they nodded agreement: they smiled, a summer heat flooded down from the blue-grey sky (What have the others got that I haven't?). (O'Brian p.7)

'This really is an astonishing October,' Gisèle Dufrène is saying: they nod in agreement; they're smiling, a summer heat floods down from the blue-grey sky (What have the others got that I haven't?) (tr. adap.)

She bit her lip. If Jean-Charles knew! In fact nothing had changed between Laurence and him. Lucien was peripheral. And besides he no longer stirs me as he used to. (O'Brian p. 20)

She bites her lip. If Jean-Charles knew! In fact nothing has changed between Laurence and him. Lucien is peripheral. And besides he no longer stirs her as he used to. (tr. adap.)

The first example from the beginning of O'Brian's translation of the novel shows how the use of the past as narrative tense combined with present tense for Laurence's unmediated thoughts creates an impression of two separate narratives, whereas the original tense sequence combines the voices in a much more ambiguous way. In the second example, where external narrative statement and Laurence's unmediated thoughts alternate, the translator, aware of how disruptive it would seem to write: 'And besides he no longer stirred her as he used to' (to translate 'Et d'ailleurs il ne l'émeut plus comme avant'), actually drops the past tense and keeps the present, but for consistency's sake is obliged therefore to change the pronouns and refer to 'me' where the French uses 'her'. The general effect of the translation is happier where Laurence's thoughts, as well as the externally voiced narrative, can be put into the past tense.[10] It is clear that tense and narrative status are important elements in *Les Belles Images*; because of the attention that my reading of the text gives to these elements, I have adapted quotations from the published translation to reflect as exactly as possible the original use of both tense and pronoun. Both the use of the present tense and the switches of pronoun are characteristic of the New Novels of the period. However, Beauvoir had already used a mixture of first-person monologue with first-person narrative of the past in the sections of

The Mandarins focusing through Anne, and had switched between present and past historic tense, first- and third-person pronouns in the chapters focusing through Blomart in *The Blood of Others*. No doubt she was encouraged to pursue these innovations by contemporary developments in the novel, but she also retains traditional elements such as a clear — if slight — plot development, and the division of the narrative into chapters, which the New Novelists eschew. Technique, for Beauvoir, remains a way of channelling meaning, an echo of both the freedom and the limitations of her characters.

One of the most obvious and important of these channels is the development of the first-person narrative voice. In the first of the four chapters of the text this voice is hesitant, querying, often enclosed in parentheses. The first-person pronouns of Laurence's unmediated thoughts emerge briefly, sandwiched between more mediated accounts expressed in the third person. In the following example the paragraph begins with a direct transcription of Laurence's thoughts: '"I don't even know the people who live on the floor above," Laurence thinks' (LBI p. 23). The speech tag 'Laurence thinks' prepares the next sentence, which begins in the third-person narrative voice: 'She's very well informed about the neighbours on the other side of the party wall: their bath runs, their doors slam, the radio pours forth songs and advertisements for Banania, the husband bawls out his wife, and after he's gone the wife bawls out their son.' However, the part of this second sentence which follows the colon seems again to be a direct transcription of Laurence's thoughts, though the avoidance of pronouns keeps this change low-key and prevents it sounding too assertively expressed in the first person. Two questions follow, which are much more clearly direct expressions of Laurence's thought, though again the pronoun is avoided: 'But what happens in the other three hundred and forty flats in the block? In the other houses in Paris?' A third-person pronoun then briefly reintroduces the external narrator, before a series of generalised statements with no pronouns again suggest a drift back towards the subjective point of view:

At Publinf she knows Lucien, Mona to a certain extent, and a few names and faces. Family, friends: a tiny closed circuit. And all those other equally inaccessible circuits. The world is always somewhere else, and there is no way of getting into it.

These generalisations prepare the burst of three first-person pronouns which end the paragraph:

> Yet it has made its way into Catherine's life, it's frightening her and I ought to protect her from it. How can I get her to accept the fact that there are unhappy people? How can I get her to believe that they will stop being unhappy? (LBI tr. adap. p. 23)

Characteristically, two of these uses of the first-person pronoun emerge as questions. It is by these kinds of constant shifts, generalisations and avoidance of personal pronouns that the first-person voice is kept muted. In the first chapter it emerges most strongly in the penultimate paragraph, where Laurence struggles with the half-buried perception that her depression five years earlier is about to resurface. But this incursion into the self is quickly halted: 'I am quite aware of the reasons for my breakdown and I have gone beyond them (. . .) I have settled accounts with myself' (LBI p. 38). This statement closes the first-person narrative, and the final paragraph of the chapter returns to the external voice ('She felt her life around her, full, warm, a nest, a cocoon'; LBI p. 28) as Laurence settles determinedly back into the security momentarily disturbed by the questioning 'I'.

The same techniques are used in the second chapter, but there is a significant development when a substantial section of first-person narrative in the past tense occurs. Again the immediate motivation for this narrative appears to be the eruption of feelings which Laurence prefers to suppress — this time, her antagonism towards her mother and her guilt at not sharing Dominique's suffering:

> there had always been a kind of baleful aura about Dominique. Even her suffering doesn't make her human. It's like hearing the grating of a crayfish, an unarticulated sound that evokes nothing, nothing except naked pain. Far more unbearable than if one could share it. (LBI p. 45)

Unable to rid herself of the sound of the grating of the crayfish, Laurence is forced into limited introspection, and the narrative slips for several pages into first-person narrative in the past. This is brought to an end as Laurence resolves, 'I must inform my daughter myself (. . .) Know how to answer her questions and even anticipate them. Help her to find out about reality without frightening her' (LBI tr. adap. p. 49). The first-person retreat here into impersonal commands (expressed in the infinitive in French), prepares the reappearance of the third-person narrative voice to inform us that 'From time to time Laurence makes these resolutions, but without really intending to keep them' (LBI adap. p. 49). Laurence's apparent incapacity to keep her resolutions is accompanied by an inability to maintain her narrative voice.

In the third chapter, there is a short stretch of first-person narrative in the past in which Laurence tries to think through the crisis of her car accident (LBI pp. 85–86); other brief returns to first-person narrative convey largely a growing sense of panic. However, the promise held out by her father in the last lines of the chapter appears to offer some hope for the development of Laurence's inner narrating self:

> At last I'll have time to ask the questions, get the answers I've been waiting for all these years. I'll get to know the savour of his life. I'll find out the secret that makes him so different from everybody else and from me, and that makes him capable of evoking that love that I feel for nobody but him. (LBI tr. adap. p. 127)

In a sense this hope is borne out, in so far as almost the whole of the final chapter is an attempt by the narrating self to grasp what has gone wrong through a first-person recapitulation of events. However, this is not achieved through the revelation of the father's secret, but, on the contrary, by the death of his significance for Laurence. Eventually the narrative reaches the point where Laurence can articulate her disillusion: 'I've been *deceived*. The word stabs her' (LBI tr. adap. p. 151). Meaning is not incarnate in the father. Far from liberating the first person, however, this discovery leaves Laurence directionless, her last value destroyed. She summons up the first person to take her stand on Catherine (who Laurence wishes to achieve as a surrogate what Laurence cannot or will not achieve for herself): 'Not Catherine. I won't let what's been done to me be done to her. What have they made of me? (. . .) this woman that I'm vomiting up' (LBI tr. adap. p. 152). Despite Laurence's effort for her daughter, the subjective 'I' cannot vomit up the socially constructed 'she'; Laurence sees that she cannot expel that part of herself which resembles those around her. Thus the novel ends with the reassertion of the external narrating voice.

The constant movement between the character's voice and the external narrating voice not only propels the narrative forward but itself represents the unequal struggle between Laurence's fragile subjectivity and the weight of social structures, of what Beauvoir increasingly comes to call the 'practico-inert'.[11] The freedom to make of herself what she will, which the heroine of *She Came to Stay* takes for granted, becomes, by the time of *Les Belles Images*, a freedom which is shaped by the individual's situation (gender, social class, personal circumstances etc.). The individual, in this case Laurence, is no longer so much what she makes of herself, but what she makes of her situation — what she makes of what has been made of her.[12] Though the individual is always something more than his or her situation for Beauvoir, always the source of freedom and of historical action (praxis), *Les Belles Images* brings into play the weight of the structures which, for Laurence, constantly threaten to submerge her subjectivity and freedom.

The final paragraph of the novel gives the measure of how far the character is able to go in the struggle for self-expression. The ritual recomposition of the social image which takes place as Laurence brushes her hair and applies her make-up is reflected in linguistic terms by her articulation of her defeat in the language of stereotype (for her, 'les jeux sont faits'; 'the die is cast'). Even her determination to act for Catherine is expressed in a generalised and clichéd form: ('les enfants auront leur chance'; 'the children will have their chance'). The semi-questioning of this phrase on which the novel closes ('What chance? She doesn't even know.') brings the narrative to an end at the limits to which the character is enabled to go.

Laurence is able to question the language of stereotype but she can substitute no more than a fragmentary voice for its pervasive presence. The linguistic universe of *Les Belles Images* is constructed through a relentless use of phrases and formulae which Beauvoir had culled from the media, from Louis Armand, from Michel Foucault and from other thinkers from whom the new bourgeoisie of the 1960s took their watchwords.[13] In her interview with *Le Monde*, Beauvoir refers to adding in at the proof stage of her manuscript some phrases inspired by her reading of Michel Foucault's *Les Mots et les Choses*. Foucault's treatment of the individual as a function of historically discontinuous systems of meaning was profoundly inimical to the existentialist emphasis on the individual as subject; Sartre attacked Foucault in an interview published in *L'Arc* in October 1966 (the same year as *Les Belles Images*), and in her December interview in *Le Monde* Beauvoir says Foucault 'suppresses history, suppresses praxis, that is *engagement*, suppresses man, so that there is no more poverty or misfortune, there are only systems. *Les Mots et les Choses* is a most useful instrument for the technocratic bourgeoisie.'[14]

The effect of the use of this language of the technical bourgeoisie is sometimes comic, sometimes brutally revelatory of its ideological function. It does not simply form a code through which the members of this group can constantly reassure themselves that their attitudes are identical to those around them, but perpetuates the myths with which the group protect themselves from potentially damaging truths. Like the October weather, everything in *Les Belles Images* is exceptionally good: Dominique is an incomparable hostess, Jean-Charles is a wonderful lover and Laurence's career is a succession of triumphs. The problems of the starving and the oppressed can be explained either as a result of the fact that 'man has lost his roots' (the traditional humanist view represented by Laurence's father) or can be solved by the fact that man is now 'rooted on the scale of the planet' (one of the constituent phrases of the myth of the future proffered by Jean-Charles and which presents technology as the answer to all ills).

The vocabulary of the technological bourgeoisie of which Laurence forms part is given both a more comic and a more savage twist in the novel than that of the traditional humanist. Dominique's suffering is comically undercut by the fact that her tears flow in the leisure corner of her sitting room; Jean-Charles's arguments are satirically deflated by his sententiously pronounced argument that the abandonment of nuclear weapons 'would mean falling outside the context of history' (LBI p. 11). A listing technique is also frequently used to comically subvert meaning in the characters' discourse, as for example in Jean-Charles's vision of the world in ten years' time with deserts 'covered in wheat, vegetables and fruit' in which 'all the children, stuffed with rice, tomatoes and oranges, beamed with delight' (LBI tr. adap. p. 26).[15] A more savage irony is apparent in the use of deforming terminology such as the term *force de dissuasion* (equivalent to 'deterrent force') to refer to nuclear weapons, and the 'incidental expenses' (LBI p. 49) which the suicide of a 12-year-old represents in Gilbert's terms, or the 'human effects' of overcrowding and automation which Jean-Charles sees as a necessary side effect of progress (LBI p. 62).

Laurence often questions this phraseology, but it invades her own speech at every turn, constantly demonstrating the extent to which she has been formed by her milieu. Tahiti is worse than St. Tropez, Dominique opines: 'It's *so* banal . . .' ('C'est d'un banal . . .'); and Laurence reacts to this phrase in irritation, remembering how it was Florence that was '*so* banal' when she was young. A moment later Laurence expresses her dislike of new housing estates: 'It's *so* depressing' ('C'est d'un déprimant!'), echoing despite herself her mother's syntax and emphasis. On some occasions she catches herself out on the point of echoing the habitual remarks of even someone she hates, like Gilbert. ' "It's a relaxation . . ." she was on the point of bringing out an automatic "it's essential" when she caught herself in time. She hears Gilbert's voice: "A relaxation that's essential", she looks at Mona's tired face, she feels vaguely embarrassed' (LBI tr. adap. p. 58). More overtly still, Laurence draws on both her father's and husband's vocabulary as the contrast between Mona's lifestyle and her own becomes clearly apparent, and she seeks a defence against the recognition of her own privileged status:

> Mona's scornful voice: what gives her the right to be so superior? She's not a communist but all the same she must go in for the mystique of the proletariat as Jean-Charles calls it; there's something of the sectarian about her, Laurence has noticed that before. ('If there's anything I hate it's sectarianism,' Papa used to say). (LBI p. 60 tr. adap.)

Having shored herself up with the formulae of her husband and her father Laurence is able to conclude that 'a little good will' is all that is needed to create universal sympathy and understanding. Here, the external presentation of the character as Laurence ('Laurence has noticed that before') is used to underline the extent to which the character is parroting her milieu.

Language, like the other elements of Laurence's socially constructed behaviour, is not posited as gratuitous but as serving a class interest. In an interview given a few weeks after the release of *Les Belles Images* Beauvoir drew attention to the use she had made in the novel of American sociologist David Riesman's book *The Lonely Crowd*, which she had first read in 1956.[16] Riesman's typology of what he calls 'social character' (which he defines as the components of personality that are learned as a result of social conditioning) includes a social type which he calls 'other-directed' and which he sees as characteristic of the 'new' middle class — the bureaucrat, the salaried employee in business — serving the needs of capitalism in an affluent urban society.[17] Riesman attempts to seek out the constituent elements of this social type in all academic objectivity (his bias if any is actually in favour of the child-rearing patterns of the 'other-directed' type, and he sees some positive benefit for the individual in the development of consumerism). Beauvoir, however, takes over certain elements of Riesman's analysis in order to lay bare the mechanisms which a social class employs to defend itself against the recognition of its own privileged status, and against social truths which it is in its interest to ignore.

In *Force of Circumstance*, completed three years before *Les Belles Images* in 1963, Beauvoir writes, 'Now I know the truth of the human condition: two-thirds of mankind are hungry. My species is two-thirds composed of worms, too weak ever to rebel, who drag their way from birth to death through a perpetual dusk of despair' (FOC p. 670). The 'truth of the human condition' explodes into the 'marvellous' world of *Les Belles Images* through the poster of a starving child, which only another child is sufficiently unprogrammed to find unacceptable. Other truths occasionally threaten to break into Laurence's consciousness: torture in the Algerian War, race riots in the United States, massacres in the Vietnam War, repression of the Communists in Greece, alienating working conditions in France. But a host of pacifying phrases and arguments are available to help Laurence push away the threat: the poster proves that 'we want things to change', technology will ensure that in the space of ten years 'everybody will have enough to eat; everybody will be much happier' (LBI pp. 26–27 tr. adap.). As for the young girls who spend all day putting pieces of carrot on herring fillets: 'It can't be quite the same for them (. . .) They've been brought up differently' (LBI p. 67). Or as Lucien puts it: 'it's lousy, certainly; but basically life is always lousy, and if it's not lousy for one reason it's lousy for another (. . .) There's the unhappiness of the poor. There's also the unhappiness of the rich. You ought to read Fitzgerald' (LBI pp. 70–71). Laurence muses that 'the conditions of the working class are not what they should be, everybody agrees on that point, although with family allowances they almost all have a washing machine, TV, and even a car' (LBI tr. adap. p. 73). For Laurence's father, the problems of the world are the result of 'aiming at abundance'; what is needed is 'a moral revolution — not a social or a political or a technical revolution — only a moral revolution would lead man back to his lost truth' (LBI p. 72). Then mankind could experience the 'austere happiness' that the poorest communities in Greece and Sardinia enjoy (LBI p. 71).

The traditional bourgeoisie in the shape of Laurence's father uses the myth of absolute moral values and an idealisation of the past to disguise the realities of the present, just as the new technocratic bourgeoisie elaborates myths of the future and of universal comprehension and conformity. Though it is the latter group which is the principal focus of Beauvoir's attack in *Les Belles Images*, much of the final chapter is devoted to the demolishing of the father — and indeed, the collapse of Laurence's belief in her father's values is the most shattering discovery of all for the character, linked as it is to the Freudian scenario of an unresolved Oedipus complex. The construction of both types owes a great deal to Riesman's analysis.

Riesman's typology includes two characterological groups which Beauvoir uses for her two classes of bourgeois value systems. The father, the traditional humanist bourgeois, represents Riesman's 'inner-directed' type: that is, a character who has acquired early in life a set of internalised goals which he takes to be absolute values and which he will continue to direct himself towards later in life. Though the inner-directed character can learn from experience he is capable of great determination in maintaining his goals and develops through strict discipline in childhood the capacity to cope with isolation and difficulties. Thus Laurence admires her father's consistent adherence to certain values ('To be in love: true worth. For him these words have a meaning'; LBI tr. adap. p. 31), together with his serenity and his apparent confidence in his inner resources. His influence on Laurence in childhood is indirect, but is supported by the directions of Laurence's schoolteacher, Mademoiselle Houchet, who instils in her pupils the values of humanism ('Be a man among men!'; LBI p. 22), of independent judgement ('Form your own opinion!'; LBI p. 37) and of absolute standards of beauty and truth. Laurence frequently recalls these injunctions, but tends to guiltily contest them. 'Never talk about what you don't know about,' Mlle Houchet used to say. But in that case you would never open your mouth' (LBI tr. adap. p. 10). 'Say what you think, Mlle Houchet used to say. Even with her father it's impossible' (LBI tr. adap. p. 31). The fate of Mademoiselle Houchet — she dies from cancer — appears to indicate the fate of her maxims. The father eventually turns out to be much more willing to compromise his ideals than Laurence had thought, but before his own dismantlement by Laurence in the final chapter, he is used in the earlier chapters to unmask certain aspects of the other group's practices.

Though Laurence's love as a child is mainly directed towards her father, her upbringing is dominated by her mother: 'it was my father I loved and my mother who formed me' (LBI p. 29). Dominique gives Laurence the upbringing that will fit her to take her place in the rich and leisured world to which Dominique fiercely aspires and which corresponds to the formation of the 'other-directed' Riesman type; thus Laurence's childhood is marked by a conflict between these two tendencies, which is doubled by being a conflict between her parents. The other-directed type, just like the inner-directed, has his or her goal implanted early in life, but the goal is constant sensitivity to the expectations and preferences of others. Laurence knows that 'You say what others expect you to say' (LBI p. 31). The other-directed character is the product of the peer group, the cosmopolitan individual liked by everyone. 'People love having Laurence, they love going to her place'; 'Does she like him [Gilbert] or not? She likes everybody' (LBI tr. adap. p. 16). The group to which the other-directed individual looks for guidance is constituted first by friends (of as identical a background to the individual as possible), and more widely by the view of their contemporaries offered to them by the mass media. Thus Jean-Charles and Dufrène are in agreement because 'they read the same periodicals' (LBI p. 79); everyone at the New Year's Eve party has seen the same television programme. Advertising and consumerism play important roles in tuning the individual's receptivity to swings in the moods and tastes of the group. Laurence's highly developed antennae account for her success in the advertising business; Jean-Charles's skills as a consumer are proved when he and Laurence are the outright winners in the competitive present-exchanging ritual which takes place at the New Year's Eve party.[18]

Laurence, equipped with all her other-directed skills, is a superb performer in her group. But her role in the novel as demystifier of certain of the group's myths derives precisely from her inability to achieve a close fit with her outward image. The conflicting messages which Laurence receives as a child from Dominique on the one hand, her father and Mademoiselle Houchet on the other, prevent her from achieving a painless adjustment; she pays a high price for her outward conformity and develops the psychosomatic symptoms which gradually build up in the novel. The centering of her crisis on Catherine focuses attention on the crucial importance of children's upbringing in the formation of social character. It seems in one sense rather paradoxical that a Beauvoir novel should centre on what is recognisably a parenting crisis; her earliest characters hardly appear to have parents and are certainly not parents themselves (Hélène puts herself through a backstreet abortion rather than risk becoming one). However, there is already some attention paid in *The Mandarins* to the mother – daughter relationship, and, both in interviews and in the later volumes of autobiography, references to the importance of the early formative years become frequent.[19] No doubt the writing of *The Second Sex* made Beauvoir more alert to the pressures of early social conditioning, and the autobiographies show that she took a strong interest in the relationship which some of her own friends set up with their children — most notably Nathalie Sorokine (Lise), whose relationship with her children is described in *All Said and Done*.

By putting a child at the centre of the discussion, Beauvoir is able to expose the mechanisms of the social formation of a class, the means by which parents effectively groom their children for their place in the world of *Les Belles Images*. At the same time the child's-eye view permits the unmasking of the ideological force of this grooming. Thus Catherine's attention to the world about her, her insistence on the here and now, have the power to explode the myth of the future or the confidence that someone else is busy doing all that it is humanly possible to do about the problem. Her capacity for feeling (demonstrated by her strong feelings for her sister, and her attachment to a friend) is a weapon against the indifference which traps Laurence, for whom people are virtually interchangeable. Catherine's friendship with a girl of a different age and a different background to herself not only points up the dangers of Laurence's isolation ('If I had a friend I could talk to her instead of lying here prostrate'; LBI tr. adap. p. 145) but forms a dangerous and potentially subversive link. In the world of *Les Belles Images*, the all-important peer group is made up exclusively of people exactly like oneself; to have meaningful contact with anyone else is to open up communication with a different viewpoint. Brigitte is not subject to any maternal influence, has free access to reading material, holds discussions with her medical student brother and is from a Jewish family. Quite apart from these specific danger signals, the simple existence of a strong friendship is likely to encourage, as Riesman points out, the development of autonomy and of parts of the personality which otherwise might lie dormant. Laurence's struggle towards autonomy is partly doomed by the absence of any such friend — by her refusal, for example, to make any genuine overture towards Mona.

Brigitte, then, is clearly dangerous. To counteract this threat, the ultimate weapon of the psychologist is deployed.[20] The expertise of the psychologist is by no means unknown to Laurence; she has studied the surveys of archetypal fantasies on which she has to draw in her work, the reduction of desire to 'smoothness, brilliance, shine; the desire for gliding, for icy perfection; erotic values and infantile values (innocence); speed, domination, warmth, security. Was it possible that all tastes could be explained by such primitive fantasies?' (LBI tr. adap. p. 36). Laurence questions this reductionism, and now resists the definition of Catherine's anxiety as an abnormality requiring the attention of a psychologist. It is Jean-Charles who suggests referring Catherine to Madame Frossard, and who reveres her powers as a 'specialist' (LBI p. 111). The task of the psychologist, as Jean-Charles formulates it, is to ensure that his daughter will 'be a success in life' (LBI p. 110). Laurence's objections are met with the accusation that she is 'downright backward' (LBI p. 111) and that her own 'sentimentality' needs sorting out by a psychiatrist. The proof of Laurence's sentimentality is that she wrecked the car rather than run over a cyclist — in other words, adopted a moral rather than a materialistic attitude. The role of the therapist is clear: Catherine and Laurence need to be cured of their moral sensibility, develop a proper view of the relative worth of a human being and a car, learn an appropriate deafness to suffering which does not directly concern them.

The complicity between the psychologist and the society of *Les Belles Images* is confirmed by the portrait of Madame Frossard: competent and rapid, perfectly and pleasantly impersonal, she ignores Laurence's hostility and advises the separation of the two friends to protect Catherine.[21] This view of psychiatric treatment as a desensitising process, designed to replace pain and suffering by a bovine lack of feeling, parallels Anne's dismay in *The Mandarins* when Paule is adjusted out of her suffering. In both novels, pain and suffering are identified as the truth — not only the truth of the individual's suffering but also, in *Les Belles Images*, as a moral and political truth. In both texts, Freudian explanations are viewed as suffering from the blanket nature of their application;

the individual, for Beauvoir, can never be mechanistically reduced to a complex.[22] This mechanistic aspect — as Beauvoir sees it — of Freudian theory is exploited humorously in the text when Laurence's father remarks,

> The castration complex! It's been so over-used to explain everything that it no longer explains anything whatever. I can just see a psychiatrist coming to attend a condemned man on the morning of his execution and finding him in tears: 'What a castration complex!' he would cry. (LBI p. 126)

Laurence and her father also enjoy a habitual joke relating to Freud's treatment of one of his female hysteric patients (LBI p. 29). Yet Beauvoir by no means completely rejects Freudian concepts; she told Jeanson in 1965 that she herself had had 'a very marked Oedipus complex and a fixation on the father, accompanied by a profound jealousy of my mother; then a *very* great disappointment at the awkward age, when my father basically "dropped" me'. She goes on to say, 'it was really a kind of lover's chagrin, a kind of break-up which took place between my father and myself, and which was very painful for me'.[23]

This conceptualisation of her relationship with her father is clearly offered in an uncritical spirit, yet when the same situation is transferred to the novel, Laurence rejects a Freudian analysis as the key to her problems: 'Oedipus not coped with properly, my mother still my rival. Electra, Agamemnon. Is that why Mycenae stirred me so? No. No. Stuff and nonsense' (LBI tr. adap. p. 150). The point is that Laurence may be prepared to admit the existence of an unresolved Oedipus complex, but that she finds this neat formula so generalised as to be virtually irrelevant. The image of the *krisses* (Malay daggers) fighting in a drawer presents the Freudian explanation as an 'ordering' system: the turmoil of words and images in her mind 'fight among themselves like Malay krisses in a closed drawer (if you open it everything is in order)' (LBI tr. adap. p. 150). When she opens the drawer (that is, applies the Oedipus explanation) the drawer is in order. But as soon as she closes it (abandons the packaged answer) the turmoil starts up again. Throughout the text Laurence is shown to be obsessive about order, constantly tidying (*faire de l'ordre*) and looking for neat answers (see for example LBI pp. 47, 70, 94). But she cannot even begin to approach the crux of her problems until she summons up the courage to go *beyond* the formula: 'I am jealous but above all, above all . . . She breathes too fast, starts panting. So it wasn't true that he possessed wisdom and joy and that his inner glow was enough for him!' The secret Laurence has counted on learning from him 'did not exist.' (LBI p. 151). This is what she discovered in Greece and has been afraid to admit to herself. The emotional disappointment is a cover for a devastating intellectual discovery: there are no values left for her to cling to. Her isolation is complete; the blackness of the mole's tunnel has no chink of light.

Like the set expressions of language, the mythologies of ancient Greece, and the 'beautiful legends' of Christianity (LBI p. 65), Freudian explanations are presented as part of ordering systems which are external to Laurence's subjective experience. In Greece, Laurence is unmoved by her visit to the site of the Delphi oracle, where Pythia, the priestess of Apollo, delivered oracles as obscure and generalised as the formulae with which Laurence struggles. Set against these is Laurence's dim perception of a different way forward for Catherine, a way which Laurence is not able to fully articulate but which is represented by the little Greek girl dancing in Delphi (thus, in a sense, Laurence does receive her oracular message). The child is spontaneous, ecstatic, completely carried away by the strength of her own response to the music, quite 'beside herself' (LBI p. 132). The English 'quite beside herself' translates the French 'l'air tout à fait folle' (literally, 'with an air of madness') which, though it does not imply here madness, has the connotation of extravagance and of something outside the norm. The term *folle* is again used when Laurence thinks about the child later (p. 146, where the translation gives, appropriately, 'out of her mind with music'). The contrast with the mother, fat, unmoved by the music and 'bovine' (the same word used of Paule in *The Mandarins* after her cure) sets up the same set of oppositions between the socially adjusted and the suffering 'deranged' individual which Anne voices in *The Mandarins*. Folly becomes a symbol of the struggle of the individual for expression.

The sight of the enraptured child pushes Laurence into the sudden realisation that Catherine is still on the side of music and feeling, can still perhaps be given the possibility of developing her own feelings. Laurence herself can no longer respond to music, can rarely recognise any feeling beyond the constant sense of preoccupation which is the 'colour of the day and the air she breathes' (LBI tr. adap. p. 133). She is shocked by the shouting and swearing which her mother uses to express her pain, and deals with her mother's distress and humiliation after Gilbert's violence towards her by giving her tranquillisers (she is tempted to take one herself), taking her out to lunch in an attempt to create a facade of normality, urging her not to think about it, to take a plane or a lover (LBI pp. 104–7). When she feels anger herself after an argument with Jean-Pierre she acts immediately to suppress it — a glass of water, exercises, a cold shower, a sleeping pill (LBI p. 101). After a second, more violent discussion she refuses herself the cold-water treatment, allows a storm of feelings to break out, but finds herself unable to cry. When Jean-Charles sends the conventional flowers, she accepts them because her feelings about her husband are 'not of the least importance. (. . .) There was no point even feeling angry' (LBI p. 115).

This repression leads, from early on in the narrative, to the inscription of her feelings in her body: she feels sick at the idea of her mother's suffering and is 'sick from emotion' when she learns that Dominique has written to Patricia (LBI p. 101). After accepting Jean-Charles's roses she finds that 'she could not swallow a thing' (LBI p. 114), and this distaste for food is given a social dimension when she discovers the scarcity of food in the Greek village of Andritsena. At the beginning of the last chapter Laurence, unable now to eat at all, is acutely aware of her lack of words to express her crisis: 'What have I failed in? I don't even know. I have no words to express my sufferings or regrets. But this lump in my throat prevents me from eating' (LBI tr. adap. p. 129). She suffers from crises of feeling but 'her body is of stone; she wants to scream out, but stone has no voice, nor tears' (LBI tr. adap. p. 148). The symbolic parallel between eating and swallowing lies becomes explicit when Jean-Charles tries to press Laurence into seeing a doctor:

> They'll force her to eat, they'll make her swallow it all; all what? All that she is vomiting up, her life, the life of the others with their phoney loves, their concern with money, their lies. They will cure her of her refusals and her despair. No. (. . .) Not Catherine. I won't let them make of her what's been made of me. What has been made of me? This woman who loves no-one, who is indifferent to the beauties of the world, who can't even weep — this woman that I'm vomiting up. (LBI tr. adap. pp. 180–81)

Not eating is the only form of revolt against manipulation by others which Laurence feels able to carry out. Yet almost immediately after this passage, Laurence does find her voice for Catherine, does express her decision with a new power and authority which stun Jean-Charles to the point that he is unable to comprehend: 'I don't understand a thing of what you're saying' (LBI p. 152). 'I'm saying what I think, that's all,' says Laurence in irritation (LBI p. 152), as though she were not doing this for virtually the first time in the book. There is no more vomiting as Laurence finds the power to say no.

An analysis of the last paragraph of the text holds out little hope that Laurence's stand will go any further than the defence of her child. At the same time it is worth noting how the character achieves a strength which, however limited, does not appear to be present at earlier moments. The key is the release of the character from the paralysing grip which her childlike belief in her father has exercised over her power to be independent. The discovery that he is not the holder of a secret is both shattering and, ultimately, liberating. A character who has been taught since childhood not to pay any attention to her own thoughts and feelings ('Don't sit there daydreaming; do something'; LBI p. 18) succeeds, after the virtual reversion to her childhood which the Greek trip represents, and the three-day retreat to her bedroom, in a kind of self-analysis which permits her to rid herself of certain illusions and draw up a balance sheet of who she is. Perhaps this effort is posed in opposition to the professional therapy advocated by Jean-Charles. The idea that this might succeed seems both optimistic in its premiss and pessimistic in its outcome, since it is apparently not to lead to the adoption of a changed lifestyle.[24] However, there is one aspect of her situation which Laurence does not explicitly identify but which can be related to Laurence's failure to act on her own behalf, which is her situation as a woman.

Many of the charades which Laurence automatically plays in the text say as much about the socialisation of a sex as of a class. Her worship of her father, for instance, the pleasure she takes in having him interpret the Greek alphabet for her, just as she asks all the men in her life (and no women) what the answer to Catherine's question is, indicate her learned dependency on patriarchal wisdom. Socially, Laurence is the perfect product of female training to constantly 'handle' people ('She models her smile upon her husband's'; LBI tr. adap. p. 23), to avoid conflict (Laurence will give Goya an extra bonus secretly because there's 'no point in upsetting Jean-Charles'; LBI p. 108), to accept male patronage ('They scarcely had the choice, Laurence dear,' said Gilbert. 'The rents in Brazilia are far beyond their reach. His mouth rounds in a slight smile, as though he were apologising for his superiorities.' LBI tr. adap. p. 10). Laurence pays a high price for marriage, but the professional view is that her intellectual regression and emotional problems are 'perfectly usual' (LBI p. 37) for a mother at home with small children. Work, when she takes it up, is less stressful than her domestic life. Her role as mother far outweighs Jean-Charles's role as father, despite the fact that they both have jobs: 'I'm the one who looks after Catherine. You do involve yourself from time to time. But I'm the one who brings her up' (LBI tr. adap. p. 152). Taking seriously the role of mother involves a heavy load of guilt: 'If my ten-year-old daughter sobs, I'm the one who's at fault. Dominique and Jean-Charles will both blame me' (LBI tr. adap. p. 22). The nascent anorexia through which she eventually expresses her crisis is a classic female method of expressing revolt.

The gender aspect of Laurence's situation is strengthened by the parallel crisis of her mother. Dominique dislikes men ('Men, I've had it up to here with them.'; LBI tr. adap. p. 70) but, despite her prestigious job, is obsessed by the perception that in the circles in which she is desperate to move, a man is an essential attribute ('I've already told you that a woman without a man has no social position; her situation looks dubious. I know that people are already saying that I have a gigolo.'; LBI tr. adap. p. 149). In losing Gilbert, Dominique feels that she has lost the peace and security which she had hoped would be her compensation for the battles and humiliations which she encountered in her struggle to reach the top ('What you have to do, what you have to put up with; above all when you're a woman'; LBI p. 96). Laurence questions this attitude when she is with her mother — but it is clear that, no more than Dominique, Laurence has absolutely no intention of trying to manage her life without a husband. No matter how brutal Jean-Charles's accusations, they are 'tied together for life' — what Laurence may think of him or what he may think of her is completely irrelevant (LBL p. 115). She has been groomed to catch a young man just like Jean-Charles and there is no question of voluntarily abandoning her socially essential husband.

The situation of the men in the novel is rather different. Whereas it is possible to feel sympathy for some of the women characters at certain moments, and some members of the female sex even carry a positive coding (Mona, Catherine, Brigitte, the little Greek girl), the men are virtually all unredeemable. It is they above all who represent the machinations and ideology of their class. Thus Dufrène explains 'that in real-estate dealings it's difficult to draw a line between fraud and speculation: one is forced into illegal practices' (LBI p. 125). As for Thirion, one of France's top barristers, his 'whole career has been made up of dirty deals and self-advertisement' (LBI tr. adap. p. 88). He tells an admiring audience that his women colleagues 'are quite charming and many are talented (generally speaking they are not the same ones). But one thing is certain: there is not one of them who will ever be able to argue a case before the assizes' (LBI p. 83). Jean-Charles blames Laurence for 'not having saved him 800,000 francs by taking the risk of killing a man' and argues that 'Everybody would have given evidence in your favour' (LBI p. 113). Even Lucien, the romantic lover, is presented as a slave to consumerism and is assimilated to Jean-Charles: 'as like as two peas' (LBI p. 59). However, the most potent representative of the rich male technocrat is Gilbert Mortier. Immensely rich and powerful (his income is 'virtually unlimited'; LBI p. 16), he heads a multinational electronics company and shares Jean-Charles's Panglossian confidence in a future world of perfection created by technology. The emergence of his egoism and brutality from beneath a thin veneer of charm and elegant manners creates the first tremors in Laurence's carefully arranged life. When he argues that his abandonment of Dominique in order to marry the 19-year-old daughter of a former mistress is perfectly justifiable because 'I don't love Dominique any more. I do love Patricia' (LBI p. 81) and because 'a woman of fifty-one is older than a man of fifty-six' (LBI p. 40), Laurence is forced into recognising the obscenity of the word 'love' in his mouth. She had taken at face value the image of the stylish couple in the Ferrari, and she has to face the reality of Gilbert brutalising Dominique, hitting her and dragging her into the bedroom by the collar of her dressing gown. The alliance of a beautiful 19-year-old girl with Gilbert despite Dominique's revelations about his past underlines the materialistic motivations beneath the formation of the couples around her, so strong as to permit the overriding of any sense of disgust.

Gilbert becomes something of a diabolical figure for Laurence, to the extent that she imagines killing him. Yet the scene in which Dominique discovers that Gilbert is to marry Patricia is juxtaposed with the scene in which Laurence breaks with Lucien — a scene which Laurence plans and plays out with a determination and lack of concern for Lucien that echoes Gilbert's tranquil egosim: 'Come on, don't make it into a big thing. There are plenty more fish . . . People are pretty interchangeable, you know,' she informs Lucien (LBI tr. adap. p. 94). The treatment that Dominique receives from Gilbert tends to emphasise the situation of woman as victim in the text — but Laurence is not posited simply as victim of a situation which is convenient and comfortable for her. 'Half victim, half accomplice' — Laurence's situation mirrors that of the quotation which prefaces the second volume of *The Second Sex*.[25] Doubly mutilated by her socialisation, Laurence remains a complicitous member of a class to which Beauvoir had become implacably hostile.

'The horror my class inspires in me has been brought to a white heat by the Algerian War' wrote Beauvoir in 1963 (FOC p. 665). Though the novel postdates the end of the Algerian War in its setting, it carries an echo of the horror which Beauvoir felt in the face of her contemporaries' dismissal of French atrocities in Algeria in the article which Laurence reads. 'Crisis between France and Algeria' — the title is given twice (LBI pp. 63, 66), and Laurence conscientiously reads the article through to the end ('once she had begun a thing she did not like to leave it unfinished'; LBI p. 68) before turning her attention to writing a text for a shampoo advertisement.[26] Hunger, torture, shampoo. The ideology which allows Laurence to turn her attention indifferently from one to the next is shown to be scarcely chipped by the events of the novel. But the text itself is 'on the side of the hungry' as Sartre puts it.[27] The technical innovations which it introduces are not employed to describe in 300 pages a suspension bridge, like the novel which Jean-Charles admires and which clearly refers to the long descriptions of objects characteristic of the apolitical New Novel. Technical innovation is used to attack the arguments and practices of a social class. Yet the text remains focused on an individual, because despite the pressures which emanate from the situation of class and gender, it is the individual who remains the site of meaning for Beauvoir — the site from which all solutions, all praxis has to come. The problem of realities such as the starving children of the Third World is essentially seen as a function of the individual consciousness.

Notes

1. See the transcript of the film *Simone de Beauvoir*, published by Josée Dayan and Malka Ribowska, p. 28. My translation.

2. Interview with Jacqueline Piatier in *Le Monde*, 23 December 1966, p. 17. In the same interview Beauvoir makes a point of drawing attention to the fact that she had borrowed the mole image used in the text for Laurence from Alain Badiou's *Almagestes* (1964). This borrowing, as well as Beauvoir's insistence on it, makes a connection between *Les Belles Images* and Badiou's highly experimental work which describes itself as an exploration of language.

3. *All Said and Done*, p. 138.

4. Francis Jeanson, *Simone de Beauvoir ou l'entreprise de vivre*, pp. 294–95. My translation.

5. 'Mon expérience d'écrivain', in Francis and Gontier (1979), p. 449. My translation.

6. The debate, in which Beauvoir, Sartre and Jorge Sembrun opposed Yves Berger, Jean-Pierre Faye and Jean Ricardou, was published as *Que peut la littérature?* in 1965.

7. See *Force of Circumstance*, p. 27.

8. Jeanson, p. 295. My translation.

9. See Gérard Genette's *Figures III*, p. 203, for the distinction between the two questions of narrative voice and narrative focus — or, as Genette puts it, between 'Who speaks?' and 'Who sees?'. It is this distinction which allows me to disagree with Irène Pagès, who does not recognise any external narrative voice in the text, arguing that 'Laurence is the narrator' (Pagès, 'Beauvoir's *Les Belles Images*: Desubstantification of reality through a narrative', p. 136).

10. Blandine Stefanson draws attention to the problems of the translation in her edition of *Les Belles Images*. However, her characterisation of the third-person narrative as 'the distant jeering author's comments' is very different from my own and conflates author and narrator. See Stefanson, pp. 29–32.

11. See for example *All Said and Done*, pp. 37, 40. In general, the practico-inert represents the inertia (thing-like nature) of the social field in which individuals try to exercise their freedom.

12. Cf. Sartre's explanation in *Le Nouvel Observateur*, 26 January 1970, that for him 'man is no longer what he makes of himself, but what he makes of what has been made of him' (my translation).

13. Beauvoir describes in *All Said and Done*, pp. 137–39, how she put together this compilation.

14. Parodic echoes of Foucault in the text include phrases such as 'the idea of what constitutes man is due to be overhauled, and no doubt will vanish; it's a nineteenth century invention, now out of date' and 'we are on the threshold of a new epoch — one in which men will become useless' (LBI p. 79). It is tempting to see the choice of architecture as Jean-Charles's profession as selected to allow a satirical use of the spatial imagery favoured by structuralists.

15. The same technique is used to remove any emotional content from the account of Lucien and Laurence's early relationship. This highly amusing set piece, reminiscent in its exaggerated gestures of an early silent movie, produces a kind of parody of a structuralist account of this relationship, comically reduced to a series of 'comings and goings and always back at the same place' (LBI p. 27).

16. Interview with Jacqueline Piatier in *Le Monde*, 23 December 1966, p. 17. The impact of Riesman's book on Beauvoir is also documented in *Force of Circumstance*, p. 385.

17. See David Riesman, *The Lonely Crowd*, p. 21.

18. In a 1983 interview Beauvoir later analyses the giving of gifts to show how a gesture which should be highly moral, should be a gesture from one freedom to another, becomes, in an alienated society, an attempt by the giver to dominate the receiver (*Libération*, 30 March 1983, pp. 26–27).

19. See for example *All Said and Done*, p. 12, and the 1965 Jeanson interview.

20. Madame Frossard, referred to in the French text as both *psychologue* and *psychiatre*, seems to be a clinical psychologist. It is clear that she is not simply testing and evaluating Catherine, since there are references to the cure that she is to carry out.

21. A further instance in the text of the favour with which the psychologist is looked upon in Laurence's milieu, is the success of the *test du passeur* (the ferryman's test) with which Laurence entertains Dominique's guests in the opening pages of the novel. This test, incomprehensibly translated by O'Brian as the test 'about the man who takes you over the frontier', and often confused by commentators (including Stefanson in her edition of the text) with a children's logical test, is in fact a fairly low-grade psychological test, which poses the problem of a woman who, neglected by a husband preoccupied by his work, spends the night with another man at his house on the other side of the river. To get back home early next morning before her husband returns from a trip, she has to recross the bridge, but a madman bars her way. She finds a ferryman but he refuses to work without being paid in advance. Her lover refuses to lend her the money, as does a bachelor friend who lives on the same side of the river; he has always idealised her and declares himself disappointed by her behaviour. After again pleading in vain with the ferryman, she decides to cross the bridge. The madman kills her. The test consists of classing the six characters of the story (in order of their appearance: the woman, the husband, the lover, the madman, the ferryman, the friend) in order of decreasing responsibility for the woman's death. There are several interesting aspects of the reference in the text to this test. First of all, its success demonstrates the interest and faith in psychology in Laurence's milieu. Secondly, the contrast between this test and the one which Laurence imagines offering the guests at the New Year's Eve party ('You have a third-party collision insurance and a cyclist darts straight across you: do you kill the cyclist or do you wreck the car?'; LBI p. 126) marks the progress in Laurence's thinking: the first test, designed to amuse and centering on sexual mores, the second designed to reveal the egotism and brutal materialism of the players. Finally, it is possible to see in the desperate supplications of the woman and the suicidal gestures into which she is led by her fear of the attitudes of those around her, an image of the fate of Laurence herself.

22. In *The Prime of Life*, published six years before *Les Belles Images*, Beauvoir explains why psychoanalysis was unacceptable to both herself and Sartre in the 1930s. They were put off Freud's texts by

their dogmatic symbolism and the technique of association which vitiated them for us. Freud's pansexualism struck us as having an element of madness about it, besides offending our puritanical instincts. Above all, the importance it attached to the unconscious, and the rigidity of its mechanistic theories, meant that Freudianism, as we conceived it, was bound to eradicate human free will. (p. 21)

Later, in *Being and Nothingness* (1943), Sartre opposed existential psychoanalysis to Freudian techniques. In existentialist psychoanalysis the individual is helped to understand the series of choices which he or she has made in their life, and to focus on the nature of their freedom. There is no suggestion of a 'cure'.

23. Jeanson, p. 253 (my translation). The terms used in the interview and the novel are remarkably similar. In the interview Beauvoir speaks of a '*very* great disappointment' ('une *très* grande déception') and the same word is insisted upon in the French text of the novel: 'J'ai été *déçue*. Le mot la poignarde. (. . .) Je suis déçue.' ('I have been *deceived*. The word stabs her. (. . .) I have been disappointed.'; LBI tr. adap. p. 151).

24. It bears a curious resemblance to the process to which Blomart submits himself in *The Blood of Others*, recapitulating his entire life in the space of a night in an attempt to seek a way forward.

25. Quotation omitted from the Parshley translation and which runs, in full: 'Half victims, half accomplices, like everyone' (J.-P. Sartre).

26. The insistent reference to Algeria is all the more significant in that Beauvoir appears to have invented this crisis. The newspaper headlines which Laurence reads earlier (LBI p. 37) are taken from the issues of *Le Monde* of 29, 30 and 31 March 1966, but there is no mention of Algeria. Laurence's confusion when faced with the articles from *Le Monde* is interpreted by Blandine Stefanson in her edition of the text as 'a mild satire on *Le Monde*'s lack of commitment' (Stefanson p. 255). In fact the front pages of these issues are devoted to the Vietnam War and to the Twenty-Third Soviet Congress in Moscow, and Beauvoir's deliberate selection of the more obscure items seems to be a comment more on the way the presentation of the news as a continuous narrative can obscure the point. The demonstrations by Buddhist monks, for example, referred to by Stefanson as relating to 'political and territorial reshuffling', is clearly referred to in *Le Monde* as a demonstration against the American presence in Vietnam.

27. In the famous interview in which Sartre declared that in the face of a child dying of starvation his novel *Nausea* counted for nothing ('ne fait pas le poids'), he went on to say that the only thing the writer could do was to be on the side of the starving, and to pose the problem in the most radical way possible. *Le Monde*, 18 April 1964, p. 13.

7

The Short Story Cycles:
When Things of the Spirit Come First and *The Woman Destroyed*

To read Simone de Beauvoir's two short story cycles together is to span the whole breadth of her published fiction, since *When Things of the Spirit Come First* was written in 1935–37, before any of her published novels, and *The Woman Destroyed* came last, written in 1967–68 after all the novels. Opening and closing Beauvoir's fictional production in this way, and separated by more than 30 years, the broadly similar form of the two works offers a unique opportunity to consider developments in Beauvoir's use of narrative strategies.

When Beauvoir wrote *The Woman Destroyed*, her first collection of short stories lay in the back of a drawer, a fate to which Beauvoir had firmly consigned the manuscript in 1938 after it had been turned down by both Gallimard and Grasset.[1] It was not until 1979, 11 years after the publication of *The Woman Destroyed*, that Beauvoir eventually published *When Things of the Spirit Come First*. It is perhaps therefore hardly surprising that Beauvoir did not consciously think back to her first short stories in her elaboration of *The Woman Destroyed*.[2] Nevertheless, the two works do have a great deal in common. Both focus on the lives of women, with male characters presented almost exclusively from a female point of view; both present women enmeshed in dilemmas and illusions from which there appears, with few exceptions, to be little hope of their escape. Both take the bourgeoisie as the social context, though *When Things of the Spirit Come First* is largely set 40 years earlier and has a much harsher social critique. The theme of the constraints of the family and the despotic powers of the mother in the mother–daughter relationship are treated in a very similar way in both — indeed, the monologue of Murielle in *The Woman*

143

Destroyed reads almost like a sequel to the monologue of the mother in the earlier story 'Anne'.

In terms of form, *When Things of the Spirit Come First* has a much firmer claim than *The Woman Destroyed* to constitute a short story cycle: its five stories are linked not only by theme but by recurring characters, and its title (or, to be more precise, its original title) is echoed in the opening line of the final story.[3] The three stories of *The Woman Destroyed*, though they were written to be published together, are much more loosely linked by theme and situation, by their single narrative focus through a woman in crisis and by the variations each offers on the theme of *The Woman Destroyed*, the title not only of the collection but of the last story. In both cycles, therefore, the last story is the source of the title of the collection, and is important to the interpretation of the cycle as a whole. Nevertheless, there is a marked difference between the conception of the cycle in the two works.[4] An equally significant difference is to be found in the range of narrative situation employed; though a very similar use is made in both of monologue and of the diary form, *When Things of the Spirit Come First* does not restrict itself to the first-person narrative employed in all the stories of *The Woman Destroyed*.

When Things of the Spirit Come First

The five short stories of *When Things of the Spirit Come First* form a strongly interlocking whole. The situation set up in the first story, 'Marcelle', is re-exploited in the final story where the effect of the arrival in the household of Marcelle's husband is explored from the point of view of the younger sister Marguerite. 'Marguerite' thus draws on 'Marcelle' and completes it, since it offers a further twist in the saga of Marcelle's relations with her erring husband. Both these stories plunge into the central character's childhood, taking us back into the pre-First World War era before focusing more closely on events taking place in the 1920s. Events of the middle three stories are kept roughly contemporaneous with the end of 'Marcelle', giving characters in each story the opportunity to react to events in the other stories of which they are made to be aware, with the last story reaching a few years beyond the other narratives and able, as a result, to offer news of the fate of the other principal characters. In this way, stories which individually appear to be left open-ended ('Marcelle', 'Chantal') are somewhat brutally closed off at the end of the cycle: 'Chantal married a wealthy physician, Marcelle has just published a slim volume of verse, and the other day an archaeological journal mentioned Pascal's name with praise. They are not discontented with their lot' (WTS p. 202). Anne's fate is closed within 'Anne' by her death, and the heroine of 'Lisa' seems unlikely to survive for long, so that only the vigorous and positive Marguerite is left with an open future at the end of the volume.

Each of the heroines is the 'more or less consenting victim', as Beauvoir puts it in the preface to the French edition, of what she calls spiritualism — in other words, of a mystical belief in a religious, intellectual or aesthetic absolute held to be superior to the material world.[5] Its practitioners essentially try to 'be' rather than to act. Such a belief necessarily involves, Beauvoir argues in the French preface, a degree of self-deception (bad faith) which in the stories tips the balance towards complicity and away from victimisation. The narrative mode, varying from the veiled irony of a somewhat supercilious external narrator to the intimate first-person voice of the prayer and the diary, also contributes to this balance.

The agents of the victimisation process are principally shown to be the bourgeoisie, the family (especially the mother), and educational institutions. The stifling world which the bourgeoisie of the period imposed on their daughters is drawn in the first story, 'Marcelle'. Even though Marcelle is relatively free from maternal despotism, she suffers from the constraints and isolation of her childhood and is led by her parents to consider herself as an exceptional person. She interprets the respectful attitude which the working-class boys at the social centre she runs adopt towards her as a homage to her personal qualities rather than as the automatic privilege of a social class. Adult life is a disappointment to someone who had expected to live amongst geniuses, and she falls easy prey to Denis Charval, the penniless poet who claims to live only for 'a few pure, precious impressions that he could not translate into words without betraying them' (WTS p. 26). When she is eventually abandoned, she draws no lesson in realism from her experience but adopts a new sublime ideal and aspires, as the reader later learns in 'Anne', to transmit to humanity through her writing the meaning of suffering.

Marcelle's self-delusions are insisted upon in the story — her belief in herself as a genius, her naive conviction that 'the barriers between the classes were brought into being by hatred and prejudice alone' (WTS p. 18), and her apparently complete inability to recognise her own strong sexuality — a failing which Denis exploits with ease. Marcelle is thus posited as a case in which complicity is strong; her sexual masochism underlines this point heavily. The external narrative stance adopted enables the degree of Marcelle's guilt to be made clear; this third-person narrative voice focuses through Marcelle to the exclusion of the other characters, but enjoys a much higher degree of autonomy than the external narrators of Beauvoir's novels, qualifying Marcelle for example from the outside as a 'dreamy, precocious little girl' (WTS p. 9) in the first line, and sweeping through long time periods without reference to the character's framework.

This rather unfamiliar narrator adopts a more formal tone and vocabulary than the narrators of the novels, and creates an air of superiority and veiled irony which are one of the main indications to the reader that Marcelle is not on the right path. In *The Prime of Life* Beauvoir describes the narrative voice of 'Marcelle' and 'Lisa' as 'employing a certain concealed irony which I had borrowed from John Dos Passos' (POL p. 223).[6] In particular, the constant use of superlatives of the type 'extraordinarily sensitive' (WTS p. 9) and 'the wonderful revelation' (WTS p. 43) indicate this ironic distance, together with the use of comic disjunctions such as the detail that of all the places Marcelle liked crying, 'she liked crying in churches best' (WTS p. 9). Though Marcelle loses her religious faith, her early religious experiences are clearly held to have prepared a fertile ground for her later illusions.

The use of this external narrator in the first story of the volume is important to Beauvoir's demystifying intentions. Having clearly established Marcelle's delusions, she is able to proceed, in the second story, 'Chantal', to a more covert and more complex approach. 'Chantal' opens with a series of diary entries covering the first seven weeks of Chantal's exile to provincial Rougement for her first teaching post. The diary is essentially a means whereby the character can construct and polish a highly indulgent (and unconsciously comic) self-image — that of the liberated, sophisticated young woman with a highly cultured approach to life. Despite her apparent independence, the rather self-consciously literary style of the diary, and the constant attempt to describe the reality around her in terms of her cultural baggage (focusing comically on a holiday in Italy) quickly make it apparent that Chantal is a sister of Marcelle in her double cultivation of estheticism and of her own persona. But Chantal's self-image is more fragile than Marcelle's; faced with a pitying letter from a Parisian friend she breaks down and admits in the last diary extract of Part 1 that she feels buried alive in the desert of Rougemont.

The second part of the story introduces an external narrator, but the ironic, distancing element of the narrative voice of 'Marcelle' has disappeared in favour of a more covert voice which focuses fairly closely on Chantal. Despite this focus, the shift to external narrator permits a more direct introduction of the two pupils, Monique and Andrée, than the diary form had allowed. In the third part the external narrator abandons Chantal for Andrée, focusing on her first from the outside ('Andrée was neither frivolous nor inattentive; she accepted reproof politely; she did not chatter in class; and she had an excellent reputation in the lycée'; WTS p. 61) before gradually moving closer and closer to the character's perspective. Chantal becomes 'Plattard' — the name by which Andrée thinks of her — and the distance between Chantal's view of herself and the view her pupils have of her comes sharply into focus. Her youth and sincerity make of Andrée a more positive character than the self-indulgent Chantal; from this point on in the story Andrée becomes a rival focus of attention and the dominant source of information about events. Part 4 offers only a brief further incursion into Chantal's diary, in which she enters the predictable but nevertheless splendid confession that 'I see my life as a novel of which I am the heroine' (WTS p. 72), before returning to the external narrator and Andrée's perspective in the fifth part. It is thus Andrée's perspective that controls the central drama of the story, which breaks in Part 5, and from Andrée's critical perspective that Chantal's reaction to Monique's pregnancy is narrated. We have to wait until the final part, in which the external narrator focuses first through Chantal and then through Andrée, to witness Chantal, badly shaken and frightened by her complete misinterpretation of events, finally succeeding in the resurrection of her own image:

> All at once her sadness vanished. At the dawn of these young lives her form would stand out forever, her slim form, so well set off in a tailored suit — a somewhat enigmatic, paradoxical form, whose appearance in an old provincial town had been so dazzling (WTS p. 87).

Chantal is once again the heroine of her own life story.

Chantal's illusions inevitably involve other people to a much greater extent than Marcelle's, since Chantal is so dependent on the opinion and admiration of others, and the variation of narrative viewpoint enables the discrepancy between Chantal's illusion of how others see her and the reality to come into play. Her careerism, social snobbery and puritanism are not motivated within the story by reference to her childhood and adolescence, as are Marcelle's traits (though some details do emerge later in 'Anne'); this lack of immediate context, together with Andrée's condemnation of the character leave Chantal as firmly denounced as by any ironical external narrator.

A strong element of 'Chantal' is the portrait offered of an institution, and its role in the fate of the two adolescent girls. The narrative follows the shape of the school year, beginning in October and ending with the annual prize-giving ceremony. The narrow lives of the teachers, the teaching methods and examination systems which stifle any element of intellectual enquiry, the constant stress given to dress and conduct, are shown to conspire in the oppression of Andrée and Monique into a sterile world from which any attempt at escape is doomed to lead, like Monique's adventure, to further entanglement.

The real tragedies of the cycle take place in the second and fourth stories, which are also linked by the presence of Chantal in both. Intervening between 'Chantal' and 'Anne' is the brief third story, 'Lisa', which continues the theme of institutional oppression. Lisa arrives in Paris as a student teacher at the Catholic college of the Institution Saint-Ange, with a robust constitution and a lively intelligence; after four years: 'Intellectual work had mined her body, and far from enriching this thin and unproductive soil, cultivation had made it barren (. . .). She would never pass an *agrégation*; she would never write a book' (WTS p. 92). This is the view of Lisa offered by Mademoiselle Lambert, in charge of the student teachers at the college; its bleak prognostications for Lisa's future are confirmed by Lisa herself. She knows that her only hope of earning a living is to study for the competitive examinations that would allow her to become a fully fledged teacher, but hates the idea of 'using one's brain as though it were a machine for grinding knowledge' (WTS p. 94). The constraints of life in the college, an institution which allows only one day a week to be spent outside its walls, and which keeps its pensionnaires in almost complete penury, make the present as bleak as the future.[7] Lisa's only escape is to the Bibliothèque Nationale — another institution, frequented by 'the scholars, the students, the cranks and the respectable tramps — the usual frequenters of the library' (WTS p. 94).

The drawing in of this oppressive context makes of Lisa a victim rather than a focus of blame, but the external narrative voice conveys more a sense of distaste for Lisa than pity. In the opening section of the story, in which the external narrator exercises a great deal of autonomy, a clearly ironical tone is perceptible at the expense of the Institute, described as 'both a money-making and a charitable concern' (WTS p. 91). After presenting Mademoiselle Lambert in a similarly sardonic tone, the narrative voice adopts the view of Mademoiselle Lambert to present the unflattering portrait of Lisa referred to above, before eventually moving to Lisa's perspective. Little is done, however, to correct the first impression. Demanding and suspicious, Lisa is shown behaving badly even with her friend Marguerite. Her obsession with Pascal, the brother of Marguerite and Marcelle, who she regards as a superior being able to perceive Lisa's own true worth, makes her into a figure of ridicule and pathos. After the disappointment of a banal conversation with him, Lisa's need for admiration is so great that she allows herself to take at face value the professional badinage of her dentist.

In the final page of the story the narrative dissolves into an incoherent monologue of sexual fantasy, in which Lisa mixes the dentist, Pascal and the figure of an archangel. The mysticism of her attitude and the vocabulary of this final section again point to the influence of a religious upbringing on the retreat into spiritualism, even for those who have lost their actual religious faith. One other interesting aspect of the story is its stress on body image. Taught not to look at her naked body in childhood, Lisa hates her appearance, and assumes it to be unattractive. When a woman mistakes her in the street for her husband's mistress, Lisa is at first amused and irritated, but later, looking at herself in the mirror, sees that with the right clothes and make-up she could be thought elegant.

'Lisa' is less than half the length of most of the other stories, and it extends in time over less than a single day. Though the characters of Marguerite and Pascal appear in it, it does not share in the strong structural relationship which the first story has with the last, or the third with the fifth, and constitutes a strangely retreating centre to the volume.[8] It is followed by 'Anne', the longest story of the collection, in which Beauvoir transposed the tragedy of her schoolfriend Elisabeth.[9] Structurally, 'Anne' resembles 'Chantal' in its use of a variety of narrative situations and its division into numbered parts. Part 1 opens on a striking use of monologue in a long prayer by Anne's mother, Madame Vignon; the blatant bad faith of this devout mother emerges strongly as she elaborates, within the structure of her prayer, her plans to shunt her eldest daughter off into an unwanted marriage, and her strategy to recover her younger daughter for herself by cutting off Anne's friendship with Chantal, her correspondence with Pascal and her contact with any form of intellectual stimulation. Her constant self-justification of her behaviour in terms of the rights and duties of motherhood ('When it is a question of her daughter's soul, a mother has the right to commit an impropriety; but even using steam it is hard not to leave a trace'; WTS p. 111), combined with an evident dislike of her daughter Lucette, strongly anticipates the claims of Murielle, the mother in one of the stories of *The Woman Destroyed* who drives her daughter to suicide whilst claiming to be a devoted mother.

At the end of the prayer an external narrative voice is introduced which, like the external narrator in sections of 'Chantal', retains a certain autonomy of exposition whilst generally focusing through a character, here Madame Vignon. In the rest of the section, Madame Vignon's absolute power is wielded to good effect, as she drives Lucette into marriage by a mixture of threats and appeals to Christian principles, and tortures the fragile Anne by throwing into question Anne's faith and morality. In Part 2 the external narrative voice switches focus to Chantal — a dramatic and interesting switch, not only because it allows us to see what has become of Chantal but because Chantal is the principal combatant, with Anne's mother, in the battle over Anne's destiny. Madame Vignon nourishes ambitions for Anne to become a saint, whilst Chantal plans to rid Anne of beliefs which she sees as preventing Anne's happiness and marry her off to Pascal.

The portrait of the mother is so malevolent that Chantal might appear as the knight in shining armour ready to take up arms in defence of her friend. However, the external narrator suffuses the text with sufficient irony for it to be immediately apparent that Chantal has her own interests at heart. The narrative slips from free indirect speech to evident ironical interpretation:

Anne must have been brought very low for her mother to have reversed her decision: it was a real stepping-down on the part of Madame Vignon. Chantal felt quite moved at the notion that she was bringing her friend treasures of hope and joy and happiness. (WTS p. 125)

Chantal turns out to be as expert in jesuitical argumentation as the mother: ' "Even from the Christian point of view passiveness and inertia have never been virtues," said Chantal. "You have told me yourself that this total submission to the divine will is often only a cover for laziness and cowardice" ' (WTS p. 132). Anne is caught between the guilt she feels if she goes against her mother's wishes, and the self-hatred she feels if she bows to them. Chantal sees this conflict as a 'stage required' (WTS p. 133) in Anne's development whilst Madame Vignon asks God to harden her heart in Anne's own interest.

The final protagonist in the battle for Anne comes into play in Part 3 of the story, as the external narrative focuses through Pascal. However, Pascal, like Madame Vignon and Chantal, fails to put Anne first, and the narrative voice retains an expository and ironical function to underline the guilt of all the major players in Anne's tragedy. When Pascal receives an urgent telegram from Anne expressing her distress, the narrator comments: 'the urgent tone of the appeal astonished him, and with Pascal astonishment was always close to reprobation' (WTS p. 139). While Anne aspires to passion and happiness, Pascal tells her gravely that 'of all the diversions men have discovered, happiness is without doubt the most illusory' (WTS p. 144); for him, the couple's 'silent, mystic communion was the highest peak a love could reach' (WTS p. 144). Anne has to go without the embrace which 'would have seemed to him too coarse to translate their hearts' inexpressible harmony' (WTS p. 145). Here, and in the explanation that in his youth Pascal 'had had some rather squalid adventures' which 'had left him with a sense of great disgust' (WTS pp. 147–48), we can clearly hear the external narrator's voice.

The fourth and final part sees the narrative focus passing from one to the other of all the main participants, as each in turn attempts to salvage his or her own interests from the wreck of their projects. The presentation of Anne entirely from other people's points of view — though her speech is frequently presented directly in dialogue with the other characters — emphasises the pressures under which she suffers and tilts the balance of responsibility away from her. There is no evidence in fact that she shares the bad faith of the heroines of the previous stories, despite the fact that her fate and her strong religious belief place her under the banner of spiritualism. The 'inseparability' of spiritualism and self-deception to which Beauvoir refers in the preface is not made clear in the story of Anne-Elisabeth, an account of a tragedy in which Beauvoir evidently retained a strong personal investment.

'Anne', the penultimate story in the volume, brings back into play the characters of Chantal, Pascal and Marcelle. Pascal plays his biggest role here. He is in fact the only man in the whole volume who is viewed from the inside, and this privileged view is far from making him appear sympathetic. Chantal's role is interesting; in a way she repeats the pattern of the earlier story, intervening in the lives of others without any real desire to see her plans through or any appreciation of the effect her behaviour might have, and demonstrating an admirable capacity to recover from other peoples' disasters. Set against the monstrous behaviour of the mother, however, Chantal appears less guilty of treachery towards her friend, and Beauvoir draws on her own experiences of a summer holiday visit to her friend Elisabeth's family to convey the character's status as disliked outsider.[10] The story also offers some indications of an unhappy, poverty-stricken childhood, which go some way towards explaining Chantal's social ambitions.

The final story, 'Marguerite', draws together again Marcelle, Pascal and Charval, and seems to take upon itself the role of tying up the loose ends, since it also gives news in the last lines of Chantal, otherwise in no way involved in 'Marguerite'. This poses something of a problem, since the narrator of the story is Marguerite herself. At the end of her fairly formal first-person narrative, after disassociating herself from Pascal and Marcelle, Marguerite declares:

> But that is a story I do not intend to tell. All I have wished to do was to show how I was brought to try to look things straight in the face, without accepting oracles or ready-made values. I had to rediscover everything myself, and sometimes it was disconcerting — furthermore, not everything is clear even now. But in any case what I do know is that Marcelle and Chantal and Pascal will die without ever having known or loved anything real and that I do not want to be like them. Chantal married a wealthy physician, Marcelle has just published a slim volume of verse, and the other day an archaeological journal mentioned Pascal's name with praise. They are not discontented with their lot. (WTS p. 202)

Marguerite seems to be not only aware of the dramas of all three characters, but actually conscious of the need to bring them all into play at the end of her narrative, as if she herself had read (or written) the preceding stories. She gives news of them almost as if they were her own fictional creatures, and concludes, 'They are not discontented with their lot' with exactly the sense of superiority and irony displayed by the external narrator in other stories. What *is* the motivation, in fact, for this first-person narrative? None is given at the beginning; the final paragraph given above, however, makes it clear that Marguerite intends her narrative to 'show' how she had come to abandon spiritualism — in other words, her narrative is addressed to a reader, the reader who she informs that there is another story which she does 'not intend to tell'. This is no journey of self-discovery, but a formally composed account with a single flow of narrative time, and in which the first lines anticipate the last. In both the French and English prefaces to the collection, Beauvoir refers to the strongly autobiographical basis of the story; the authority and powers lent to Marguerite's voice presumably originate in this identification between character and author, both motivated by the desire to 'show' their revolt against the spiritualism of which they themselves had been the prey.

With the exception of Andrée, whose fate is left uncertain, Marguerite is the only positive heroine of the volume, neither victim nor self-deceived, standing for 'the real' and for 'acts' in the place of dreams, for courage and self-reliance in the place of 'cowardice' and 'hypocrisy' (WTS pp. 201–2). On her way to this discovery, Marguerite easily rejects Marcelle's cult of beauty, and Pascal's cult of 'the inner life' (WTS p. 159), but has considerably more difficulty in rejecting Denis's mysticism, his cult of the bizarre and the immoral. The sections set in the bars of Montparnasse amidst prostitutes and pimps see Marguerite ecstatically worshipping vice, just as in her childhood she had approached the Holy Sacrament: 'in my own way I too was serving the things of the spirit,' writes Marguerite (WTS p. 173), evidently delighted by the audacity of her parallel. The temptations of sexuality, strongly outlined in 'Marcelle' and suggested in 'Lisa', are however beyond the ken of this would-be practitioner of vice; accepting invitations from strange men and sharing the bed of a lesbian, Marguerite takes flight when 'acts' threaten. In the 1970s Beauvoir suggested to Alice Schwarzer that sexual relations could be a great trap for women, and indicated that the frigid woman in her view was perhaps fortunate in being less vulnerable to this trap.[11] Forty years earlier in *When Things of the Spirit Come First* there is already a strong feeling that female sexuality can work against women, as the puritanical Chantal and Marguerite are found faring considerably better than Marcelle or the schoolgirl Monique.

The cycle thus ends on a positive, almost edifying note. Marguerite seizes the pen to write her success story in a way that no woman character in Beauvoir's novels ever achieves. In stylistic terms, Marguerite's use of a formally composed first-person narrative does not reappear either; instead, the narrative forms of bad faith — the diary, the interior monologue of the prayer — are taken up and developed in *The Woman Destroyed*. The external narrative voice is purged of its irony, its autonomy, its distance and its formality when it reappears in the novels. *When Things of the Spirit Come First* shows a concern and a desire for experimentation in narrative voice and structure that looks forward to later developments in Beauvoir's fiction.

The Woman Destroyed

The Woman Destroyed is the last of Beauvoir's fictional works. Published in 1967, only a year after *Les Belles Images*, it has much in common with this novel as well as with the much earlier *When Things of the Spirit Come First*. The heroines of *The Woman Destroyed* are the older sisters of Laurence and of the young women of *When Things of the Spirit Come First*, not only in terms of the illusions with which they struggle, but also in terms of the largely bourgeois milieu in which they are situated.

Beauvoir has described the three stories as presenting 'the voices of three women who use words in their struggle with a situation in which all exits are blocked'.[12] The struggle with words, already apparent in *Les Belles Images*, where Laurence intermittently formulates her 'I', takes place in *The Woman Destroyed* without the presence of an external narrative voice. Each woman produces a monologue, each of a different type but each performing essentially the same function, which is to provide her with an erroneous and self-justified reading of her situation. Reality breaks into these discourses in varying degrees; the forms and strategies of Chantal's diary and Madame Vignon's prayer are re-adopted and elaborated to present the reader with the materials of a detective story: 'I hoped that people would read the book as a detective story; here and there I scattered clues that would allow the reader to find the key to the mystery,' writes Beauvoir of one of the stories in *All Said and Done* (ASD p. 140). Since the subject of each story is essentially a demonstration of the ways in which each woman produces a self-justifying discourse in the face of a mountain of evidence against them, the wider issue of the relationship of women to language is also approached.

Though each story is kept formally closed in on itself, the adoption of the title of the last and longest of the three stories as the title of the volume produces a particular pattern of expectations about the cycle. There is a two-way process in which the reader feels that the first two stories are a preparation for the last, and that, in reverse, the reading of the last story may reveal something affecting the decoding of the stories as a whole. Another rather striking aspect of the title is the way in which it draws attention to the sex of the narrator-protagonists; the fact that the stories are about women, and about women in difficulties, is underlined from the outset. Finally a third, less immediately apparent aspect, is that the title permits the direct expression of an authorial view; a glimpse all the more interesting since the use of monologue within the stories themselves does not offer any scope to overt comments by an author or narrator. Unlike *When Things of the Spirit Come First*, the title of *The Woman Destroyed* (*La Femme rompue*) offers no indication of the source of the characters' problems; instead, it offers a categorisation, a use of a conventional statement with a rather dismissive definite article, which fixes the characters inescapably into place and carries at least a hint of an ironic distancing between the author and her three *femmes rompues*.[13]

'The Age of Discretion'

Within the volume itself the first story also has a title employed with ironic intention, though the object of the irony is not necessarily the woman. The title of 'The Age of Discretion' ('L'Age de discrétion') sets up a conventional view of old age which is exploded during the course of the story.[14] The woman narrator is supremely confident that retirement is the last pleasant phase of a happy and successful life; behind her in her mind's eye she sees a successful career, a long and happy relationship with her husband, and an exemplary devotion to her son, whose education and career she has personally guided. Gradually, the discrepancy between the woman's affirmations about the success of her retirement on the one hand, and the realities of old age on the other, force her monologue into question. The present, she discovers, cannot be defined by the past even when the past stretches out much further than an inevitably short future; she cannot rely on communication with her husband as she has always done because he too is growing old; worst of all, she cannot count on laying claim to the future through her stake in her son's life, as she has to give up the role of possessive and dominating mother. Even the aging of her body, which she imagines she has come to terms with, eventually disrupts her view of herself and forces itself upon her attention.[15]

However, the focus of the story is not so much on these problems in themselves as on the woman's mythmaking resistance to recognition of them. Of the three stories of the volume, the monologue of 'The Age of Discretion' is the most conventionally organised. It is divided into three narrative blocks, based on three narrative moments: the opening block begins with the woman looking at her watch and consists of her reflections as she awaits the arrival of her son in her flat, ending just before his actual arrival (TWD p. 18); in the second block she goes over her son's visit and connected problems in her mind while lying awake in bed the following morning (the narrative moment is TWD pp. 26–27); the third and most substantial block is less clearly situated in terms of narrative time and does not return to a narrative present until the series of questions which close the story. Each block therefore consists in principle of a block of interior monologue, but in practice the feeling of interior monologue is considerably reduced by the strong element of narrative of events. Though each block begins and ends in the present tense, with narrative and story time coinciding, each block quickly moves into the past tense (the perfect tense nevertheless in the French text, not the past historic) to offer a clear and consecutive account of events. The use of three separate narrative blocks instead of one also tends to reduce the feeling of interior monologue, since it draws attention to an organising presence external to the character; however, the spaces between the blocks permit the development of events which eventually force the narrative into question.

'The Age of Discretion' demands rather less of the reader than the other two stories in the sense that the narrator herself eventually begins to admit some of her own errors — and the reader is clearly invited by her doubts and admissions to seek out further flaws in her analyses. As in *When Things of the Spirit Come First*, the first story of the cycle thus invites a reading practice which will serve in the other stories. However, the woman's narrative begins to look suspicious long before she makes any admissions. Early clues largely centre on discrepancies between the level and tone of her vocabulary on the one hand, and her claims on the other. Thus, for example, her claim to have come to terms with retirement is undermined by her commentary on the sound of the word retirement (*la retraite*); the word, she muses, had always struck her as sounding just like on the scrap heap (*au rebut*) (TWD p. 10). A few lines later she adds that retirement is one of those lines in life which once crossed has the rigidity of an iron curtain.

Other illusions are signalled by the categorical tone in which the woman rehearses her convictions. She declares of a book on the subject of communication between people: 'What a bore, all this going on about non-communication! If you really want to communicate you manage, somehow or other' (TWD p. 7). Equally firmly fixed in her mind is her feeling that the book she has just completed is her best yet. Dismissing her husband's doubts she declares, 'I know he is wrong. I have just written my best book and the second volume will go even further' (TWD p. 16). The reader can hardly be surprised when, later in the story, the woman falls into a morass of misunderstandings with those around her and eventually asks in disbelief, 'Might all one heard about non-communication perhaps be true, then?' (TWD p. 44). More shattering still is what she finally has to admit about her book: 'I had produced nothing new, absolutely nothing. And I knew that the second volume would only prolong this stagnation. There it was then; I had spent three years writing a useless book. Not just a failure (. . .). Useless. Only fit for burning' (TWD p. 53).

In the example of the book what is immediately noticeable is the tone of the woman's new version of the truth; it is no less categorical than her earlier view, and the reader is all the more inclined to view it with suspicion now that the woman has already proved to be wrong. Where else can the reader now turn for evidence to bolster these suspicions? The views of other characters have to be treated with caution, since we only know what the woman believes them to say or think. Nevertheless, a number of other characters do serve as a corrective to the woman's illusions. Martine, the former pupil, is used to deliver the truth about the merits of the woman's book ('an excellent synthesis' but 'nothing new'; TWD p. 50). Manette, embodying the appetite for life which has made of her retirement 'a delight' (TWD p. 18), counterbalances the image of the horrors of old age which the woman posits on the last page. Even Irène, the daughter-in-law straight from the world of *Les Belles Images*, serves to point up the absolutism of the woman's social and political values ('Anyone would think he had become a burglar'; TWD p. 32).

However, other characters apart, there is a further clue embodied in the text to the mechanisms which operate in the woman's construction of her self-deceiving discourse, and this is what might be termed the degree of literarity of the text. Words are naturally crucial to the woman's construction process, firstly through the very frequent recourse which, as a teacher of literature, she has to literary works, and secondly through her habit of using words in a heightened manner to construct both her idylls and her disappointments. Both these factors are present in her contrasting views of the past, exemplified in the following two extracts. In the first, taken from the opening passages of the story, the woman has just prepared the couple's breakfast tea:

> I poured out the China tea, very hot, very strong. We drank it as we looked through our post: the July sunshine came flooding into the room. How many times had we sat there opposite one another at that little table, our very hot, very strong cups of tea in front of us? And we would be sitting there again tomorrow, and in a year's time, and in ten years' time . . . That moment had the sweet taste of memory, and the warmth of a promise. Were we thirty or sixty? (TWD tr. adap. p. 7)

In the second, she goes to meet her friend Martine:

> As I came into the gardens the smell of cut grass wrung my heart — the smell of the Alpine pastures where I had walked, a haversack on my back, with André, a smell so moving because it was the smell of the fields of my childhood. Reflections, echoes, reverberating in infinity: I have discovered the pleasures of having a long past behind me. I haven't got time to recount it to myself, but often, quite unexpectedly, I catch a glimpse of it, a luminous background to the present; a background that gives the present its colour and its light, as rocks and sand are reflected in the shifting, glistening mirror of the sea. (TWD tr. adap. p. 14)

Both of these extracts are highly polished mythical moments

which the woman constructs for herself to maintain her illusion that time passes with no destructive effect, that she and her husband remain the same at 60 as they were at 30, that the past is a kind of sunny country walk which she can choose to take at her leisure. If the highly literary nature of the writing in these passages were not sufficient to alert us to their suspect nature, further clues emerge from the way the woman perceives the subject through a screen of literary culture. This teacher of literature values nothing more highly than culture, and, like Chantal of *When Things of the Spirit Come First*, she draws on it to bolster her myths, quoting Valéry, Hugo, Montesquieu, Sainte-Beuve, Bachelard, Freud, Hans Christian Andersen and others. In the tea-drinking cameo quoted above it is difficult to miss the allusion to Proustian privileged moments. When these images of the nature of the past are eventually counterbalanced by apparent 'discoveries' of illusion, the new position is expressed in terms as mythical and self-consciously literary as the original image. Thus, after an attempt to literally return to the scenes of her childhood, the woman is faced with the shattering of her polished image of the past; she therefore replaces her image of 'the sweet taste of memory' and the sunny countryside walk by Chateaubriand's phrase, 'the desert of time past' (*le désert du passé*) to express her rejection of the past as no more than a series of stereotypical images, which fade with use. The sunny countryside or the desert? Proust or Chateaubriand? At the end of the story the woman appears to have completely abandoned her view of pleasant retirement; in the last paragraph she replaces her ideal of a period in which values, relationships and preoccupations remain essentially unchanged by a vision of a future of increasing withdrawal from others and from the world, a future dominated by mental and physical decay.

Has the woman abandoned her illusions for realism? Or has she simply gone from one extreme to another, substituting an impossibly black view for an overly rosy one? The period which the woman spends alone in the flat, painfully confronting her attitude to her work and to her son, appears to indicate her progress towards realism. Regretfully, she rejects the comfort of the phrase that an adult is no more than 'a child puffed with age' (TWD p. 47), and accepts that the age of her privileged relationship with her son is over. The adjustment to her body is less successful. Convinced that she made the adjustment to her physical ageing ten years earlier, the woman actually copes with the loss of attractiveness by failing to identify with her body, describing it as 'an old friend who needed my help' (TWD p. 17). On the swimming expedition with André this apparent tranquillity is exploded by her shame at her 'ghastly' old woman's body and by her anger at not being able to take the climb back up the path as easily as she used to (TWD p. 59). She concludes in disgust that her body is 'letting me down' (TWD p. 60), and a strong element of her nightmarish vision of the years ahead with which the story closes is the notion of physical decay.

The most positive element of the end of the story is the re-establishment of the woman's dialogue with André; the two are shown reacting very differently to their age, but they manage to reaffirm the things they have in common. The re-establishment of this dialogue is closely linked to communion with nature and a reconfirmation of the value of culture. Earlier in the story the woman had found that language was breaking down, 'words came to pieces in my mind' (TWD p. 55), that paintings, books and museums no longer had anything to offer her (TWD pp. 54, 64–65). Now, citing a line from the thirteenth century *Aucassin et Nicolette*, the woman gazes at the moon and feels re-united with the world as it was centuries ago. ' "That's the great thing about writing," I said. "Pictures lose their shape; their colours fade. But words you carry away with you" ' (TWD p. 68). Literature is re-established as a privileged activity. Thus, although many of the woman's assumptions are challenged in the story, others are reconfirmed: the value of the couple, of communication and of the woman's commitment to her work and to culture remain. Though she has faced up to a certain number of her illusions and declares herself determined to face reality, she remains enmeshed in a special use of words.

'Monologue'

The title of the second story, together with the epigraph from Flaubert ('The monologue is her form of revenge'), focuses the reader's attention from the beginning on the use of interior monologue, thus reinforcing the tendency of this narrative mode to emphasise by its very nature the narrative itself. In strong contrast to 'The Age of Discretion', the second story, 'Monologue', immerses the reader in a single stretch of interior monologue. Ignoring the rules of punctuation and the syntax of written

French, largely observed in the first story, 'Monologue' proceeds by the logic of associations and transitions dependent on the flow of consciousness. Sudden changes of subject and unexplained references to new characters and events constantly hinder the reader and prevent identification with the speaker. The violence and crudity of the language appear designed to alienate from the first line; at times the text engages not only in a challenge but virtually an assault on the reader, most notably when the speaker Murielle begins to shout, 'I'm sick of it I'm sick of it sick sick sick . . .' TWD p. 83), where sick is then repeated on the page 81 times. The reader is left embarrassed, bewildered, confronted with the responsibility as reader and uncertain whether to conscientiously read the words, contemplate them on the page or fall back on counting them (a surprisingly frequent reaction).

Procedures such as this inevitably draw attention to the highly self-conscious nature of the interior monologue. Both the title and the story's epigraph also underline the narrative mode itself. Though the title simply identifies it in a neutral way, this neutrality is balanced out by the epigraph ('The monologue is her form of revenge'), through which the author is able to establish the link between language and violence in her text. Despite the violence and apparent chaos of the narrative, however, the 'Monologue' gradually assumes structure and meaning; the crisis of desperation expressed by the monologue is gradually understood by the reader to be an anticipation of the visit of Murielle's son Francis and her second husband Tristan, during which she plans to try to persuade them to set up house again with her. Much of Murielle's unconnected ramblings are in fact a rehearsal of the arguments which she intends putting to Tristan, and a rebuttal of the charges which she knows her family level against her over the death of her daughter Sylvie. Whilst she prepares her case in her mind, her neighbours and people outside in the street celebrate New Year's Eve; the passing of time during the evening and the part of the night which the monologue lasts is marked out by the stages which the festivities reach outside and in the flat above. Inside Murielle's flat her desperation is also patterned by a series of crises. The first, fed by a macabre vision of herself dying alone in her flat, leads her into the wave of self-pity which reaches its height with the series of 'sicks' (TWD p. 83). Shortly afterwards, she makes her first gesture towards the outside world as she tries to ring Tristan, driven to seek human contact by her memories of her daughter's funeral. The lack of any reply plunges her deeper into her guilt and pain at Sylvie's death and she tries to contact her own mother, who thrusts her back into solitude by putting the phone down (TWD p. 90).

A long passage of the monologue then circles round her mother, and mother – child relationships, with her thoughts inevitably returning again to Sylvie. Reliving all the details of the circumstances of Sylvie's death, and the reactions of others to it, she concludes with an absolute affirmation of her own innocence: 'Looking deep into the eyes of my seventeen-year-old girl they murdered I say, "I was the best of mothers." You would have thanked me later on' (TWD p. 98). A break in the monologue follows (unfortunately not indicated typographically in the English translation) as Murielle cries. After this break she appears calmer, snaps back into battling mood and takes the decision not to wait until the following morning but to telephone Tristan and put her case at once. Her 'dialogue' with Tristan is the only sustained contact Murielle makes within the story — but it does not permit escape from the monologue. The reader does not hear Tristan, and nor, it seems, does Murielle, as she launches into an unstoppable tirade. When Tristan too cuts the contact, Murielle enters into a paroxysm of rage and hysteria which brings the monologue to a close.

Within this structure, the theme of the mother – child relationship is constantly returned to. 'A child needs its mother' (TWD p. 75) — Murielle pronounces the maxim which she regards as the central plank of her case for her husband and son to take up life with her again on the first page of her monologue. It is repeated many times in the story, in varying forms, and the unmasking of Murielle necessarily implies the unmasking of this truism, deliberately embedded in a context which subverts it. In the interests of producing this context, Murielle is established as a highly unreliable narrator and as a person whose behaviour towards her children (in contrast to her claims) has been alarming in the extreme. 'A kid deprived of his mother always ends up by going to the bad he'll turn into a hooligan or a fairy,' declares Murielle of her son at one moment (TWD pp. 79 – 80), whilst threatening to commit suicide in front of him at another. In the case of Sylvie, the daughter who committed suicide, Murielle is prepared to defend the fact that she was in the habit of reading her daughter's diary ('I look things straight in the face'; TWD p. 81), and searching her room for letters ('I was doing my duty as a mother'; TWD p. 84); that she called the police when Sylvie tried to go and live with her father ('Was I supposed to put on kid gloves?'; TWD p. 84), inter-fered in a friendship which Sylvie had with a woman teacher at school ('these brainy types are all lesbians'; TWD p. 85, tr. adap.), punished her when Sylvie refused friends of Murielle's choosing and finally, when the girl was driven to suicide, tore up the suicide note addressed to the father ('it didn't mean a thing . . . a mother knows her own daughter'; TWD p. 96).

Murielle's behaviour is *so* appalling, her justifications so clearly inadequate, that the kinds of ambiguities about the truth which subsist in the first story appear to have little place in this one. The reader is in no doubt that it is their task to contest Murielle's assessment of herself as 'the best of mothers' (TWD p. 98) by uncovering the gaps and discrepancies in her discourse and unravelling the plot, or perhaps one should say series of sub-plots (What were the circumstances of the death of Murielle's daughter? What was the traumatic incident which occurred one 14 July in Murielle's childhood which appears to have had a traumatic effect on her? Why is the day following the monologue one of such importance to Murielle?). The stance that the reader is invited to adopt is demanding but clear. Having once adopted this detective stance, however, we find ourselves investigating, amongst all the other evidence of Murielle's illusions and unreliability, a network of maxims and ideas about the relationship of a mother to her children which are so much a part of accepted wisdom that the reader might well be inclined to pass over them or even positively accept them if they were not so insistently formulated by a character whom we have been led to profoundly mistrust.

Murielle frequently vaunts her disciplinary system which 'breaks in' children as one might an animal.[16] Her ideal of a child is Jeanne — a tearful, timid, affection-starved little girl who has been slapped by her mother into submission, and who is willing to run all the little errands which Murielle demands. The child is viewed as a kind of clay for the mother to model as she thinks fit: 'I'll make a splendid child of Francis they'll see what kind of a mother I am,' she says of her son (TWD p. 93); and of her daughter's death she declares in even more extreme terms, 'My life's work gone up in smoke' (TWD p. 90). Murielle's elaboration of the power which society accords to the mother into a demagogic system, her erection of her idea of herself as a mother into a self-justifying role in life, constitute the key threads of a discourse which we are invited to unpick and which, despite its exaggeration, is based on perfectly commonplace ideas ('A mother knows her child'; 'A boy needs his mother a mother can't do without her child'; TWD p. 86; 'From an educational point of view it's disastrous for one parent to side against the other'; TWD p. 89, tr. adap.)

In one of the last images of the 'Monologue' Murielle calls on God to prepare a paradise for her in which she can walk hand in hand with her children whilst the rest of the world burns in hell. To what extent can Murielle's obsession with creating an image of herself as the perfect mother be seen as a *response* to her situation, to what extent can her notions of motherhood be seen as having been responsible for *creating* her situation? In other words, where is the balance made to come down between victim and accomplice? Like that other authoritarian mother, Madame Vignon, it is not easy to elicit the case for Murielle's defence from the story. She does face problems of solitude, low social status as a divorced woman in the France of the 1960s, and financial problems. Her discourse of herself as perfect mother could be read as a terrified response to the harsh verdict generally returned by society on the mother who reveals herself to be less than perfect, and of which she is well aware. The very notion that her monologue is the discourse of revenge, suggested by the epigraph, in itself implies that Murielle has been wronged. She is the only one of the three women of *The Woman Destroyed* for whom a childhood background is drawn in — an element which suggests that a connection between her situation and her childhood is to be sought. The traumatic July 14 experience in which the brother is lifted up on the father's shoulders while she is left on the ground 'squashed between them just at prick level and that randy crowd's smell of sex' (TWD p. 76), suggests in one the secondary status of the girl in the family situation and the problematic assumption of sexuality by the girl, caught between the father and the mother. In her monologue, Murielle feels the need to present herself as disinterested in sex, pure as the white blackbird, and to project an image of purity and cleanliness onto external objects like the moon and her domestic surroundings. Yet her whole vision is crudely sexual, her monologue vulgar and obscene in a way which Beauvoir's earlier 'negative' women characters barely approach.

The story does contain, therefore, the bones of a 'situation'. Murielle is not presented as unintelligent and it is possible to sympathise with her criticisms of a society which can devise a moon rocket programme but not a satisfactory central heating system, or with her concern about pollution. But possible points of contact with Murielle inevitably break down. For her, fear of pollution extends to not wanting to breathe air that others have breathed; a well-founded scepticism about the real meaning of terms such as the 'progress' and 'prosperity' of humanity leads her to see the massacre of children as an answer to the overcrowding of the planet (see TWD p. 88). Not only what she says about herself as a mother, but virtually everything else she says is subverted within the narrative as her maxims are exploded, her ideas of what is 'normal' or 'natural' turned in on themselves and shown to be in direct contradiction to reality. Nowhere does this monologue succeed in opening out to a dialogue with reality or with others.

There is a point in her narrative at which Murielle imagines writing a book about herself — a book which will force 'the others' to accept her version of events.[17] In the same way she imagines having a photograph of herself in which she would look perfect published in *Vogue*. Her monologue derives from the same need to impose an image of herself, to use words to impose herself on others. Like Chantal in her diary, like Monique of the last story, Murielle uses words to create herself. The power and rage of the character is directed into a discourse of folly and delusion, of violence and sexual fantasy which the reader is forced to embrace all the better to reject it.

'The Woman Destroyed'

The reader's approach to the last and longest of the stories is inevitably pre-ordered by the experience of the first two. We expect the woman of the third monologue to have things in common with the first two, and indeed she does. Like them, she is in crisis, like them she weaves a web of specious interpretations and mystifications in an attempt to protect herself from an unpalatable truth: in this case the fact that her marriage is at an end, that her children are grown up and no longer need her, and that she herself has a large burden of responsibility to bear for the ruins of her life which she contemplates lying about her.

However, there is a difference in the status of her discourse in the sense that she produces not simply thoughts or words but a written narrative in the form of a diary, covering not hours or weeks but just over six months of her life. Monique is the first woman in Beauvoir's fiction since *When Things of the Spirit Come First* to achieve the status of writer-narrator, and arguably the only character for whom the process of writing itself eventually brings about a measure of change. The use of the diary form inevitably brings to the fore the subject of the activity of writing, since the diarist is perceived by the reader — and perceives herself — as writer, as the source of the narrative as well as its subject. Monique is aware of the highly self-conscious nature of diary writing, a writing which she had already used as an adolescent and which she calls in the first entry a writing that is 'just for myself'. By the fifth entry she is more or less able to admit that her desire to write is connected to her unease about her relationship with Maurice and notes, 'What an odd thing a diary is: the things you omit are more important than those you put in' (TWD p. 111).

The crisis breaks in the very next entry, confirming the reader's suspicion that a great deal has not been put in, and from this point on Monique herself begins feverishly using the diary to construct a series of shifting hypotheses, on two fronts. One series concerns the images she constructs of Maurice's liaison with Noëllie — images which are necessarily hypothetical and which are clouded by both Monique's desire to minimise the relationship as much as possible, and by the fact that Maurice continues lying to her even after he has begun telling the truth. Monique is thus forced to adjust her readings as each further bit of truth emerges. On a second front, Monique uses the diary to 're-examine' her life with Maurice, making small admissions and concessions but largely devoting herself to the construction of an image of herself and Maurice as a perfect couple, easily able to withstand the pressure of an unimportant liaison, and to the reinforcement of her self-image as a loving, genuine person — a person of 'quality' whom no one in their right mind would reject in favour of the 'superficial' Noëllie.

However, an important shift of position occurs in the diary entry of 15 January. Up to this point, Monique sees herself primarily as narrator, as producer of what is essentially discourse. When, like the woman of the first story, she spends a period in the wilderness alone in the flat while Maurice is away with Noëllie, Monique does not like the earlier woman simply review certain of her attitudes in her own mind — she re-reads her diary. At a stroke, Monique is able to perceive herself not only as producer, as narrator, but as actor in what has gradually become a story with characters and a plot (*récit*).[18] Monique as reader is stunned by the evidence of the flagrant self-deception of her narrated self: 'There is not a single line in this diary that does not call for a correction or a denial (. . .) Is it possible to be so mistaken about one's own life as all that? Is everybody as blind as this or am I a half-wit?' (TWD p. 194). The main functions of the diary for Monique have been to tranquillise herself, to let as little as possible of the truth about the affair between Noëllie and Maurice filter through to her consciousness, and to confirm her self-image. As reader she perceives this, and incidentally, indicates to us as reader the position we should take up. How can she then continue writing, knowing to what purpose she has put it? 'I have taken to my pen again not to go back over the same ground but because the emptiness within me, around me, is so vast that this movement of my hand is necessary to tell myself that I am still alive' (TWD p. 194). The creation of a sense of identity has become an urgent problem, and writing is seized on as a possible means to achieve this. As she sinks further into the vacuum of loss of identity the diary entries falter. In an undated entry for February she writes:

> There was once a man who lost his shadow. I forget what happened to him, but it was dreadful. As for me, I've lost my own image (. . .) Maurice had drawn it for me. A straightforward, genuine, 'authentic' woman, without mean-mindedness, uncompromising, but at the same time understanding, indulgent, sensitive, deeply feeling, intensely aware of things and of people, passionately devoted to those she loved and creating happiness for them. A fine life, serene, full, 'harmonious'. It is dark: I cannot see myself any more. And what do the others see? Maybe something hideous. (TWD pp. 207–8)

With her values Monique loses the vocabulary inherited from her father and her husband; terms she has valued such as 'authenticity', 'sincerity', become empty; and with the collapse of her values comes the disintegration even of her sense of self. In the past, Monique has allowed her idea of herself to coincide with the view of her which she had supposed Maurice to hold, and to be couched in terms of Maurice's values and vocabulary ('authentic', 'harmonious'). Maurice's valorisation of the ambitious, showy, liberated Noëllie explodes this vocabulary, explodes the values which Monique had thought she shared with him, explodes Monique's sense of self. 'Maurice has murdered all the words,' (TWD p. 218), Monique writes after the psychiatrist persuades her to take up the diary again 'trying to get me to take an interest in myself, to reconstruct my identity for me' (TWD p. 208).

Monique's crisis of identity is closely bound up with Noëllie — in fact, in some ways, one could say that the central thread of the narrative becomes Monique's encounter with Noëllie as Monique's values are increasingly held up against and thrown into question by those of her rival and counterpart. In existentialist terms, Noëllie takes on the menacing face of the Other who obliges Monique to take cognisance of her image, just as Xavière does for Françoise in *She Came to Stay*. Maurice becomes a go-between through whom Monique is led to discover first another woman, and then herself. Noëllie has a career, works hard, is ambitious, is interested in what is going on in the world around her. She tries to teach her daughter 'to manage by herself, and to stand on her own feet' (TWD p. 154). Faced with this contrast, Monique becomes aware of her own intellectual stagnation, of her immersion in domestic matters, of the egotistic aspect of her desire to 'create happiness for those around me'. Worse still, she sees that she has not even succeeded in this aim, that instead of equipping her daughters with the means to make lives of their own, that she has weighed heavily on them, and pressed one into conforming to her own image, the other into rebelling and moving away. Like the woman of the first story, the temptation for Monique is to replace one extreme self-image by another: 'Perhaps a kind of leech that feeds on the life of others (. . .) An egoist who will not let go (. . .) Completely phoney through and through' (TWD p. 207). Other characters, particularly the realist daughter Lucienne, are used to counteract this assessment, and to prevent the slide into self-indulgent guilt. 'You've always had a very exaggerated notion of your own responsibilities,' comments Lucienne crisply (TWD p. 218).

It is clear from the narrative that Monique is credited with many errors — she forced Maurice's hand on marriage with a pregnancy, which she more or less engineered because she found the realities of a medical career too much to take; she tried to confine her husband in a career which she herself describes as 'unexciting, run-of-the-mill, poorly paid' (TWD p. 119); she has been a dominating and possessive mother. Bolstering herself up with her image of herself as the perfect wife and mother, she has refused to interest herself in things outside the home, refused to face up to her deteriorating relationship with her husband, and clung to memories of the past. Realising despite herself that her memories are 15 years old, Monique asks herself in desperation, 'What do fifteen years count? Twice two is four. I love you, I love you alone.'

Truth cannot be destroyed, time has no effect on it' (TWD p. 114). Monique's desperate attempts to refuse to see that truth is not indestructible and that time does change everything, her attempt to build a myth of the couple in which Maurice would be her husband in the same necessary sense in which Colette is her daughter, closely resemble the illusions of the women in the first two stories. It is in this sense that the theme implicit in the first two stories of the use and abuse of language, the analysis of the mechanisms of the myth-making discourse which is itself a form of 'writing', becomes more explicit in 'The Woman Destroyed'.

However, the diary is not just the record of Monique's errors — it is also the record of her pain, and this brings us to the crux of the problem of reading this story. Many readers, after immersion in Monique's narrative, emerge more with a strong sense of sympathy for a suffering fellow human being than with the sense that Monique ought not to have got herself into the position where she can declare to her husband, 'Here I am at forty-four, empty-handed, with no occupation, no other interest in life apart from you' (TWD pp. 178–79). Instead of seeing Monique as an object lesson in failure, an indication of how women weave myths to work themselves into the stereotype of the abandoned wife, many readers have preferred instead either to see Monique as the blameless victim of a wicked husband, or to deliberately reject the object lesson, pointing to the collusion which the husband and society itself offer to a woman like Monique who asks nothing more than to live her life through others. In *All Said and Done*, Beauvoir recorded her astonishment at the enormous post which she received on publication of her stories:

> I was overwhelmed with letters from women destroyed, half-destroyed, or in the act of being destroyed. They identified themselves with the heroine; they attributed all possible virtues to her and they were astonished that she should remain attached to a man so unworthy of her (. . .). They shared Monique's blindness. (ASD p. 142)

On the more feminist front, Beauvoir defends her choice not to use positive heroines before adding that 'There is no reason at all why one should not draw a feminist conclusion from *The Woman Destroyed*' (ASD p. 144).

What elements of the story might be used for this feminist conclusion? How clearly are the victimising forces so apparent in

When Things of the Spirit Come First drawn in here? A great deal turns on the portrait of the husband. Like the other characters, he is viewed only through Monique's eyes, and by keeping Monique in love with Maurice to the last, Beauvoir inevitably tilts the portrait towards the favourable. Yet the facts of his behaviour are made less than attractive — benefiting from Monique's support and work in the home while he has built up his career, he has waited ten years while Monique continues to be of need as a home-maker before announcing that he no longer loves her. Ten years earlier, Monique would have had a much better chance of remaking her life, and, as she says, would have agreed to take a job if she had known why Maurice was pressing her to do so (TWD p. 179). His lies about the seriousness of his relationship with Noëllie only encourage Monique not to face the truth. There is evidence of his manipulation of Monique's state of mind to suit himself. It is he who begs her to see a psychiatrist and allows her to recover some strength before announcing his departure from their flat (see TWD pp. 206, 210). Maurice's inability to face up to his own guilt seems to make him incapable of admitting the whole truth to Monique, except when he is angry and loses control. There are many parallels with Henri's treatment of Paule in *The Mandarins*, and Beauvoir seems just as indulgent. Maurice has the right to make a new life, she said in an interview in 1985, and in the story only two of the many people Monique consults express even a whisper of blame for Maurice (Marie-Lambert is critical of Maurice's silence and Colette blames Maurice's angry attack on Monique).[19] Monique herself underlines Maurice's own suffering as frequently as she blames him, despite his persistent manoeuvres and lies. Other friends, both male and female, appear all to agree that Maurice's behaviour is 'perfectly usual' and that 'a faithfulness lasting twenty years is an impossibility for a man' (TWD p. 164); these claims are not questioned or extended to women within the narrative.

The possibilities in the story for placing blame on Maurice have clearly not been much exploited. However, there are two — perhaps three — elements which can be used for the feminist reading of the story to which Beauvoir refers. The first is the confrontation Monique's experience brings about with the traditional wisdom of what one might call the women's magazine ethic: 'This evening I am going out with Maurice. The advice of Isabelle and of Miss Lonelyhearts column — to get your husband back, be cheerful and elegant and go out with him, just the two of you'

(TWD p. 117). It becomes painful to witness Monique endeavouring to hide her anger, to be 'more understanding, more detached, more full of smiles' (TWD p. 128), visiting the beauty parlour and worrying that she should have gone to the hairdresser more often, should have kept her weight in check, should have tried to revive (single-handedly) the couple's sex life.[20] As she consults her stars in the newspaper and sends off handwriting extracts to a graphologist, a chasm opens up between the futility of all these activities, all based on the notion that women must use their guile and charms to hook their man and then to keep him on the leash, and the increasingly evident truth that the game is not worth the candle. The other couples in the story seem little happier than Monique and Maurice; at times Monique begins to question the whole notion of the couple as a romantic ideal (at the Club 46, for example; TWD p. 189).

A second element derives from Beauvoir's strategy in choosing a negative heroine — the reverse of a role model — in both this and the other two stories. To posit women as helpless victims is to do nothing to transform the attitudes of women themselves. In choosing to emphasise the element of complicity rather than the element of oppression Beauvoir is working on the elements of their situation which it is within women's own power to change. To accuse her of being unsympathetic to women in these stories is to fail to see that Beauvoir is *always* extremely severe with women because she regards as criminal the encouragement which women are habitually offered to flee their freedom and their responsibility.

A third basis, finally, for a more positive reading of this story is the hope offered by the progression of the narrative itself. Monique discovers the power of words, and after using them to weave her myths in the first part of the diary, moves cautiously towards using them to face reality and construct a new, more independent identity. 'I am afraid,' declares Monique in the last line of her diary, but like Marguerite at the end of *When Things of the Spirit Come First*, she knows that she has to look things in the face and to depend only on herself.

Monique's writing closes the cycle of *The Woman Destroyed* in which three women blocked into situations with no immediately discernible exit elaborate discourses to conceal their situations from themselves. Taken separately, the sources of their errors may appear individual; taken together, however, the ways in which these three women use words to build myths about their roles as wives and mothers, to conceal from themselves the passage of time, to cover over the difficulties that they have in relating to their bodies, becomes an insistent pattern — an indication of a common 'situation' as women. The fate of the woman of the first story may appear the most optimistic, as she comes to terms with certain elements of her life, and is not alone.[21] However, there is a dependence on the husband and a bitterness about the loss of her maternal illusions about her son which hang heavily over the woman's future. Her book is a failure and she retains her habit of using words and culture to create mythical moments. The second story is the bleakest portrait of a woman anywhere in Beauvoir's fiction. Murielle's power and anger precipitate her into folly; the madness and delusions at the centre of this volume provide a chilling image of the madness which stalks so many of Beauvoir's women characters, and of which the retreat into the flat of each of the women of *The Woman Destroyed* is the shadow.[22] There is no communication for the woman of 'Monologue', no use of words to work towards reality. Monique's case is more banal than the other women's situation — more banal and more familiar, as the response in Beauvoir's postbag showed. More than the other women, Monique is the traditional representative of the middle-aged, middle-class woman who believes in the couple, who aspires to be a perfect wife and mother, and who succumbs to the appeal of the security of domestic preoccupations.[23] Monique's struggle with writing is the formalisation of the struggle with labels like 'mother' which all three women undergo, with the formulae based on the 'common sensical' and the 'normal' to which Murielle clings, with the cultural screen which the woman of 'The Age of Discretion' interposes between herself and reality. Monique's pain is intense, but the passage to writing seems to permit a hesitant move beyond the myth-making discourse, beyond the words which Maurice has 'murdered' to words which more nearly approach her own reality. Monique both closes the cycle of the woman destroyed, and opens it up.

Notes

1. See *The Prime of Life*, p. 328.
2. In my interview with Beauvoir (1985) in reply to the question, 'When you wrote *The Woman Destroyed* did you think back to the short-story collection which had been refused at the beginning of your career?' Beauvoir replied, 'Oh no, not at all. I didn't think about that at all.'
3. The original title of the collection, as Beauvoir reminds us in the

French preface, was *La Primauté du spirituel* (The primacy of the spiritual) — intended to be an ironic reference to a work of that title by Catholic philosopher Jacques Maritain, which argues for the primacy of the spiritual in human affairs. Maritain's book refers sympathetically to both Maurras and Mussolini. I refer to the French preface because it is not the same as the preface to the English translation.

4. Forrest Ingram defines a short-story cycle as 'a set of stories so linked to one another that the reader's experience of each one is modified by his experience of the others'. See *Representative Short Story Cycles of the Twentieth Century*, p. 9. Beauvoir confirmed in my 1985 interview with her that she did write the three stories of *The Woman Destroyed* to be published together.

5. By 'spiritualism' Beauvoir is not referring to the belief that the spirits of the dead can make contact with the living, which is one of the senses of the English word.

6. See also A.-M. Celeux, *Jean-Paul Sartre, Simone de Beauvoir: Une expérience commune, deux écritures*, p. 49.

7. Beauvoir based the story on her knowledge of the Institut Sainte-Marie, which she attended before going on to the Sorbonne. The names of the original model for Lisa, and of Mademoiselle Lambert, are not even changed. See *The Prime of Life*, p. 222.

8. The account given of the collection in *The Prime of Life* (p. 222) suggests that 'Lisa' was in fact originally the first story of the cycle.

9. Recounted in *Memoirs of a Dutiful Daughter*, pp. 349–60.

10. See *Memoirs of a Dutiful Daughter*, pp. 254–59.

11. See Alice Schwarzer, *Simone de Beauvoir aujourd'hui*, p. 81.

12. In her presentation of the novel in the Gallimard 1967 edition (also noted by Anne Ophir in *Regards féminins*, p. 60).

13. Although the phrase *la femme rompu* is not in itself a recognisable cliché — or was not before Beauvoir used it — the word *rompu* is frequently used metaphorically to mean 'worn out'. The element of destruction foregrounded in the English title represents only one of the meanings of *rompue* which also has associations with being 'broken in' — an association permitting a rather different perspective since it points to the social pressures on women to conform to their allotted role.

14. In French as in English, the term 'discretion' encompasses both the positive meaning 'discernment' or 'judgement', and the more ambiguous qualities of tact, self-effacement — even 'silence'. Conventional wisdom seems to have it that age will bring, paradoxically, both these things about.

15. Many of these themes are taken up in Beauvoir's essay *Old Age*, published in 1970 (see my Chapter 1). The problems of health and the body, sexuality, relationship with time, and the problem of creativity treated at length in *Old Age* are all raised in 'The Age of Discretion', sometimes in such similar terms that it is clear that the story is a source of the essay, or a dramatisation of aspects of the subject which Beauvoir had already thought out.

16. In the French text Murielle uses the verb *dresser*, for which 'train' is offered in the English text. However, whereas *dresser* is not an acceptable word in French to describe the bringing up of children, English 'train' is

acceptable in some contexts. A more accurate translation would therefore be 'break in' or 'bring to heel'.

17. See Ophir, p. 42. Anne Ophir's analyses of all three stories are perceptive and suggestive.

18. See Valerie Raoul, *The French Fictional Journal*, p. 10, for a theoretical discussion of the transformation of *discours* into *récit* in the fictional diary form.

19. When I suggested to Beauvoir that the story appears to approve Maurice's desire to leave Monique and find another woman she replied, 'Yes, he might have his reasons. Another more outgoing woman . . . Yes, of course.'

20. The escape of her body from Monique's control is accentuated when she begins to experience continual bleeding: 'I was afraid of my blood, and the way it flowed from me' (TWD p. 208).

21. Beauvoir herself suggests this in *All Said and Done*. The text of the autobiography is ambiguous because Beauvoir writes that 'in the last tale the failure is overcome' (ASD p. 141), but when I asked her which story she meant she replied, 'Oh it was "The Age of Discretion"'.

22. Monique's suspicions that there are 'plottings that go on behind my back' (TWD p. 208) begin to resemble Murielle's delusions of persecution.

23. See Anne Ophir (p. 60), who sees Monique as a kind of generic woman destroyed.

8

Points of Departure

There are no arrivals anywhere, there are only points of departure.
— Simone de Beauvoir

From the point of view of narrative structure and voice, Beauvoir's fictional narratives fall into a number of distinct groups. *When Things of the Spirit Come First*, the earliest text as far as composition goes and which has an experimental quality, produces the widest range of approaches. Four of the text's five stories are spoken (in total or in part) by an external narrative voice whose stance varies from the overtly judgemental and ironic to the discreetly covert silent. The number of characters acting as narrator or as focus of narration varies between one (as in 'Marcelle'), two (as in 'Chantal') and three (as in 'Anne'). Of the nine characters who play this role, eight are women. Three women accede to a narrative voice: Madame Vignon in her long prayer, Chantal in her diary, Marguerite in her more formal past-tense narrative of her life. The female voice is thus largely dominant, and does at times escape the control of the external narrator — most notably in the case of the positively coded Marguerite.

The story of the rest of Beauvoir's fictional writing is the story of an ever increasing reduction of this plurality of voice, and a loss of the authority conceded to the female voice. In the first published novel, *She Came to Stay*, the external narrator remains as the main voice of the text, but gives up the irony and judgement sometimes exercised in *When Things of the Spirit Come First* to adopt the covert stance which remains the lot of the external narrator throughout both this and the next four texts, before disappearing altogether. Three characters act as focus of narration in *She Came to Stay*, of

175

which two are female and one male. The dominance of the female character noted in *When Things of the Spirit Come First* remains, since Françoise's narrative is by far the most important of the text, and the male character's contribution amounts only to a few pages. No character narrates in the first person, though their 'I' enters the text through the long dialogues and through frequent direct transcription of the characters' thoughts.

In terms of narrative organisation, *She Came to Stay* can be seen as a transitional work, since it begins a refining process of a basic structure which is used with only minor variations in each of the following three novels. In *The Blood of Others, All Men Are Mortal*, and *The Mandarins*, the number of narratives is reduced from three to two; in each novel one of the narratives is voiced by a character-narrator in the first person (Blomart, Fosca and Anne respectively), and one is voiced in the third person by a covert external narrator focusing through a single character (Hélène, Régine and Henri respectively). The strong balance towards the male narrative in *The Blood of Others* and *All Men Are Mortal*, in which the first-person male narrative dominates the text as a whole, becomes an equal balance between male and female in *The Mandarins*, the text in which a female character is entrusted with a first-person narrative for the first time since the early short stories.

A further structural element common to these three novels is the pattern of the argument which they dramatise: the structure of 'preference', in which charaters take up an absolute position, then abandon it in the face of its drawbacks before returning to their starting point and re-adopting their initial position in the full knowledge of all its difficulties, is enacted in all three texts. In the first two, *The Blood of Others* and *All Men Are Mortal*, this enactment is carried out by the figure who is also the dominant narrative power in the text, the male character whose narrative is voiced in the first person. To the extent that these characters not only voice their narratives (using the authoritative past historic as well as the more personal perfect tense), but themselves enact the structure of preference and articulate its meaning to the reader, they become figures of considerable power and authority in the text. Reinforcing this authority is the time structure of their narratives; the flashback structure, enclosed in the narrative time of a single night in which the character narrates his life story in order to draw a message from his experience, is an important channel of meaning in the text.

When we come to *The Mandarins*, in which the character who

escapes the control of an external narrator and voices the narrative in the first person is a woman, we find that this authority has been removed. Though part of Anne's narrative is narrative of the past, expressed in the past historic tense just as if she shared the status of her predecessors, this narrative of the past is constantly invaded by a present-tense monologue which does not so much narrate events as raise perspectives of suffering and death. The structure of preference is articulated not by character-narrator Anne but by Robert, and is supported not by a flashback structure but by the general invasion of the structure into all the diverse strands of the text.

Despite this loss of authority by the character-narrator in *The Mandarins*, all three of these novels are clearly organised to allow the channelling of meaning either through the character's voice, or through the patterning of themes and events, or through the time structure, or through all three. *The Mandarins*, already a deviant in the pattern with its diminution of the character-narrator's power, closes this structural pattern and a new one emerges in the final two texts, *Les Belles Images* and *The Woman Destroyed*. The most obvious change is again the element of reduction. The thick volumes of the earlier novels are reduced first to the brief narrative of *Les Belles Images*, and then to the short stories of *The Woman Destroyed*. The double narrative of the previous three texts is replaced by a single focus: first that of Laurence of *Les Belles Images*, with her fragmented first-person voice which fades for long stretches of the narrative behind that of the external narrator each time that Laurence retrenches into her social persona. Then the three women of the short stories, the unnamed woman of 'The Age of Discretion', Murielle of 'Monologue' and Monique of 'The Woman Destroyed', each in turn take the narrative stage with their uninterrupted monologues. The external narrator vanishes. The past historic tense, dominant in all of the other novels, also disappears completely in the final two texts, replaced by the perfect and, above all, by the uncertainties of the present tense. The character-narrators or centres of narrative focus no longer bestow meaning, no longer act as the reader's guide. Instead, they are offered up to us for investigation and, ultimately, disapproval. The reader becomes the detective, the character-narrator the criminal.

Why does the authority of the character-narrator or centre of narrative focus fade in this way? Is there a connection with the fact that this role is increasingly played by women? From *The*

Mandarins onwards, where Anne accedes to the first-person voice, power and authority no longer reside automatically in the character-narrator. But what about Françoise of *She Came to Stay*? She imposes meaning, even if she does not have the first-person voice; she achieves a powerful act and interprets it for us. The question then, is not so much is the character-narrator or focus of the narrative a woman but, rather, what kind of woman is she?

Françoise and Hélène, who act as narrative focus in *She Came to Stay* and *The Blood of Others*, are in both cases partly defined by what they are not. Thus Françoise is *not* Elisabeth (negative, failed artist, overwhelmed by her sexuality — Elisabeth). Hélène is *not* Denise (negative, failed writer, victim of breakdown — Denise), though Hélène does inherit the troubled sexuality of the negative woman, and is subjected to an abortion which reveals her body as obscene and grotesque. Anne of *The Mandarins* is a turning point. She has charge of her own narrative (which Françoise and Hélène do not) and uses monologue to express her suffering as well as offering an account of recent events in the past historic. Anne also has a negative double in the suffering Paule who, like Denise, fails when she tries to write and is driven into temporary insanity. But Anne is both *not* Paule and at the same time *is* like Paule; Anne remains a reliable narrator, using words in a way the reader is expected to trust and not the myth-making language of Paule. But Anne approaches the breakdown which Paule experiences, and comes to the brink of carrying out the suicide which Paule had planned. The character-narrator woman is, in other words, coming more and more to resemble the negative woman, the mad woman who misuses words.

With *Les Belles Images*, the merger is complete. The negative woman with her mythical language emerges in the foreground and invades the narrative. Laurence's use of carbon-copy echoes of the reassuring slogans of her class and her profession is coupled with her breakdowns and her anorexia; all three women of *The Woman Destroyed* elaborate a self-deceiving discourse and are plunged into a crisis of suffering; one is despatched to the psychiatrist and another passes over the line between suffering and paranoia. In both texts, folly and the misuse of words replace the reliable powerful narrator. Power passes to the reader, whose status has been gradually rising whilst that of the character-narrator has been falling. The delusions of the suffering woman, hitherto contained in the failed writing and painting of an Elisabeth, a Denise, a Maria and a Paule, now constitute the narrative. In the last short stories, the function of this narrative for the woman — that is, the creation of a mythical discourse intended to protect the woman from the truth — is clearly the same function as writing held for Paule and Denise. Murielle uses the monologue in place of the book she dreams of writing which would be a complete self-justification. Monique's diary is in a way the complete emblem of everything that these women have wished to do.

How can this connection between women, folly and the abuse of words be accounted for? Why is the monologue form, the use of 'I' by women so consistently linked with suffering and delusions, from Chantal in *When Things of the Spirit Come First* to Murielle of *The Woman Destroyed*? Must women fail when they write — must they be mad to write? It has become almost a routine observation to point to the splitting of the female character so often observable in women's writing. Gilbert and Gubar, noting the dichotomy often set up in the nineteenth-century women's novel between monster woman and angel woman, interpret this splitting process as dramatising the anxiety felt by the woman author about entering through writing what she perceives as a male-dominated domain. Thus, they argue, through the twin faces of the mad and violent Mrs Rochester and the conformist angel-figure Jane Eyre, the woman writer expresses her anxiety about engaging in the subversive activity of writing as a woman, by both embodying her revolt in the mad woman and by punishing it. There is a reductionist tendency in this kind of analysis, especially in the danger of identifying character and author, as Toril Moi has pointed out.[1] Nevertheless, the point that women writers have to engage with a largely male tradition in writing at all is an important one. When we turn back to Beauvoir's fiction, the evidence that she shared the perception of fiction as a male domain and that she had little sense of connection to a female tradition of writing is unmistakable. We have seen that in the early stages of Beauvoir's writing before she published anything she admired a number of writers who served in different ways as models: Dostoyevsky, Hemingway, Dos Passos, Faulkner. All are male. In her autobiographies, Beauvoir draws attention to these influences, creating an implicit context for her own writing. *She Came to Stay*, *The Blood of Others* and 'Monologue' formalise this process a step further by carrying epigraphs from, respectively, Hegel, Dostoyevsky and Flaubert, which not only serve to place her texts in a tradition but act, ultimately, as a kind of guarantor for the text.[2] Here we are dealing with writers who Beauvoir admired, but another manifestation of the desire to situate her work is the way in which her texts sometimes take as reference point writers who she did not admire, writers who, precisely, she wished to contest through her own writing. Thus the title of *When Things of the Spirit Come First* is borrowed from Jacques Maritain with ironic intent (as Beauvoir is careful to stress in the French preface to the stories) and the text of *Les Belles Images* parodies Foucault (as well as borrowing in a more positive spirit an image from Alain Badiou's *Almagestes*). Beauvoir stresses all these influences, borrowings and contestations with care. It is plain that she did see writing as a male tradition, and that she sought to place her work within it. Does this imply an anxiety about writing as a woman?

Beauvoir was perfectly well aware of the factors which conspire to stop women writing and discussed them herself both in *The Second Sex* and elsewhere.[3] When writing or speaking about her own fiction, Beauvoir often insisted upon what she calls the 'universal' aspect of fiction — the aspect which, for her, prevents writing from being simply 'anecdotal'. In 'My Experience as a Writer', a lecture given in Japan in 1966, she took the writing of her first novel *She Came to Stay* as an example. The text, she explained, was first and foremost the result of a 'concrete psychological experience' (in other words of the trio she had participated in with Sartre and Olga); but she could not write her novel, she said, until she had 'found a way to pass from this particular experience to a universal level'. She achieved this when she 'realised that it was the relationship to the consciousness of others which was tormenting me'.[4] Beauvoir then repeats several times with evident satisfaction how pleased she was to have found this 'universal' aspect. Here we have the explanation of Hegel and the whole philosophical superstructure of the text: Beauvoir only felt able — only dared — to dramatise her own experience when she had found a way of making it acceptable to herself as writing. What this actually meant was that she had found in philosophy and in Hegel a way of placing her work in an authorised, male, tradition.

There are other aspects of Beauvoir's fiction which express an anxiety of authorship. Amongst the most evident are the puzzlingly ironic ring of so many of Beauvoir's novel titles (most notably *The Mandarins* and *The Woman Destroyed*), betraying her fear of identifying fully with her works, and the extraordinary eagerness with which she criticises her own work in her autobiographies, as if to ward off the inevitable criticism from others. One might also note her attribution of her own writing in *The Mandarins* to a male character, and the insistence with which Beauvoir constantly attacked the narrowness of the 'housewife' writing which she seemed so anxious to avoid.[5] However, the question should also be posed of whether Beauvoir was not right to fear that if she did not take care to place her work in this specifically male tradition that it would be much more difficult to get it taken seriously. When she changed tack and wrote about women's experience of pain without a philosophical lens in *The Woman Destroyed*, her text was greeted by newspaper critics in France with dismissive glee. The subtleties of the text were overlooked in the rush to condemn this woman writer whose pretentions to a 'universal' writing had been at last unmasked — the comparisons with Françoise Sagan are instructive.

The development — one might almost say the dissolution — of narrative structure in Beauvoir's fiction and the loss of authority of the narrator-character or character focus of narration, can be seen to be closely associated with the gradual emergence of the figure of the 'negative' mad woman, who moves in stages from the background to the foreground of the texts, eventually taking over the narrative voice completely. The figure of Murielle of *The Woman Destroyed*, with her violent and powerful monologue, heavily marked by folly and by sexuality, is the extreme point of this process. As this woman moves into prominence, so the narrative forms change and dissolve. The tone and form of Anne's monologue is inherited by the later women; even its ending — 'Who knows? Perhaps one day I'll be happy again. Who knows?' (TM p. 763) — is echoed in the final words of Laurence of *Les Belles Images* and the woman of 'The Age of Discretion'.[6] The origin of this association, I have suggested, can be sought in Beauvoir's own attitude to writing as a woman. But we still have to try and account for why this woman and her narrative forms are increasingly allowed to take the stage. One factor that could well be significant is the writing of the authobiographical texts which took place in the long gap in Beauvoir's fictional production, between 1945 and 1966 (between the production of *The Mandarins* and *Les Belles Images*). Writing about her life in this direct way not only allowed Beauvoir to focus on the individual without the same degree of concern for the 'universal' (though she still defended the 'narcissistic' practice of writing about herself in terms of its universal application), but forced her (or permitted her?) to write as a woman. In the autobiographies, she told the audience at one of her Japanese lectures, 'this "I" that I pronounce is the "I" of a woman'.[7] When she returns to fiction writing after the production of *Memoirs of a Dutiful daughter*, *The Prime of Life*, *Force of Circumstance* and *A Very Easy Death*, with their use of the female 'I', the male narrative voice disappears.

Another factor which has to be considered is that of historical moment, and of Beauvoir's growing awareness of historical context. It is striking that the early self-deceived women characters of *When Things of the Spirit Come First* with their monologues, diaries and special use of words, are, like the women of the last two works of fiction, firmly embedded in a social context. The removal of this context in *She Came to Stay* — where characters seem to float free of family and social context, is clearly connected to the absolute sense of freedom which Beauvoir experienced in the period of her life where she had the feeling of living 'like Kant's dove, supported rather than hindered in flight by the resistant air' (POL p. 15). Having fought free of the bourgeoisie in which she had been brought up, she failed, temporarily, to understand that she had simply exchanged one social status for another. She said in 1966:

> What we don't know has as much weight in a life as what we do know. I mean that for example between 1929 and 1938 I was apolitical; well! if I had to rewrite *The Prime of Life*, I would emphasise this indifference much more; it defines me as a French middle-class intellectual of the era, since most French intellectuals were at that time outside politics.[8]

I have suggested that *She Came to Stay* (written at the end of this apolitical period) can be read as above all an ostrich attempt precisely to avoid any discovery of politics, of the interrelation of the individual and the wider stage of history. However, with the approach of the Second World War came the eventual discovery of the individual's historicity and the elaboration of the structure of persuasion which the structure of preference and the double-narrative organisation really is. Introduced for the first time in *The Blood of Others*, written during the German occupation of France, it permitted the inscription of the message of commitment into the structures of the text itself. The same can be said, in differing degrees, of *All Men Are Mortal* and *The Mandarins*, in which the same basic structure operates and in which Beauvoir is still caught up in the impact which the Second World War, and its aftermath in the Cold War, had on both her and her fiction. Of course it remains the case that even in these texts, in which the narrative structures are most strongly pressed into service to articulate a message, this official meaning is subverted or relegated to the sidelines by other elements of the text. The powerful narrators of these texts who articulate the concept of commitment and who are to be trusted by the reader are again curiously free of social constraints. Blomart has to shake off a wealthy background, but this is rapidly achieved — we know very little of the background of the characters of *The Mandarins*, and Fosca is inevitably a completely ahistorical figure. It is only after the 1954–1966 gap that there is a return in *Les Belles Images* to a strong emphasis on social class, coupled with a new set of narrative structures.

We have already taken note of the writing of the autobiographies in this gap, but the period was also marked by the impact of the Algerian War on Beauvoir and her direct involvement in political action. 'The horror my class inspires in me has been brought to a white heat by the Algerian War' (FOC p. 665); the connection between class and history is made with the return of the focus on the sins of those who fail to act (instead of on the dilemmas of those who do act), no doubt also assisted by the greater sympathy for Marxism to which Beauvoir came round in the early 1950s. The Algerian War made the weight exercised on events by those who do not act clear to Beauvoir. The use of Riesman's theories in *Les Belles Images*, the implicit context of the socialisation of women in *The Woman Destroyed*, produce a much greater emphasis on the situation, on the weight of class, gender and upbringing on the individual. The return to the weight of the situation meant a return to the modes by which individuals try to hide from their situations; the creation of comfortable myths and the abuse of language analysed in *When Things of the Spirit Come First*, but pushed into the background in the middle novels, come full circle and return in *Les Belles Images* and *The Woman Destroyed*.

The narrative forms of bad faith (the monologue, the diary and a mythmaking use of words) are effectively identified as those of a class as well as of a sex. Monologue, myth, the weight of the bourgeoisie are made to interlock on the one hand; dialogue (the double narrative), a proper use of words and a reliable narrator on the other. Femininity and the bourgeoisie seem here to be wrapped up with each other; the need to confirm her escape from these two forms of 'social character' learned in childhood is a powerful force in Beauvoir's texts, strongly marked in their narrative organisation.

'There are no arrivals anywhere, there are only points of departure' writes Simone de Beauvoir in *Pyrrhus and Cinéas* (p. 288). The identification of narrative structures in a text is only a point of departure. It leads to the posing of new questions about meaning and not its foreclosure. I have tried to suggest relations between narrative structure and voice on the one hand, and Beauvoir's attitude as a woman to writing and to certain of her female characters on the other. I have also tried to look at changes in narrative organisation in terms of the impact which historical events had on Beauvoir's perception of the individual's relation to history, and on the growing weight given in the text to the constraints of gender, class and individual circumstances.

Other points of departure could be made, other links suggested. Beauvoir saw that narrative structure is a powerful means of persuasion at the author's disposal, but it is also a tool which can turn against its creator and allow rival meanings to spring up unbidden. One of the rival meanings which I have drawn attention to is the way in which the use of narrative voice betrays a fear that woman's voice, woman's writing is an abuse of words. In later life, Beauvoir came to admire the novels of Doris Lessing, but her work is situated at the antipodes of Lessing's admonition in *The Golden Notebook*: 'I tell you, there are a great line of women stretching out behind you into the past, and you have to seek them out and find them in yourself and be conscious of them.' Beauvoir sought to place her writing in a masculine intellectual tradition, and to respect the 'extraordinary power of words', but, almost despite herself, the treacherous woman's word creeps to the fore, and makes her writing part of the tradition of 'a literature of our own'.[9]

Notes

1. See Sandra Gilbert and Susan Gubar, *The Madwoman in the Attic: The Woman Writer and the Nineteenth Century Literary Imagination*, pp. 77–78. Moi, *Sexual/Textual Politics*, p. 61.

2. In his analysis of the function of the epigraph in *Seuils* (1987), Genette describes the epigraph as a 'password of intellectualism' and as an attempt by writers 'to choose their equals, and thus their place in the Pantheon' (p. 149).

3. Notably in 'Woman and Creativity', a lecture given in Japan in 1966 of which the French text is given in Francis and Gontier (1979), pp. 458–74, and which appears in English in Moi's *French Feminist Thought*, pp. 17–32.

4. 'My Experience as a Writer', in Francis and Gontier (1979), pp. 440–41.

5. See, 'My Experience as a Writer', pp. 449–50, and Alice Schwarzer, *Simone de Beauvoir aujourd'hui*, pp. 123–24.

6. Cf. Laurence; 'What chance? She doesn't even know' (LBI p. 154, tr. adap.) and the woman of 'The Age of Discretion': 'Will that make it bearable for us? Let us hope so. We have no choice in the matter' (TWD p. 71).

7. 'My Experience as a Writer', in Francis and Gontier (1979), p. 450.

8. Ibid., p. 452.

9. Quotation from Doris Lessing's *The Golden Notebook* borrowed from Elaine Showalter (p. 298), to whose book *A Literature of Their Own* I also refer in my last line.

Biographical Notes

9 January 1908   Born to middle-class Catholic parents, Françoise and Georges de Beauvoir. The family live in a flat on the boulevard du Montparnasse (no. 103).

1910   Birth of her sister Hélène (Poupette).

1913   Begins school at the Cours Désir.

1914–16   Writes 'Les malheurs de Marguerite' (Marguerite's Misfortunes) and 'La Famille Cornichon' (The Cornichon Family). The latter is copied out into a handsome volume by her Aunt Lili.

1914–18   First World War.

1918   Meets Elisabeth 'Mabille' (Zaza).

1919   Family moves to a cheaper flat at 71 rue de Rennes.

1922   Loses her belief in God.

1925–27   Studies mathematics, philosophy and literature at the Institut Catholique and the Institut Sainte-Marie.

1928   Begins postgraduate studies in philosophy at the Sorbonne and at the Ecole Normale.

1929   Meets Sartre. Succeeds in the *agrégation* examination. Rents a room at her grandmother's house in the rue Denfert-Rochereau. Does some private teaching and works on a novel. Death of Zaza.

1931   Takes up a teaching post in Marseilles. Begins another novel about a friendship between two women (completed in 1932). Sartre teaching in Le Havre.

1932   Teaching post in Rouen. Meets Olga Kosakievicz, Colette Audry.

1933   Begins a novel about a brother and sister, Pierre and Madeleine Labrousse.

1934   Visits Sartre in Berlin. Introduced to phenomenology.

1935   Begins work on *When Things of the Spirit Come First* (completed 1937). Trio with Olga and Sartre (until 1937).

1936   Spanish Civil War. Teaching post in Paris. Meets Jacques Bost.

1937   Hospitalised with a lung infection. Affair with Bost. Gallimard and Grasset turn down *When Things of the Spirit Come First*. Sartre also teaching in Paris — the couple take rooms on adjoining floors in a hotel in Montparnasse. Begins work on *She Came to Stay*.

September 1939   Outbreak of Second World War. Sartre mobilised then in prisoner-of-war camp.

June 1940   Germans occupy Paris. Beauvoir joins exodus south but returns to Paris within weeks. Meets Nathalie Sorokine ('Lise' in the autobiographies).

1941   Return of Sartre to Paris — he and Beauvoir organise a short-lived Resistance group. Death of Georges de Beauvoir. *She Came to Stay* accepted for publication by Gallimard. Begins work on *The Blood of Others*.

1943   Sartre publishes *Being and Nothingness*. Beauvoir publishes *She Came to Stay* and completes *The Blood of Others*. Writes *Pyrrhus et Cinéas* and begins *All Men Are Mortal*.

1944   Writes *Les Bouches Inutiles*. Paris liberated. Editorial board set up for *Les Temps Modernes*. Gives up teaching.

1945   Visits Spain and Portugal. *The Blood of Others* published. Label 'existentialist' henceforth applied to Beauvoir and Sartre.

1946   *All Men Are Mortal* published. Starts work on *The Second Sex*.

1947   Lecture tour of the United States January – May. Meets Nelson Algren. Returns to Chicago to visit him in September. Publication of *The Ethics of Ambiguity*.

1948   RDR founded. *America Day by Day* and *L'Existentialisme et la sagesse des nations* published. Visits Algren May – July. Moves to a furnished room in the rue de la Bûcherie. Finishes vol. 1 of *The Second Sex*: extracts start appearing in *Les Temps Modernes*.

1949   RDR breaks up. Publication of *The Second Sex*. Algren comes to Paris. Begins work on *The Mandarins*.

1950   Korean War (ends 1953). Spends two months with Algren at Lake Michigan.

1951   Return visit to Lake Michigan. End of liaison with Algren. Buys her first car. In Norway with Sartre he reads the first version of *The Mandarins*.

1952   Operation for removal of non-malignant tumour. Begins living with Claude Lanzmann.

1953   Moves closer to Marxism. Finishes *The Mandarins*. *The Second Sex* published in English.

1954   French defeat in Vietnam. Algerian hostilities begin. Publication of *The Mandarins*. Awarded the Goncourt Prize.

1955   Visits China and Moscow. Publication of *Privilèges*. Buys (with the proceeds of the Goncourt Prize) a studio in the rue Schoelcher, overlooking the Montparnasse cemetery.

1956   Summer in Rome — she and Sartre return every summer for many years. Begins writing her autobiography.

1957   Publication of *La Longue Marche*. Reading manuscripts for *Les Temps Modernes* documenting French atrocities in Algeria.

1958   Publication of *Memoirs of a Dutiful Daughter*. Engages in militant protest action against the Algerian War. Separates from Lanzmann.

1960   Publication of *The Prime of Life*. Visits Cuba. Signs the 121 Manifesto (against the Algerian War). Meets Sylvie Le Bon. Protests with Gisèle Halimi over the torture of Djamila Boupacha.

1962   End of the Algerian War. Invited to Moscow by the Union of Soviet Writers, she returns frequently to the Soviet Union over the next few years. Assumes joint authorship with Hamili of *Djamila Boupacha*.

1963   Visits Czechoslovakia. Publication of *Force of Circumstance*. Death of Françoise de Beauvoir.

1964   Publication of *A Very Easy Death*. December: Participates in debate with supporters of the *Tel Quel* tendency about the role of literature (published as *Que peut la littérature?*).

Autumn 1965   Begins writing *Les Belles Images*.

1966 Gives three lectures in Japan. Publication of *Les Belles Images*.

1967 Participates in the Russell Tribunal examining American war crimes in Vietnam. Completes *The Woman Destroyed* in May; extracts appear in *Elle* with illustrations by Hélène de Beauvoir. Special edition of the text with illustrations published.

1968 Publication of *The Woman Destroyed*. Supports the most militant students in the May events.

1970 Publication of *Old Age*. Defends *La Cause du Peuple* and assumes the editorship of *L'Idiot International*. Participates in the MLF pro-abortion demonstration.

1971 Investigates the Rochel accident for *J'Accuse*. Signs the pro-abortion 343 manifesto in *Le Nouvel Observateur*.

1972 Declares herself a radical feminist in an interview with Alice Schwarzer in *Le Nouvel Observateur*. Publication of *All Said and Done*. Making of the film *Sartre par lui-même*, largely filmed in Beauvoir's studio and with considerable participation by her. President of Choisir (pro-abortion group). Participation in Bobigny affair (abortion trial).

1973 Launches new column on everyday sexism in *Les Temps Modernes*.

1974 President of the League for Women's Rights. Special number of *Les Temps Modernes* on the women's struggle.

1975 First television interview (18 February). Works with Sartre on a television series on France 1905–1975, abandoned after censorship problems. Accepts the 1975 Jerusalem Prize.

1977 Works on television adaptation of *The Woman Destroyed* with Josée Dayan.

1978 Making of the film *Simone de Beauvoir*, with Sartre, Olga, Bost, Lanzmann and others.

1979 Publication of *When Things of the Spirit Come First*.

April 1980 Death of Sartre.

1981 Publication of *Adieux: A Farewell to Sartre*.

1983 Publication of Sartre's *Lettres au Castor et à quelques autres*, edited by Beauvoir.

1985 Her last press interview (in *Le Matin de Paris*), given to dissociate herself from the biography of her written by Francis and Gontier, which she had assisted them with. 'Everything in it is false.'

14 April 1986 Death in hospital after a short illness. Buried on 19 April in the Montparnasse cemetery, with Sartre. Lanzmann reads out a page of *Force of Circumstance*.

Bibliography

Major works of Simone de Beauvoir

The original French edition is given first, followed by the English edition (where there is one) to which my text refers.

L'Invitée (Paris: Gallimard, 1943). *She Came to Stay*, trans. Yvonne Moyse and Roger Senhouse (London: Fontana, 1984).

Pyrrhus et Cinéas (Paris: Gallimard, 1944).

Le Sang des autres (Paris: Gallimard, 1945). *The Blood of Others*, trans. Yvonne Moyse and Roger Senhouse (Harmondsworth: Penguin, 1978).

Les Bouches Inutiles (Paris: Gallimard, 1945). *Who Shall Die?* trans. Claude Francis and Fernande Gontier (River Press, 1983).

Tous les hommes sont mortels (Paris: Gallimard, 1946). *All Men Are Mortal* (Cleveland, OH: World Publishing, 1955).

Pour une morale de l'ambiguïté (Paris: Gallimard, 1947). *The Ethics of Ambiguity*, trans. Bernard Fretchman (New York: Philosophical Library, 1948).

L'Existentialisme et la sagesse des nations, including 'Idéalisme moral et réalisme politique', 'Littérature et métaphysique' and 'Oeil pour oeil' (Paris: Nagel, 1948).

L'Amérique au jour le jour (Paris: Morihien, 1948). *America Day by Day*, trans. Patrick Dudley (London: Duckworth, 1952).

Le Deuxième Sexe, 2 vols. (Paris: Gallimard, 1949). *The Second Sex*, trans. H. M. Parshley (Harmondsworth: Penguin, 1986).

Les Mandarins (Paris: Gallimard, 1954). *The Mandarins*, trans. Leonard M. Friedman (London: Fontana, 1982).

Privilèges, including 'Faut-il brûler Sade?', 'La pensée de droite aujourd'hui' and 'Merleau-Ponty et le pseudo-sartrisme' (Paris: Gallimard, 1955).

La Longue Marche (Paris: Gallimard, 1957). *The Long March* (London: Deutsch, 1958).

Mémoires d'une jeune fille rangée (Paris: Gallimard, 1958). *Memoirs of a Dutiful Daughter*, trans. James Kirkup (Harmondsworth: Penguin, 1987).

La Force de l'âge (Paris: Gallimard, 1960). *The Prime of Life*, trans. Peter Green (Harmondsworth: Penguin, 1986).

Brigitte Bardot and the Lolita Syndrome, trans. Bernard Fretchman (London: Four Square, 1962).

La Force des Choses (Paris: Gallimard, 1963). *Force of Circumstance*, trans. Richard Howard (Harmondsworth: Penguin, 1985).

Une Mort très douce (Paris: Gallimard, 1964). *A Very Easy Death*, trans. Patrick O'Brian, (Harmondsworth: Penguin, 1969).

Les Belles Images (Paris: Gallimard, 1966). *Les Belles Images*, trans. Patrick O'Brian (London: Fontana, 1983).

La Femme rompue (Paris: Gallimard, 1968). *The Woman Destroyed*, trans. Patrick O'Brian (London: Fontana, 1985).

La Vieillesse (Paris: Gallimard, 1970). *Old Age*, trans. Patrick O'Brian (Harmondsworth: Penguin, 1986).

Tout Compte Fait (Paris: Gallimard, 1972). *All Said and Done*, trans. Patrick O'Brian (Harmondsworth: Penguin, 1987).

Quande prime le spirituel (Paris: Gallimard, 1979). *When Things of the Spirit Come First*, trans. Patrick O'Brian (London: Fontana, 1986).

La Cérémonie des Adieux and *Entretiens avec Jean-Paul Sartre* (Paris: Gallimard, 1981). *Adieux: A Farewell to Sartre*, trans. Patrick O'Brian (London: Deutsch, 1984).

Lettres au Castor et à quelques autres, 2 vols, ed. Simone de Beauvoir (Paris: Gallimard, 1983).

Lectures, interviews and articles by Beauvoir referred to in text

'Interview de Simone de Beauvoir par J. F. Rolland', *L'Humanité-Dimanche*, 19 December 1954. Reprinted in Francis and Gontier 1979 (see below), pp. 358–62.

Contribution to a 1964 debate on literature published in *Que peut la littérature?* ed. Yves Buin (Paris: Union Générale d'Editeurs, 1965), pp. 73–92.

'Mon expérience d'écrivain' (1966), lecture given in Japan and published in Francis and Gontier (1979), pp. 439–57.

'La Femme et la création' (1966), lecture given in Japan and published in Francis and Gontier (1979), pp. 458–81. An English translation ('Women and Creativity', trans. Roisin Mallaghan) appears in Toril Moi (ed.), *French Feminist Thought* (Oxford: Blackwell, 1987), pp. 17–32.

Preface to Jean-François Steiner, *Treblinka* (Paris: Mayenne, 1966).

'Simone de Beauvoir présente *Les Belles Images*', by Jacqueline Piatier, *Le Monde*, 23 December 1966, p. 17, reprinted in Stefanson (see below), pp. 55–61.

Interview in *Vinduet*, 22 August 1968, translated from the Norwegian and reprinted in Francis and Gontier (1979), p. 233.

Letter to *Le Monde*, 20 October 1970, reprinted in Francis and Gontier (1979), pp. 87–88.

'La Femme révoltée par Simone de Beauvoir', interview by Alice Schwarzer, *Le Nouvel Observateur*, 14 February 1972, pp. 47–54. Reprinted in Schwarzer, *Simone de Beauvoir aujourd'hui* (see below), pp. 27–51.

'Marriage is a very dangerous institution' and 'Happiness is a snare when the world is a horrible place', two article-interviews by Caroline Moorehead, *London Times* Wednesday, 15 May 1974, p. 9, and Thursday, 16 May, p. 11.

'Sex, Society and the female dilemma', dialogue with Betty Friedan, *Saturday Review*, 14 June 1975, pp. 14–19, 56.

'Entretien avec Simone de Beauvoir', by Pierre Viansson-Ponté, *Le Monde*, 10–11 January 1978, pp. 1–2. Reprinted in Francis and Gontier (1979), pp. 583–92.

'Interview with Simone de Beauvoir', by Alice Jardine, *Signs* (Winter 1979): 224–36.

'En France aujourd'hui on peut tuer impunément', *J'Accuse*, 15 February 1981, reprinted in Francis and Gontier (1979), pp. 475–81.

Interview in *Libération*, 30 March 1983, pp. 26–27

'Interview de Simone de Beauvoir' (1983), by Anne-Marie Celeux in her *Jean-Paul Sartre, Simone de Beauvoir: Une expérience commune, deux écritures* (see below), pp. 75–81.

'Interview with Simone de Beauvoir' (1984), by Hélène V. Wenzel, *Yale French Studies*, no. 72 (1986): 5–32.

Preface to Claude Lanzmann, *Shoah* (Paris: Fayard, 1985).

Secondary texts referred to

Ascher, Carol. *Simone de Beauvoir: A life of freedom* (Boston, MA: Harvester Press, 1981).

Astruc, A., and M. Contat. *Sartre. Un film réalisé par A. Astruc et Michel Contat* (Paris: Gallimard, 1977).

Atack, Margaret. 'The Occupation in Fiction: a study of changing narrative structures, 1940–1945' (Doctoral thesis, University of London, 1985).

Audet, J.-R. *Simone de Beauvoir face à la mort* (Lausanne: L'Age d'homme, 1979).

Badiou, Alain. *Almagestes* (Paris: Seuil, 1964).

Barnes, Hazel. *The Literature of Possibility: a study in humanistic existentialism* (London: Tavistock, 1961).

Blanchot, Maurice. *La Part du Feu* (Paris: Gallimard, 1949).

Burnier, Michel-Antoine. *Les Existentialistes et la politique* (Paris: Gallimard, 1966).

Cayron, Claire. *La Nature chez Simone de Beauvoir* (Paris: Gallimard, 1973).

Celeux, Anne-Marie. *Jean-Paul Sartre, Simone de Beauvoir: Une expérience commune, deux écritures* (Paris: Nizet, 1986).

Chapsal, Madeleine. *Les Ecrivains en personne* (Paris: Julliard, 1960), pp. 17–37, on Beauvoir.

Cohen-Solal, Annie. *Sartre 1905–1980* (Paris: Gallimard, 1985).

Contat, Michel, and Michel Rybalka. *Les Ecrits de Sartre* (Paris: Gallimard, 1970).

Cottrell, Robert. *Simone de Beauvoir* (New York: Ungar, 1975).

Danto, A. C. *Jean-Paul Sartre* (New York: Viking Press, 1975).

Dayan, Josée, and Malka Ribowska. *Simone de Beauvoir. Un film* (Paris: Gallimard, 1979).

Descubes, Madeleine. *Connaître Simone de Beauvoir* (Paris: Editions Resma, 1979).

Evans, Martha Noel. 'Murdering *L'Invitée*: Gender and Fictional

Narrative', *Yale French Studies*, no. 72 (1987): 67–86.

Evans, Mary. *Simone de Beauvoir: A Feminist Mandarin* (London: Tavistock, 1985).

Fallaize, Elizabeth. 'Narrative structure in *Les Mandarins*', in *Literature and Society. Studies in ninteenth and twentieth century French literature*, ed. C. A. Burns (Birmingham: Goodman, 1980).

Fitch, Brian. *Le Sentiment de l'étrangeté chez Malraux, Sartre, Camus et Simone de Beauvoir* (Paris: Minard, 1964).

Foucault, Michel. *Les Mots et les choses. Une archéologie des sciences humaines* (Paris: Gallimard, 1966).

Francis, Claude, and Fernande Gontier. *Les Ecrits de Simone de Beauvoir* (Paris: Gallimard, 1979).

—— *Simone de Beauvoir* (Paris: Librairie Académique Perrin, 1985).

Friday, Nancy. *My Mother/My Self. The Daughter's search for Identity* (London: Fontana, 1979).

Gagnebin, Laurent. *Simone de Beauvoir ou le refus de l'indifférence* (Paris: Fischbacher, 1968).

Garcia, Irma. *Promenade Femmilière* (Paris: Editions des Femmes, 1981).

Genette, Gérard. *Figures III* (Paris: Editions du Seuil, 1972).

—— *Seuils* (Paris: Editions du Seuil, 1987).

Gennari, Geneviève. *Simone de Beauvoir* (Paris: Editions Universitaires, 1958).

Gilbert, Sandra M., and Susan Gubar. *The Madwoman in the Attic. The Woman Writer and the Nineteenth Century Literary Imagination* (New Haven, CT: Yale University Press, 1979).

Ingram, Forrest. *Representative Short Story Cycles of the Twentieth Century* (The Hague: Mouton, 1971).

Jeanson, Francis. *Simone de Beauvoir ou l'entreprise de vivre* (Paris: Editions du Seuil, 1966).

Joyaux, G. J. 'Le problème de la gauche intellectuelle et *Les Mandarins* de Simone de Beauvoir', *Kentucky Foreign Language Quarterly* 3 (1956): 120–28.

Kanapa, Jean. *L'Existentialisme n'est pas un humanisme* (Paris: Editions Sociales, 1947).

Kaufmann-McCall, Dorothy. 'Simone de Beauvoir, *The Second Sex* and Jean-Paul Sartre', *Signs* (Winter 1979): 209–23.

Keefe, Terry. *Simone de Beauvoir. A study of her writings* (London: Harrap, 1983).

—— *French Existentialist Fiction: Changing Moral Perspectives* (London: Croom Helm, 1986).

—— 'Heroes of our time in three of the stories of Camus and Simone de Beauvoir', *Forum for Modern Language Studies*, no. 17 (1981): 39–54.

Lasocki, Anne-Marie. *Simone de Beauvoir ou l'entreprise d'écrire* (The Hague: Nijhoff, 1971).

Le Bon, Sylvie. 'Un positiviste désespéré: Michel Foucault', *L'Arc*, no. 30 (October 1966): 1299–1319.

Leighton, Jean. *Simone de Beauvoir on Woman* (London: Associated University Presses, 1975).

Lukacs, Georg. *Existentialisme ou Marxisme?* trans. E. Kelemen (Paris: Nagel, 1960).

Marks, Elaine. *Simone de Beauvoir: Encounters with Death* (New Brunswick, NJ: Rutgers University Press, 1973).

Maritain, Jacques. *Primauté du Spirituel* (Paris: Plon, 1949).

Merleau-Ponty, Maurice. *Sens et Non-Sens* (Paris: Nagel, 1948).

Michel, Henri. *Paris Résistant* (Paris: Albin Michel, 1982).

Moi, Toril. *Sexual/Textual Politics: Feminist Literary Theory* (London and New York: Methuen, 1985).

—— 'Existentialism and feminism: the rhetoric of biology in *The Second Sex*', *Oxford Literary Review* 8 (1986): 88–95.

—— 'She came to stay' (review article), *Paragraph*, no. 8 (1986): 110–20.

—— (ed.) *French Feminist Thought. A Reader* (Oxford: Blackwell, 1987).

Okely, Judith. *Simone de Beauvoir. A Re-Reading* (London: Virago, 1986).

Ophir, Anne. *Regards féminins. Condition féminine et création littéraire* (Paris: Denoel/Gonthier, 1986).

Pagès, Irène. 'Beauvoir's *Les Belles Images*: desubstantification of reality through a narrative', *Forum for Modern Language Studies* 11 (1975): 133–41.

Poster, Mark. *Existential Marxism in Postwar France* (Princeton, NJ: Princeton University Press, 1975).

Raoul, Valerie. *The French fictional journal* (Toronto: University of Toronto Press, 1980).

Riesman, David. *The Lonely Crowd* (New Haven, CT: Yale University Press, 1950).

Robichon, J. *Le Défi des Goncourt* (Paris: Denoel, 1975).

Sartre, Jean-Paul. *Situations I* (Paris: Gallimard, 1947).

—— *Situations III* (Paris: Gallimard, 1949).

—— *Les Carnets de la drôle de guerre* (Paris: Gallimard, 1983).

—— *Lettres au Castor et à quelques autres*, 2 vols. (Paris: Gallimard, 1983).

—— 'Jean-Paul Sartre répond', *L'Arc*, no. 30 (October 1966): 87–96.

—— *L'Être et le néant* (Paris: Gallimard, 1943). *Being and Nothingness*, trans. Hazel Barnes (London: Methuen, 1984).

Schwarzer, Alice. *Simone de Beauvoir aujourd'hui. Six entretiens* (Paris: Mercure de France, 1984). *Simone de Beauvoir Today: Conversations 1972–82* (London: Chatto and Windus, 1984).

Showalter, Elaine. *A Literature of Their Own. British Women Novelists from Bronte to Lessing* (Princeton, NJ: Princeton University Press, 1977).

Simons, Margaret. 'Beauvoir and Sartre: The philosophical relationship', *Yale French Studies* 72 (1986): 165–79.

Stefanson, Blandine (ed). *Les Belles Images* (London: Heinemann Educational Books, 1980).

Suleiman, Susan. *Authoritarian Fictions. The Ideological Novel as a literary genre* (New York: Columbia University Press, 1983).

Wardman, Harold. 'Self-Coincidence and Narrative in *L'Invitée*', *Essays in French Literature*, no. 19 (1982): 87–103.

Warnock, Mary. *The Philosophy of Sartre* (London: Hutchinson, 1965).

Whitmarsh, Anne. *Simone de Beauvoir and the Limits of Commitment* (Cambridge: Cambridge University Press, 1981).

Wurmser, André. 'Henri Monnier chez Marie-Chantal', *Les Lettres Françaises*, 8 December 1966, p. 7.

Index